FUNDAMENTALS OF HUMAN COMMUNICATION

FUNDAMENTALS OF HUMAN COMMUNICATION

An Interpersonal Perspective

James C. McCroskey
Virginia P. Richmond

Department of Communication Studies
West Virginia University

WAVELAND
PRESS, INC.
Prospect Heights, Illinois

For information about this book, write or call:
Waveland Press, Inc.
P.O. Box 400
Prospect Heights, Illinois 60070
(847) 634-0081

CONTENTS

SECTION 3 Psychology of Communication

SECTION 4 Messages in Communication

SECTION 5 Interpersonal Communication Relationships

PREFACE

The purpose of this book is to introduce the student with little or no background in the formal study of human communication to the fundamental content of this field, hence the title of the book— *Fundamentals of Human Communication: An Interpersonal Perspective.* Just because a college student has not engaged in formal study of communication, of course, does not mean he or she knows nothing about communication. Human beings begin their informal study of communication shortly after birth. By the time young people reach college age, many presume they already know all they will ever need to know about communicating with others. Unfortunately, that usually is not an accurate perception.

Children begin to learn about communication in much the same way they begin to learn about most everything else—through trial and error. In the absence of formal instruction about communication, this base of trial-and-error learning is likely to stay with and guide the person through childhood and throughout the remainder of the person's life. It will, of course, be modified over the years by continued trial-and-error experiences.

Unfortunately, the trial-and-error process often involves a lot of errors, and many of those errors will not even be recognized as such. As a consequence, much of what is learned is simply wrong and leads the person to be a less effective communicator. When children are introduced to the formal study of communication in elementary school, this instruction usually focuses on reading and writing. These aspects of communication, although certainly important, represent only a minuscule portion of the child's, and later the adult's, communication with others. Oral interpersonal communication (which accounts for over 90 percent of an adult's total communication in everyday life) is virtually ignored in most elementary and secondary schools; hence, it should not come as a surprise to learn that most people have very little understanding of how the overwhelming majority of the communication in which they will engage throughout their lives actually works (or, more likely, fails to work). Adults in this culture are incompetent communicators because our educational system does not even try to teach them how to be competent.

When any oral communication is taught in the elementary and secondary schools, the focus usually is on speaking and listening performance skills—such things as public speaking, oral reading, book reports, current event reports, "show and tell," and pronunciation and articulation skills. What is left untaught is the basic understanding of the human communication process—how it actually works. Hence, people are taught to believe that communication is nothing more than a set of oral skills that needs to be mastered. That simply is not correct. Unfortunately, learning how to talk and how to listen, skills that certainly are worth acquiring, does not mean one has learned to communicate.

It is our view that the most important organ for communication is the human brain. If one has a cognitive grasp of how communication functions, it is possible to use the other organs of communication effectively. If one's head is not on straight, if one does not understand the communication options he or she has, or if one clings to false knowledge about the process of human communication, one's likelihood of being a successful communicator is greatly diminished. It is these cognitive skills that are addressed in this book.

The chapters of this book are divided into five sections. Section 1 includes four chapters, the first three of which focus on the basic elements involved in the communication process. These chapters view human communication from an interpersonal perspective, one which also is predominant in the remaining sections of the book. Most of the communication situations in which we participate in our everyday lives involve interpersonal, dyadic (two-person) contacts. Hence, that is the most appropriate foundation to begin one's study in this discipline.

Chapter 4 concerns mediated communication. While most human communication involves live, person-to-person interaction, an increasing amount of communication today involves some form of media linking people across space and/or time by means of print or electronic systems. As mediated communication increases in both amount and importance, it is critical that we understand how the introduction of media impacts the process of human communication.

Section 2 includes three chapters devoted to people's orientations toward communication and their effectiveness. Chapter 5 is concerned with the extent to which people want to communicate, while chapter 6 is concerned with the fears and anxieties that many people confront when they need or wish to communicate. Chapter 7 addresses interpersonal communication competence.

The third section includes four chapters concerned with the psychology of communication. To understand communication one must also understand how people perceive others (chapter 8), how people form and change attitudes and beliefs (chapter 9), the processes of selectivity and attribution in communication (chapter 10), and how individuals' personalities both impact and are reflected in their communication behavior (chapter 11).

Section 4 includes three chapters that center on a critical aspect of communication—messages, both verbal and nonverbal—and how these messages are associated with meanings and relationships. Section 5 addresses interpersonal and relational concerns—developing interpersonal relationships (chapter 15), interpersonal influence (chapter 16), managing interpersonal conflict (chapter 17), intercultural communication (chapter 18) and gender (chapter 19). A central aspect of understanding the communication process is understanding the contexts of communication, and culture and gender are two of the critical aspects of all communication contexts.

Unfortunately, this small book will not be able to teach you all you ever need to know about human communication. It is designed to get you started in the right direction. Many other books are noted in the references that will permit you to go beyond these beginnings. It may well be that, when you have finished this book, you will have more questions about communication than you had before you began. If so, we have accomplished at least one of our major objectives in writing this book.

We wish to acknowledge the special efforts of Brenda Cox, who taught us how to use WordPerfect (through numerous iterations) and then used her skills to make our work presentable to others. Her assistance was invaluable.

J.C.M.
V.P.R.

BASIC ELEMENTS OF THE COMMUNICATION PROCESS

Section 1

THE PROCESS OF HUMAN COMMUNICATION

1

Communication has become one of the most commonly used words in the English language. Communicating with others is a very important reality. There are now *three* things that are certain in life: death, taxes, and communication. Of these, only communication may be expected to enhance our lives.

Humans must communicate with each other to survive. Simply communicating with others is not enough, however. As potentially harmful as no communication can be, if we express the wrong thing, or the right thing in the wrong way, we might be much better off not communicating at all. Unfortunately, many of us do not know how to communicate effectively in many situations.

Frequently our ineptness at communicating is rooted in our lack of understanding of what communication is and how it works. Because we must communicate to carry on our lives, we need to understand communication. The purpose of this chapter is to consider some basic matters that provide the necessary foundation for developing an understanding of communication. First, we will look at the two general ways in which people use this word and discuss how we will use it—our definition of human communication. Next we will discuss three types of communication as they relate to our definition. Finally, we will examine two models of communication.

Definitions of Communication

What communication means to you and what it means to the person sitting next to you may be very different. What communication means to one communication *professional* may even be different from what it means to another communication professional! Communication is like any other word: It means whatever people who use it think it means. When we take a careful look at how people generally use the word, however, we find that people use "communication" in only two very different ways. One way refers to the process of transferring messages from place to place, in which case it is often used in the plural form (that is, communications). Beaming television signals from Los Angeles to New York City via a communications satellite is an example of this meaning. Telephone companies also use this meaning when they advertise their "office communications systems." All of electronic and print "communications" industries make use of the term in this way.

The second way of using the word refers to the process of stimulating meaning in the mind of another person by means of a message. This is how we will be using "communication" in this book. We will define human communication as *the process by which one person stimulates meaning in the mind(s) of another person (or persons) through verbal and nonverbal messages*. Unlike the first use of communication, which emphasizes the exchange of messages, this definition of the term emphasizes *meaning*. This definition also encompasses a concern for three types of communication: accidental, expressive, and rhetorical.

Types of Communication

Accidental Communication

Each of us probably has had the experience of having a close friend or relative tell us something unexpected about ourselves. For instance, if you have always considered yourself reserved and quiet, imagine how surprised you might be if your friend revealed an admiration for how talkative and outgoing you are! Your surprise results from your lack of awareness that you come across to your friend in such a way. In essence you have *accidentally* communicated this talkative, outgoing aspect of your personality to the other person. We are often totally unaware of much of what we communicate to other people. In fact, there are times when we are completely unaware that we are communicating anything at all, although we are. There are, of course, other times when we are very much aware that we are communicating and of what we are communicating. This is purposeful or intentional communication; we are consciously in control of sending messages to the other person. Accidental or unintentional communication, on the other hand, happens when we do not have that conscious control. Even when we do not intend for them to, most of our actions and words stimulate some meaning in the minds of other people. In short, people attribute meaning to our behavior even when we have no intention of stimulating meaning in them.

Accidental communication and purposeful communication are very much alike in their essential processes. Both are the result of one person stimulating meaning in the mind of another person through some type of message. The difference is that accidental communication can often interfere with what we *want* to communicate to another person. A humorous, but potentially tragic, example of this was given by former Vice-President Richard Nixon when he stepped out of a plane in South America and extended to the awaiting crowd the hand signal "OK." Mr. Nixon obviously intended to express a positive and warm greeting to the crowd. Unfortunately, in much of South America that particular hand gesture has roughly the same meaning for people as a right hand with an extended middle finger does in North America! Vice-President Nixon accidentally communicated an insult to his South American greeters. A similar example is provided by E.T. Hall in his book *The Silent Language* (1959). Hall notes that some Latin Americans differ greatly from North Americans in how closely together they stand in everyday conversations. When people from these two different cultures stand and talk with each other, the North American continually backs away from the Latin American, and the Latin American continually moves toward the North American. Both individuals are trying to establish and maintain what is for them a comfortable conversational distance, and they do so unconsciously. At the same time each person may be accidentally communicating certain feelings and attitudes to the other. The North American may perceive the Latin American as pushy and aggressive, while the Latin American may perceive the North American as cold and unfriendly. Neither person intends to express these feelings to the other; rather, they are communicated "accidentally" by the respective actions of each person.

These two examples of accidental communication imply that nonverbal messages can have a very strong impact on interpersonal interaction. This impact often is stronger than that of verbal messages. Although it is important to remember that communication can be accidental, in this book we are more concerned with purposeful communication. Thus, unless otherwise stated, when we use the term *communication* from this point on, we mean the process by which one person *intentionally* tries to stimulate meaning in the mind of another person.

Expressive Communication

If we are sitting quietly in a library and we hear a loud noise of books falling on the floor behind us, we will probably turn toward that sound. We may then hear a person near those books muttering something we probably should not print here! That person is exemplifying *expressive* communication. This type of communication is characterized by messages that *express* how the sender feels at a given time. More simply, expressive communication suggests a person's emotional state. Intention, or purposefulness, is a common, but not an essential, characteristic of expressive communication. For instance, when we want to communicate affection to another person, we do so by intentionally saying certain things ("I enjoy being with you") and performing certain behavior (patting the person on the back). When taking a test, we may unintentionally communicate frustration by blurting out a four-letter expletive in response to running out of ink or breaking a pencil tip. While this may not be our purpose, our outburst will stimulate meaning in the minds of others in the class.

Another framework in which to view expressive communication is the ***content*** and ***relational*** levels of messages (Watzlawick, Beavin, & Jackson, 1967). The content level of a message is simply what we say: It is the words comprising the message. The relational level is an expression of how we feel about the other person or our relationship with the other person. It suggests to the other person how he or she should interpret our message. For example, your instructor might say, "The class average on this exam was seventy-four," imparting to the class an explicit bit of information. There can be a relational level as well to your instructor's spoken words. Based on this you may interpret your instructor's message, "I am very disappointed in your work." If this were the way you interpreted the person's message, it would stimulate in your mind some meaning about the nature of the relationship between your instructor and you and your classmates. Of course, the relational level can often result in accidental communication. Communicating that she or he is really upset with the class may be purely unintentional on your instructor's part; but the way in which the instructor looks at the class and uses the voice and arms when speaking could be misconstrued as anger. Fortunately we do have control over much of our expressive communication. We can reword an utterance or regulate our voice and movements to convey our emotional state without causing accidental communication.

Rhetorical Communication

This type of communication is exemplified by the salesperson attempting to persuade a customer to buy a particular product, by politicians trying to solicit votes from the citizens of their district, and by your parents when they attempt to get you to spend less money while you are away from home. The major difference between rhetorical communication and accidental and expressive types of communication is it is goal-directed. That is, through rhetorical communication our intent is to produce a specific meaning in the mind of another individual. Therefore, the salesperson, the politician, and your parents communicate rhetorically with a ***specific*** goal in mind. They communicate to persuade you to buy a new TV, cast a vote, or save money.

When we read or hear the words ***"rhetoric"*** and ***"rhetorical communication,"*** our first response may be to think of a public-speaking situation, a congressional filibuster, or a defense lawyer briefing a jury. Although rhetorical communication is often associated with these kinds of situations, it is also an integral part of interpersonal situations. Hardly a day passes without our communicating rhetorically with at least one individual. Our goal may be as trivial as getting someone to pass the butter at the dinner table. It may be as urgent as talking our neighbor into giving us a ride to work or school when our car won't start. In either case the process that allows us to reach that goal is rhetorical communication.

Rhetorical communication assumes that we have intent to achieve a certain goal by stimulating a specific meaning in the mind of another person. This suggests that rhetorical communication cannot be accidental but only purposeful. It does not suggest, however, that we will always achieve our goal by communicating rhetorically. Often when we try to change another person's mind about something, or attempt to get the person to do something for us, we may continue transmitting different messages until we discover one that accomplishes our goal. On the other hand, we might learn that nothing we say will bring the results we want, so we give up. There is nothing accidental about this process, only an intention that was either successful or unsuccessful.

It is useful to distinguish between the terms *"influence"* and *"persuasion."* When we "influence" someone, we cause that person to alter his or her thinking or behavior. This may occur because of accidental, expressive, or rhetorical communication. On the other hand, when we "persuade" someone to alter her or his thinking or behavior, we do so with conscious intent. Thus, persuasion always involves rhetorical communication. The two terms are frequently used interchangeably.

Rhetorical communication can take an expressive form. Often we play on the emotions to stimulate a specific meaning in the mind of another person. We often do this by communicating sadness or pleasure, liking or love, even anger or fear. Our intent is to make the other person feel that if we don't get what we want or need, our positive feelings will cease or our negative feelings will linger. Younger children often seem expert at communicating rhetorically in this fashion. When they desperately want something, they can be as sweet as honey. Deny them their request and they can throw a temper tantrum to end all tantrums. The "sweetness" expressed in the former case is, of course, one way the child has of saying "Please." The violent outburst in the latter case is one way (often a successful one) of expressing displeasure with our decision.

Now that we have discussed accidental, expressive, and rhetorical types of communication as covered by our definition of human communication, we can consider that definition in a bit more detail. We defined communication as **the process by which one person stimulates meaning in the mind(s) of another person (or persons) through verbal and nonverbal messages**. In order for us to comprehend this definition fully, a few of its parts need some clarification. The word "process" implies that communication is dynamic and changing. Berlo (1960) suggests that communication is much like the river spoken of by the Greek philosopher Heraclitus. Heraclitus said that you can't step in the same river twice—from the moment you take your foot out of the water until you put it back in, the river changes so much that it really isn't the same river. As we change as individuals over time and from event to event, our communication with others also changes. Therefore, it may be axiomatic that we can never communicate in the same way twice.

In the preceding definition the words "stimulates meaning" emphasize that it is through communication with others that we develop, cultivate, share, expand, and reshape ideas. Rare is the occasion on which we develop an idea completely on our own. The very thoughts which lead to an idea are the fruit of our experiences of talking with others, reading various literatures, and simply observing the world around us. Such ideas or combinations of ideas are the meaning stimulated through the verbal and nonverbal messages that are exchanged interpersonally. By "verbal messages" we mean language. Language, simply put, *is a system of symbols or codes used to represent certain ideas or meanings*. The use of these symbols is regulated by a set of formal rules, which we call grammar and syntax. We transmit these messages either in spoken or in written form. Finally, "nonverbal messages" refer to *any messages other than verbal*. These messages include such things as tone of voice, eye movements, hand gestures, and facial expressions.

This examination of our definition accentuates the complexity of communication. It is little wonder that so much intellectual and scholarly energy has been and continues to be expended in endeavors to learn more about this human phenomenon. The past four decades have witnessed many endeavors aimed at explaining the process of communication in pictorial or diagrammatical form. In the next section we turn our attention to two diagrams or "models" of communication, each of which depicts a different view of what the process is.

Models of Communication

The Rhetorical Communication Model

The Rhetorical Communication Model (McCroskey, 1993) illustrates intentional communication. This model (figure 1.1) includes the source, channel, and receiver as essential elements in the process. The model distinguishes what occurs during communication from what occurs in the source before communication and in the receiver following communication.

A source, before communication, undertakes what is referred to in the model as the "investigation process." Through this process the source must conceive an idea, decide her or his intent, and select some

1964

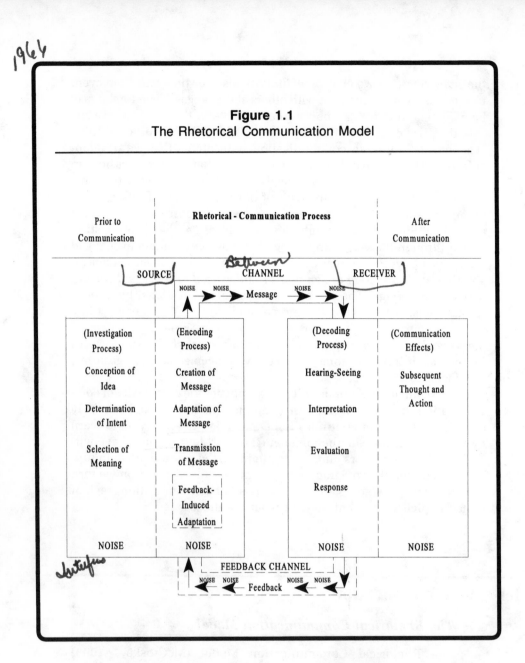

Figure 1.1
The Rhetorical Communication Model

meaning to be stimulated (intentionally) in the mind of the receiver. During the actual process of communicating, the source undertakes an "encoding" process. This process involves creating a message, adapting it to the receiver, and transmitting it across some source-selected channel. Also during the actual communication process, the receiver undertakes a "decoding" process. This entails sensing (for example, hearing or seeing) the source's message, interpreting it, evaluating it, and responding to it. Feedback is the receiver's response to the source's message. More will be said about this and other components in the next section of this chapter and in chapter 2. After communication, certain "communication effects" result for the receiver. These effects are any thoughts or actions on the receiver's part that occur after communication with the source. If the subsequent thoughts and actions of the receiver are those the source wanted, then the source has succeeded in her or his intent: Rhetorical communication has taken place.

Finally, this model includes *noise*—any physical or psychological stimulus which distracts participants from focusing on the communication processs. Note that noise can occur at any point during, and even before or after, the exchange of messages. Noise is not restricted to the channel.

The rhetorical communication model considers many elements of the communication process. Specifically, by looking at what happens before, during, and after communication, this model includes such elements as encoding, decoding, and feedback. The model illustrates that by communicating in a specified and intentional way, the source produces a certain response from the receiver.

The Interpersonal Communication Model

The basic model of interpersonal communication below was first presented by McCroskey, Larson, and Knapp (1971). Figure 1.2 depicts communication as it occurs between two people; it is thus a *dyadic*

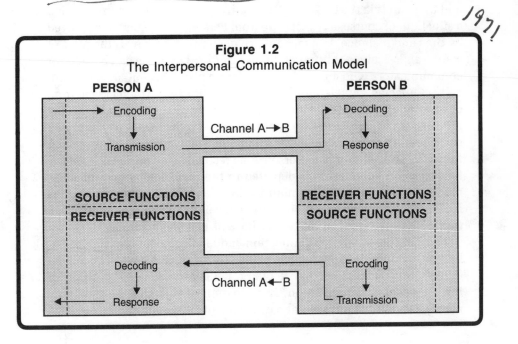

Figure 1.2
The Interpersonal Communication Model

model (as can be the rhetorical model of communication). A most important feature of this model is its treatment of both participants as both source and receiver. Also included in the model are the components of encoding, transmission, channel, decoding, and (although not labeled as such) occurrences before and after communication.

We can begin an analysis of this model by starting where Person A forms an idea. Person A encodes this idea into a message and transmits it across channel A ⟶ B to Person B, who initially plays the role of receiver. Person B decodes the message and emits a response, which contributes to subsequent idea formation in Person B. The process of idea formation in Person B may cause this person to function as a source. He or she then encodes a message and transmits it across channel A ⟵ B to Person A. Now, Person A begins to serve as a receiver by decoding the message from Person B and emitting a response to it. This response may affect Person A's idea formation, at which point he or she may again begin to serve as a source. Thus, the process depicted by this model is essentially a perpetual and cyclical one. In this sense, communication as illustrated by this model is truly a process, susceptible to change at any given point. Moreover, to the extent that each person can serve simultaneously as both source and receiver, we may say that this is a transactional model. Time and proximity play important roles in the interpersonal communication model. If Person A and Person B are separated by 2,000 miles and several time zones, Person B may encode and transmit (via the U.S. Mail) a lengthy message to Person A. In such a situation, of course, any response from Person A to Person B is delayed by time and distance. In a face-to-face encounter, however, the roles of source and receiver shift much more rapidly. The same can be said for communicators who are separated by great distances but are electronically connected via telephone or computer linkage. Any message from one person is responded to almost immediately by the other person. Any message that is received by either person from the other may alter any subsequently transmitted messages. In figure 1.2 the communication from Person B as source to Person A as receiver may be considered the feedback component that is depicted in the rhetorical communication model. In interpersonal communication the person who starts out as receiver is unlikely to remain only a receiver in the communication transaction—at some point he or she will become a source.

The interpersonal communication model illustrates the process of human communication, which is the focus of this text. The model depicts this process so that it offers a diagram of our definition of interpersonal communication. Examination of this and the rhetorical model has pointed out several basic concepts inherent in interpersonal communication. Although most of these ideas have been mentioned in our discussion to this point, the next chapter will treat each individually by focusing on its role in the human communication process.

References

Berlo, D. K. (1960). *The process of communication.* New York: Holt, Rinehart & Winston.

Hall, E. T. (1959). *The silent language.* Greenwich, CT: Fawcett Publications.

McCroskey, J. C. (1993). *An introduction to rhetorical communication* (6th ed.). Englewood Cliffs, NJ: Prentice-Hall.

McCroskey, J. C., Larson, C. E., & Knapp, M. L. (1971). *An introduction to interpersonal communication.* Englewood Cliffs, NJ: Prentice-Hall.

McCroskey, J. C., Richmond, V. P., & Stewart, R. A. (1986). *One on one: The foundations of interpersonal communication.* Englewood Cliffs, NJ: Prentice-Hall.

Watzlawick, P., Beavin, J., & Jackson, D. D. (1967). *Pragmatics of human communication.* New York: W. W. Norton & Co.

CRITICAL COMPONENTS OF HUMAN COMMUNICATION

2

Both of the models of communication we examined in the previous chapter have as essential components the *source*, the *receiver*, the *message*, and the *channel*. Except for channel, these components are also part of our definition of communication. *Feedback* is an essential component in the rhetorical communication model and is an implied component in the interpersonal communication model. Two other critical components of the interpersonal communication process that we have not considered are *goals* and *context*. A basic understanding of these seven components is critical to an understanding of human communication, and interpersonal communication in particular.

The Source

The source is the person who originates a message. In a broader view of communication, the source could be any individual or collection of individuals. The following are examples of the above: one person (an individual who wants to persuade a friend to go to a movie), a dyad (a couple who wants another couple to come to dinner), a group (a city council that wants to explain to its constituents a new municipal tax), or even an organization (a national food chain that wants to explain to consumers why its food is better than its competitor's). Whether an organization, group, dyad, or individual, the source has three functions in communication: (1) to decide what specific meaning is to be communicated; (2) to encode that meaning into one or more messages; and (3) to transmit the message(s). In interpersonal communication, it is typical that one individual does all three of these functions, but it is not uncommon to see each performed by a different person. Consider this example. Tom is having some problems in his relationship with his supervisor (Lisa). He has a specific idea and meaning to communicate to Lisa. He goes to his friend, Nicole, to ask advice on how best to state the message. Then he goes to his and Lisa's mutual friend, Casey, to ask her to carry the message to Lisa.

We used the word "encoding" in both the rhetorical and interpersonal models, and here we note it to be a major task of the source. Perhaps this term needs further clarification. As we will show in the next chapter, and as you may already have inferred from the models of communication, meaning cannot be transmitted; only messages can. When it is our intent to stimulate a specific meaning in the mind of another, we attempt to convey that meaning by transmitting a message that we feel represents that meaning. Thus, borrowing directly from McCroskey and Wheeless (1976, p. 24), encoding "*is the process of creating messages that we believe represent the meaning to be communicated and are likely to stimulate similar meaning in the mind of a receiver*." More simply, encoding involves translating ideas and information into messages. Encoding requires some degree of accuracy and precision in order for effective communication to take place. Inaccurate and imprecise encoding often can lead to accidental communication or, worse, total confusion. It is, therefore, very important that as sources we select messages that have similar meanings for us and our receiver.

The Receiver

The source in interpersonal communication is the person who originates a message, and the receiver is the person for whom the message is designed. Like the source, the receiver can be an individual, dyad, group, or large organization. Also, like the source, the receiver has three functions in human communication. These are: (1) receive the source's messages; (2) decode those messages into some meaning; and (3) respond to the messages. Again, it is typical in interpersonal communication for one person to do all three of these functions. However it is not uncommon for more than one person to be involved. For example, Bonnie could receive Dean's message, have Joan interpret it for her, and have Don respond to it.

In a discussion of the receiver, the term "decoding" needs some explanation. Because meaning cannot be transmitted, neither can it be received. We must receive messages that are transmitted to us and assign meaning to them. Decoding, then, is the translation of a message into ideas or information. The meaning we assign to a given message depends to a great degree on previous messages we have received from the source and on our previous experiences. Often the meaning we get from or assign to a specific message may be nothing close to the meaning intended by the source. For communication to be effective, it is necessary for us as receivers to consider our background and experience compared with the background and experience of the source. This may require that we "put ourselves in the other person's shoes."

The Message

By now you probably have developed a good idea of what a message is. To be on the safe side, though, we want to make another try at stimulating in your mind what we mean by "message." We noted earlier that our major concern in communication is meaning, not messages. So what is the difference between a message and a meaning? Simply put, a message is any verbal or nonverbal stimulus that evokes meaning in a receiver. Whatever it is that Chris wants to convey to Jan (whether or not other people are included in the process) will be conveyed through some message. As our definition of human communication states, the message can be either verbal or nonverbal.

The easiest way to distinguish between verbal and nonverbal messages is to think of verbal messages as being composed of words. The nonverbal messages are anything else that can stimulate meaning. This oversimplifies the distinction a bit, but it makes a good starting point. The fact that verbal messages are composed of words tells us a great deal about them. We know by this characteristic that any given word has the potential for stimulating meaning in a receiver. We can even make up a word, like "chudnuk," and assign some meaning to it, like "irresponsible person"; we can then share this word and its meaning with a friend. Later both of us will know that when either of us uses the word "chudnuk," we mean "irresponsible person." In essence, what the word chudnuk has become for us, is a *code*. We can now use that word, that code, together with other words to construct various messages aimed at eliciting certain meanings in our friend (for example, "that chudnuk will never be on time for the game!"). We could not use chudnuk when talking with other people, however, because they would not know what we meant when we used it. It would not be a *shared* code. We can only use *shared* language codes to communicate effectively. If two people know different languages, say one knows English and the other knows Russian, they will have very difficult problems communicating. This is because they do not have a shared language code.

Nonverbal messages are more difficult to characterize. All we know from the word "nonverbal" is that such messages are not verbal. This tells us what nonverbal messages are *not* but not what they *are*. Nonverbal messages are *any stimuli other than words that can potentially elicit meaning in the mind of a receiver*. As concrete examples, such behavior as winking, pointing with the index finger, fidgeting with a pencil, tugging at your hair, twiddling your thumbs, sighing, sticking out your tongue, wrinkling your nose, being late for class, and sitting with your right ankle resting on your left knee, may stimulate meaning in the mind of an observer (a receiver) and thus are nonverbal messages. Some of these examples raise an important point: Not all messages, particularly nonverbal messages, are consciously encoded. Very seldom do we intentionally, consciously sit at our desk fidgeting with our pencil; nevertheless, this behavior may be seen by someone else as a message and it may communicate many things to that other person.

The Channels

Messages are not self-mobilizing; they are carried from the source to the receiver by one or more channels. A channel, then, is ***the means by which a message is carried from one person to another***. Channels come in many forms. Apparently any of our five senses can function as channels. In interpersonal communication we typically think of sight and sound (or light waves and sound waves) as the most common channels of communication. There are many instances, however, when we send and receive messages through the channels of touch, smell, and taste. Moreover, in most of our face-to-face interactions, we use a combination of these channels: We hear each other's voices and see each other's movements. We also tend to touch each other at various times during our interaction. We may even take note of how pleasant (or unpleasant) each other smells. The messages conveyed over each of these channels give us a much broader repertoire of stimuli to which we can assign meaning, therefore potentially allowing us more understanding of the particular communication event.

Communication channels often occur in forms other than our physiological senses. In organizations, for example, supervisors function as channels for upper management by carrying management's messages to lower-line employees. There are mass-mediated channels, such as television, radio, film, and billboards, which carry messages from one or more sources to many receivers. On an interpersonal level, the postal system can be considered a channel through which written messages are carried. Electronic channels allow interpersonal communication via telephone, FAX, and computer. Even music and art function as channels for messages, often expressive ones. A source can create a message which reaches receivers centuries later or contemporaneously. To reiterate, a channel is ***any*** means by which a message gets from a source to a receiver.

Feedback

Feedback is a receiver's observable response to a source's message. Such responses may take the form of specific verbal messages, such as "I don't agree with that." Even more commonly, however, feedback messages are nonverbal. A frown, a smile, turning away, crossed arms, or nervous fidgeting may all be taken as responses to the source's message. For the electronic media (radio and television particularly) there is normally a time lag for feedback to reach the source. If eventually there are no positive responses, that will be taken as the strongest feedback of all! That is, if audiences do not respond favorably, the programs will no longer air.

Feedback is very important in all communication but particularly so in interpersonal communication. The source can carefully observe the receiver's responses to judge the success of the messages being sent. When feedback is negative, and is observed by the source, new messages can be formed in an attempt to improve the chances for successful communication. Feedback in interpersonal communication is the method we use to regulate the messages we send and those that are sent to us.

Goals

One component of communication, which we have referred to primarily in the realm of rhetorical communication, is goals. In our discussion of rhetorical communication we noted that the source who communicates in this way does so with the intent of stimulating a specific meaning in the receiver—this is the source's goal. Generally there are three major goals in interpersonal communication: developing interpersonal relationships, gaining compliance, and gaining understanding. We will first consider each of these goals individually and then discuss their interrelationship.

A fundamental goal of interpersonal communication is the development of relationships with others. Communication not only is essential to relationship development but, some argue, it *is* the relationship. In his book *Social Intercourse*, Knapp (1978) notes that interpersonal communication contains the forces that "bring people together, keep people together, and divide and separate them" (p. vii). Most people have a very basic need to like and be liked by others. The fulfillment of this need is one reason we develop relationships. We also develop relationships out of needs of companionship, sharing, and love. Sometimes we may feel we are not receiving what we need from a relationship, or we cannot put into it what the relationship requires. We are thus motivated to end the relationship. Whether our goal is to develop and maintain a relationship or to end it, we must communicate to achieve that goal.

Another fundamental goal of communication is to gain the compliance of others; in other words, we attempt to influence their actions in some way. By "compliance-gaining" we simply mean getting another person (the receiver) to engage in some behavior that is wanted by the source. Our motivation to gain another person's compliance derives from our desire or need for changes in our environment, in the immediate situation, and in our relationships. For example, if it is your turn to wash the dishes but you have a very important test to study for, you may try to get your roommate to wash them. You will try to convince your roommate to comply with your request. You could simply ask your roommate to wash the dishes; you could demand or threaten consequences; or you could offer your roommate something in return. Your only goal in this instance is to get your roommate's compliance in doing the task. To obtain compliance, you must communicate in a way that fulfills your intentions and meets your goal.

A third fundamental goal of communication is to gain understanding. We all have a need to know and understand. To know and understand, we need information. To get information, we must engage in communication. Thus, our need to find information, so that we can know and understand something, may motivate us to communicate with others. If you are not reading this textbook only because you have to, you are probably reading it to gain some information about communication. Possibly you hope that by having this information you can get a better understanding of how and why people communicate with each other. We talk to other people to get information, clarify certain issues, expand our knowledge of events, and understand why the world operates as it does. Other people talk to us for the same reasons.

Although relationship development, compliance-gaining, and gaining understanding are three separate goals of communication, it is a rare occurrence when they are achieved independently. In other words, to achieve one of these goals usually requires that the other two also be achieved. Relationship development is a good example. When we first meet someone, we often need or want to know how the other person is going to respond to us. Our desire for this knowledge may motivate us to communicate with the person. Berger and Calabrese (1975) have termed this process "uncertainty reduction." Our desire to know how another person will behave toward us in a given interaction creates a need for information. This need can be met only by communicating with that person. When we have gained that knowledge, we have reduced our uncertainty about that person and his or her actions. In this way the goals of relationship development and gaining understanding function together in motivating us to communicate with the other person.

To maintain, or even to end, a relationship often requires compliance-gaining. For example, in any relationship we are routinely faced with interpersonal differences, many of which can threaten the survival of the relationship. Perhaps the person is not spending as much time with us as we would like. While our primary goal is to save the relationship, our secondary goal is to get them to spend more time with us. This goal motivates us to communicate in a way that will gain the other person's compliance. Maybe the other person wants to end the relationship, but we do not. Their goal may be to get us to leave them alone; thus they spend less time with us, hoping that we will "get the message." Theirs is a relatively cruel, but often successful, compliance-gaining tactic. You can think of other examples that illustrate the interconnections among relationship development, compliance-gaining, and gaining understanding. It is nearly impossible to think of one occurring without the others. All three are potentially powerful motivators for communication. Our primary goal may be the achievement of only one of them, but accomplishment of that goal virtually requires the achievement of the other two as well.

Context

We will conclude our discussion of the critical components of communication and focus on the "context" of communication. We use context to refer to the circumstances within which communication takes place. Context is an important concern in communication. It is important because we do not communicate in exactly the same way with different people in a given situation or with the same person in different situations. Thus, even when we are communicating with a particular person, how and what we communicate is likely to change as the context in which we communicate changes.

Context centers on two important variables: *roles* and *rules*. That is, how and what we say to another person in a given situation or context depends on (1) the roles each of us takes on in that situation, and (2) the rules that govern our interactions according to those roles. For example, we interact with classmates and instructors in the role of student, with certain friends in the role of boyfriend or girlfriend, with doctors in the role of patient, and with servers in the role of customer. Each of these different interactions involves a different communication context.

It is not only the different people and different locations of each interaction that distinguish contexts but also each interaction is regulated by a unique set of rules. These rules are unique for a given context of interaction in that they are associated with our particular role within that context. Rules of this sort are not always of the "written on paper" variety. They are grounded in social and cultural norms. Some people maintain that how and what we express in any conversation is decided entirely by such rules. For example, when we are in the role of patient interacting with a doctor, the "rules" say that we should communicate in a more formal and stylized manner than when we interact with a friend in the role of roommate. Thus we might say that the function of roles and rules is to help us make predictions about how to behave in a given context. They help us to reduce uncertainty about the other person and the situation. They help us to coordinate the meaning of our messages with the meaning of the other person's messages.

We can get a clearer picture of how roles and rules affect interpersonal communication by considering five different contexts of communication in which we all have been or eventually will be involved. These are family, peers, school, work, and intimate relationships. Rather than treating each of these separately, we will look at their relation to each other compared with the roles and rules of interaction that each calls for.

In the family context, all of us take on the role of child, usually the role of sibling, and most of us will someday take on the role of mother or father, husband or wife. Depending on which role we are in, our communication with other family members is governed by certain rules. Some rules are unique to individual families, others are common to most families in our culture. As children, we interact with siblings differently from the way we interact with parents, and with a sister differently from the way we interact with a brother. As parents, our interaction with our spouse will be quite different from our interactions with our children. We will probably interact differently with each child depending on her or his age, order of birth, individual needs, and personality.

Whatever our family roles, the rules of interaction will change when we talk with peers. We can easily draw from our own experiences many examples of how our communication with friends differs from that with members of our family. Try to imagine what conversations are like between your mother and other mothers, or your father and other fathers. Perhaps you have overheard such conversations. They are vastly different from the conversations we are accustomed to having around the family dinner table. The difference may lie primarily in the change of roles and rules as we move from the family context to interacting with peers. We simply say and do things with our peers that we do not say and do with members of our family. Most of our communication in this context involves social matters and many interests that form the basis of our friendships.

The school context also requires that we take on roles that are different from our family roles. Many of our peer roles, however, may be most active in the school setting. When we are enrolled in the same class as a friend, we may interact with that person in the role of friend but with other members of the class in the role of student. As the roles change, so do the rules of interaction. Even in the classroom, communication with a friend may involve our mutual social interests. With another classmate, the interaction may center on only class-related topics. Our interaction with instructors is highly rule-oriented. As the instructor enters the classroom, we tend to cease any ongoing interactions and focus our attention on that person. Communication in the classroom is typically quite ritualized and flows according to the instructor's individual teaching style. Even when we interact with an instructor one-on-one, we tend to avoid communicating on a "social" level. This interaction limits our conversation to the subject matter and needs as a student.

Interactions on the job are similar to those in the school setting. We may have peers at work whom we consider to be good friends, and we communicate with them on a social level at work. With other co-workers our interactions may depend entirely on our work roles and the rules associated with them, so that most of our communication with those people is task-related. Moreover, organizational rules, and even some societal rules, dictate that we interact with co-workers differently than we interact with superiors, and with superiors differently than we interact with subordinates. Often organizational rules and roles totally restrict us from interacting one-on-one with certain others in the organization. For example, although the president of your college or university may follow an "open door policy" in her or his office, it may be highly unlikely that you could visit at any given time. Your role as individual student is simply too far removed from the role of university president.

Finally, there is the intimate context. By this we mean a context that is highly conducive to sharing with another person our private and confidential thoughts, feelings, and attitudes. We can much more easily conceive of such a context occurring with family and peer contexts than with school and work contexts. We often tell very private information about ourselves to certain family members and not to others, and discuss other confidential information with close friends outside our family. That is, we reserve intimate information about ourselves for those people we can trust and for those contexts in which trust is least likely to be violated. We also expect in an intimate context for the other person to share themselves with us and to have a mutual degree of trust in us. Our role in intimate contexts may be close friend, confidante, or lover.

We emphasize context to underline the fact that what and how we communicate with others is dependent on our roles in a given interaction and on the rules associated with these roles. Communication is a dynamic and change-oriented process. Changes manifest themselves in the differences in communication across contexts and with various people. Although we have discussed only five contexts, there are myriad other contexts in which communication takes place (for example, the dating context, the religious context, the political context, and so on). If we could accurately and completely list these contexts, we could find the task of investigating and explaining interpersonal communication much easier.

Culture is the largest, and often the most important, aspect of context. It is very important that you understand the context in which this book is being written. We are writing from the position of the general culture of the United States. Therefore, many readers will need to adapt what is presented in the following chapters to the cultural context in which they live. What are norms or rules in one culture may be very different in another culture. The constant is that all cultures have norms and rules. People learn the norms and rules of their culture informally, by living within that culture. When one needs to talk with people from a different culture, it is essential to study that culture extensively. Just as language codes must be shared to facilitate communication, so must other aspects of culture be understood.

References

Berger, C. R., & Calabrese, R. J. (1975). Some explorations in initial interaction and beyond: Toward a developmental theory of interpersonal communication. *Human Communication Research, 1,* 99–112.

Berlo, D. K. (1960). *The process of communication.* New York: Holt, Rinehart & Winston.

Hall, E. T. (1959). *The silent language.* Greenwich, CT: Fawcett Publications.

Knapp, M. L. (1978). *Social intercourse: From greeting to goodby.* Boston: Allyn & Bacon.

McCroskey, J. C. (1993). *An introduction to rhetorical communication* (6th ed.). Englewood Cliffs, NJ: Prentice-Hall.

McCroskey, J. C., Larson, C. E., & Knapp, M. L. (1971). *An introduction to interpersonal communication.* Englewood Cliffs, NJ: Prentice-Hall.

McCroskey, J. C., & Wheeless, L. R. (1976). *Introduction to human communication.* Boston: Allyn & Bacon.

Pearce, W. B. (1976). The coordinated management of meaning: A rules-based theory of interpersonal communication. In G. R. Miller (Ed.), *Explorations in interpersonal communication.* Beverly Hills: Sage Publications.

Watzlawick, P., Beavin, J., & Jackson, D. D. (1967). *Pragmatics of human communication.* New York: W. W. Norton & Co.

THINKING ABOUT COMMUNICATION

3

Thinking straight about communication is the most important communication skill a person can develop. Unfortunately, most people in contemporary society have been taught some very fuzzy thinking about communication. People reading their first book or taking their first course in communication often bring this fuzzy thinking to those tasks.

Try to recall a time when you took a course in a subject to which you had very little previous exposure. Perhaps the course was in psychology, art, or chemistry. Whatever it was, you probably entered the course with certain ideas about the subject to be studied. As the course progressed, you realized that many of your earlier conceptions had been inaccurate. Most academic courses are like that. You are likely to discover that this course is also one for which you have many misconceptions. Don't feel alone. Most people have some inappropriate notions about what communication is, how it is supposed to work, and what it is supposed to do. This chapter will attempt to clear up some very common misconceptions about communication.

Ten Common Misconceptions [1]

1. Meanings Are in Words

The idea that meanings are in words is perhaps the most common misconception about communication. The most important and vexing problem with this misconception is that it can lead to much misunderstanding between two people and can thwart the effectiveness of communication. What a particular word means to us may not be what it means to someone else. The word stimulates a meaning in our mind that is different from the meaning it stimulates in the mind of our receiver. Many examples of this derive from the jargon used in various industries and academic disciplines. Thus, *communication* means one thing in the telecommunications industry and something much different in the social sciences or in biology. Even the word *science* has different meanings for people in different fields, as exemplified by what it means to physical scientists as compared to social scientists and behavioral scientists. Even within the field of human communication, researchers and scholars often have different meanings for some ideas.

The point we wish to make about words and their meanings is that *no word has meaning apart from the person using it.* Because of the way we are educated about words from early in life, we fail to understand that words are merely codes or symbols for meanings we have in mind. The meanings we have for words are the products of our culture, ethnic group, social class, and experiences. Thus, no two people share precisely the same meanings for all words, because no two people share the same background and experiences. *Meanings are in people, not in words.* For effective communication to occur, therefore, we must realize that what we say to others may not stimulate in their minds the meaning we want or intend to stimulate. This requires us to adapt our ideas to the background and experiences of our receivers so that they can adapt to our ideas. When we can successfully make these adaptions, we are more likely to create shared meanings for words (also nonverbal symbols and actions). As our definition of communication implies, shared meaning is what communication is all about.

2. *Communication Is a Verbal Process*

When people think about communication, they typically think about words, either written or spoken. Our focus on communication as a verbal process is due in large part to our educational experience. From preschool education up through college, much attention is paid to verbal learning and language usage. Many children's television shows, like *Sesame Street* and *Mr. Rogers*, emphasize the learning of words and language, and often these programs allude to the importance of words for communication. However, despite what formal and informal educational systems have taught and continue to teach us about words (and what they teach is correct in many respects), communication is **more** than a verbal process. It is also a nonverbal process. We may go as far as to say that most of our communication behavior is nonverbal in nature. This is particularly true of oral communication in interpersonal contexts.

What we say or write (the verbal message) is important to communication. How we say it and the nonverbal context in which we say it are of equal and often greater importance. Recall the discussion of expressive communication and the content and relational levels of communication. It is our nonverbal behavior that comprises much of our expressive communication and the relational aspects of our messages. To a very large extent our nonverbal behavior is **the** determining factor in whether the words we use convey the meanings we want them to. Thus, *the process of communication is both verbal and nonverbal*. This is why our definition of communication emphasizes "verbal and nonverbal messages" and why we devote the bulk of three chapters of this text to nonverbal elements of communication.

3. *Telling Is Communicating*

Many people believe that simply saying something is communicating it. This is an unfortunate misconception, and it is the basis for much conflict and misunderstanding. Communicating with someone involves far more than just telling. As our model of interpersonal communication illustrates, encoding a message and sending it (telling or saying something) are merely the beginning of the communication process. People have the "telling is communication" misconception because they fail to acknowledge the active role played by the receiver in communication. Again, meaning is the crucial variable. Telling does not consider that the meaning assigned to a source's message by the receiver is determined by the receiver's own background and experiences. In writing this book, for example, the authors realized that you probably have little technical knowledge about human communication theory. However, you have had much practical experience in actual communication. Therefore, we had to encode and structure the information to be communicated (the content of this book) to the background and experiences of its intended receivers (college and university undergraduates). This was done so that the information is relatively basic while both practical and applicable to these receivers. Had we attempted to achieve the goal by simply telling (writing) you what communication is and how it functions without considering your probable knowledge and experience in communication, the book would be difficult, at best. Even so the meanings that you assign to our messages may not be the meanings we intended to convey. We can never expect to achieve shared meaning by telling alone. If anything, *telling is only half of communicating*.

4. *Communication Will Solve All Our Problems*

At one time or another each of us has been told that to solve our problems all we need to do is communicate. Delegates from the United States meet with delegates from Iran in Geneva, Switzerland, with the idea that "if we can just sit and talk with each other, we can iron out our differences." Similarly, so-called "management communication consultants" sometimes give business managers and executives the idea that if they would just open lines of communication with subordinates, production and profits would automatically increase steadily.

Whether our problems are interpersonal, international, or organizational, it is a misconception that those problems can be solved by communication alone. The basis for this misconception is that many of us believe that *whether* communication occurs is more important than *what* is communicated.

Obviously the occurrence of communication is essential to any of our problem-solving efforts. Yet often communication itself is the spark and fuel that ignited many of our problems. For example, presume you suggest to a friend that he or she should change hairstyles. Your motive for making that suggestion may be purely for your friend's own good. However, communicating that suggestion could easily be the source of much interpersonal conflict. Although communication does occur in this instance, and although its intention is positive, *what* is communicated can be misconstrued by your friend as a cheap shot. By the same token, whenever two people, or groups, or even countries have irreconcilable differences, any communication between the two parties may serve only as a catalyst to bring these differences to the surface. This may result in more problems than were there at the start. Furthermore, communication may emphasize some insignificant differences between two parties; the recognition of which may escalate minor differences into serious problems. Thus, effective communication may allow us to solve some problems, but it cannot be expected to solve all problems. Ineffective communication often creates more problems, or inflates current problems and is thus more detrimental than no communication at all. *Communication can either create, escalate, or help solve problems*.

5. Communication Is a Good Thing

Ask any politician, community leader, or school administrator and chances are they will tell you that communication is a good thing. This misconception is ominously pervasive in our society. It probably stems from the misconception described above—that communication will solve all our problems. As we have already noted, however, it will not solve all our problems. Moreover, communication is neither a good thing nor a bad thing. *Communication is a tool*. Like any tool, communication can be used for good or bad purposes. Take a chalkboard eraser, for instance. If we use this tool for its intended purpose—to clean chalkboards—we can say that it is a very useful device. However, put that same eraser in the hand of an angry adolescent who throws it at another student. Has the eraser become a bad thing? Not really. It is simply being used in a bad way. Similarly, communication can be misused, and even abused, so that it appears bad. Nevertheless, it isn't communication that has become bad; it is the way it is used which is bad.

If a teacher were to ask a failing student to visit the office to discuss the student's academic plight, one of two things could happen. The teacher could openly and sympathetically point out where the student needs to focus attention to improve her or his grades. If this meeting (which would probably be more complex and involved than depicted here) were to result in marked improvement on the student's part, we could say there was good communication between teacher and student. More appropriately, we should say that the student and teacher used their communication with one another well. Conversely, if during their meeting the teacher were to degrade and chastise the student for doing so poorly, it is likely that the student will do no better and maybe do worse. Then we might say that there was bad communication between teacher and student. More appropriately, we would say that the teacher misused communication with the student so that the results were bad. Therefore, **communication is neither good nor bad; it is a tool** we can use to help us solve our problems and to get along better with others.

6. The More Communication, the Better

A common stereotype concerning the value of communication in American society leads to the fact that the more a person talks (up to a point) the more positively that person will be viewed by others. The talkative person is perceived to be more competent, more friendly, more attractive, more powerful, and a better leader than the less talkative person. This is a fact that has been confirmed repeatedly by many laboratory and "real-world" research studies. In our society, it seems, the people who talk a lot are seen as the better people. Nevertheless, it is a misconception that the more communication, the better.

The problem arises in that people tend to equate quantity (more) with quality (better). Although more may be better in many of life's endeavors, there are many instances in which more is worse. One instance is golf— the more shots you take, the worse your score. In golf, it is the quality of your shot that counts. Thus, the better you shoot, the fewer shots you have to take and the **lower** (or better) your score.

In many ways, communication is like the game of golf. Often it is not how much we say or for how long we say it, but the quality of what we say that counts. Often it is not **how much** people communicate but **what** they communicate that is essential. In communication **quality is more important than quantity**.

7. Communication Can Break Down

Perhaps the most socially prevalent misconception about communication is that it can "break down." We consistently hear the phrase "communication breakdown" whenever people feel a need to place blame for their poor communication. Blaming our failures on communication breakdowns is a copout. Communication **cannot** break down. People can be ineffective and poor communicators, but their communication will not break down. Machine communications (like telephones) may break down, but human communication does not.

When people refer to communication breakdowns, they are usually implying that communication is unsuccessful and has been stopped. However, in many such situations communication has been highly successful. Each party involved may have developed an excellent understanding of how the other person thinks and feels. The parties just don't agree. In other situations the breakdown refers to circumstances where communication was attempted but really was a failure. In either instance, the people involved may stop talking to one another. This does not mean that communication has stopped (much less "broken down"). The absence of talk often communicates more than talking itself. In a very real sense **one cannot not communicate**. The double negative is intentional. It illustrates a very important idea about communication. The absence of verbal communication only emphasizes the importance of nonverbal communication. Remember, communication is both a verbal and a nonverbal process.

8. Communication Is a Natural Ability

Very few basketball coaches will state a person is born with the ability to be an effective outside field-goal shooter. Shooting field goals from anywhere on the basketball court, let alone from beyond fifteen feet, is a learned ability. We are born with the **capability** (the potential) to become an effective field goal shooter. However, the **ability** is learned through years of observation, coaching, and, as the saying goes, "practice, practice, practice."

Communication, like shooting a basketball, is not a **natural** ability; it is a **learned** ability. Barring any pre- or postnatal maladies, we all are born with the capability to become effective communicators. We are born with the senses necessary to transmit and receive messages. As we mature and develop, we can expand our mental and physical capacities to decode and encode various interpersonal and environmental messages. This process is one of acquiring the intellectual, psychological, emotional, and physical skills that allow us to communicate with others. It is the process of shaping our natural communicative capabilities into learned communication abilities.

The misconception that communication is a natural ability is attributable in some part to educational and governmental entities. For most of this century, the three Rs have been recognized as basic skills that every child needs to learn. Hardly anyone will argue that reading, writing, and arithmetic are **natural** abilities! Only in the last decade or so have speaking and listening been recognized as essential basic skills to be included among the three Rs. We note that, while it may be obvious to most of us (it isn't to some educational and governmental leaders), reading, writing, and even arithmetic are communication skills. Recognizing them as such, and including speaking and listening along with them, will enable our schools to better prepare children **and** adults to become more effective communicators. Most children are born with the capacity to learn these skills. Careful instruction, personal observation and experience, and "practice, practice, practice" are required for the child to develop much ability in any one of them. That many of us may be lacking in our communication abilities is thus more a result of previous educational (and perhaps interpersonal) inexperience in these areas than of some innate limitation. One purpose of this text is to help you overcome any deficit you may have in communication skills. The most important communication skills are those relating to analyzing and understanding how communication works and determining appropriate behavior for a given communication context. No one is born with those skills.

9. *Interpersonal Communication = Intimate Communication*

A common idea is that interpersonal communication and intimate communication are the same; whenever we communicate interpersonally, we communicate intimately. This, of course, is not always true. Obviously not all interpersonal communication is intimate. When we ask the service station attendant (if we can find one!) to "fill it up" or ask the telephone operator for a particular phone number, we are communicating with those people interpersonally but not intimately. When we communicate one-on-one with someone we know well, as with one of our parents, we are engaging in interpersonal communication, but not necessarily in an intimate way. Most of our daily communication with others is of an interpersonal nature, and little of it is truly intimate. On the other hand, whenever we communicate intimately with someone, we are communicating interpersonally. The idea we wish to express here is *some* interpersonal communication is intimate, but most is not. It is important to distinguish among the various *levels of communication*. We can communicate with others at a cultural, a sociological, or a psychological level. When we communicate with others at a *cultural* level, we adapt our message sending and receiving processes to predictions we make based on the culture to which they belong. When we are introduced to someone from a foreign country and begin to get acquainted with that person, much of our communication is at first based on what we know (or what we *think* we know) about people from that individual's nation. We can predict with some certainty that if the person is from a Persian Gulf country, she or he most likely has religious and political beliefs very different from our own. We can also state that this person's beliefs are probably very different from those of someone from Colombia, South America, whose values we can predict are also unlike our own.

In our American culture, we share many common beliefs, values, and characteristics that are unique to us. This shared identity allows us to communicate among ourselves as a cultural entity, and it helps to distinguish us from other cultures. We can talk, write, and sing about Old Glory, baseball, and apple pie so that they stir our emotions and patriotism; the same words simply will not have the same effect on the citizens of New Guinea. This process also operates within subcultures surrounded by the larger American culture. These subcultures arise from such diverse areas of the country as Appalachia, a Sioux reservation, the Louisiana Bayou, and the beaches of Southern California. Individuals from each of these subcultures share common beliefs and values. These are different from those of other subcultures, and this sets them apart as unique even within the American culture. Effective communication on the cultural level requires that we make accurate predictions of commonalities among persons in these cultures. We should attempt to adapt our encoding and decoding processes to these predictions. When we are communicating at this level, we usually are operating with cultural stereotypes, a very dangerous basis upon which to attempt to communicate. Nevertheless, in the initial stages of many communicative relationships, this is the only level open to us.

At the *social* level of communication, the predictions we make about other persons, which we use to make our encoding and decoding decisions, are based on our perceptions of the sociological subgroups to which people belong. At this level our concern is with the various social institutions that comprise a society. Some of these are professions, occupations, political associations, religious affiliations, sororities, fraternities, and even more discrete roles like students, professors, children, and parents. When we talk with others at the social level, we communicate with them according to their roles in society. The predictions we make at this level about people are based on commonalities they share with others who act or function in the same societal role. While we are still operating with stereotypes, these stereotypes are less likely to cause us serious problems than those based on culture alone. We communicate with one teacher, one police officer, or one doctor in pretty much the same way we would communicate with any other teacher, police officer, or doctor. We expect bank tellers to behave in certain ways, ministers to hold specific values, and politicians to have particular beliefs; we say things to each of these people and interpret their messages according to their respective roles. Obviously we may communicate differently with different people who function in the same role. However, effective communication at the social level requires that we make accurate predictions of commonalities among persons in the same societal roles. We adapt our message-sending and receiving processes to those predictions.

When we communicate with others at the *psychological* level, our communication is adapted to the unique characteristics of each person. It is only at this level that we move beyond generalities. Our predictions about a person's beliefs, values, and behavior transcend cultural and social expectations and derive from the person's unique psychological, emotional, and personality traits. To communicate with another at this level requires that we know the person as an individual. Effective communication at the psychological level requires that we adapt our messages to the individual and interpret that individual's messages based on her or his uniqueness. While we have two good friends, both of whom are students at the same school, our communication with each friend at the psychological level will be adapted to each one as a unique individual, despite their affiliations and national origin. It is at this level, and this level only, that intimate communication occurs. Intimate communication involves *knowing* each other through *revealing* to each other private and personal information about ourselves. However, note that reaching the psychological level often is possible only after we have recognized and shared with each other our cultural and social commonalities. It is for this reason that not all interpersonal communication is intimate. Intimate communication comes about only after we have shared through other levels of interpersonal communication our broader and more basic common characteristics, beliefs, attitudes, and values. For this reason, most of us communicate intimately with very, very few people. We may get to know many people well enough to communicate at the psychological level. We will choose not to go so far as to become intimate in our communication with most of them.

10. Communication Competence = Communication Effectiveness[2]

We have used the term *effectiveness* several times in the first three chapters of this text. Many of us may speak or write and hear or read the word with little thought given to what it may mean. That is, *effectiveness* is one of those words we take for granted, believing that everyone has pretty much the same meaning for it. Like most words, however, effectiveness means different things to different people. This variety of meanings manifests itself in another misconception about communication, namely that communication competence is the same as communication effectiveness. We want to dispel this myth. First, there is a very real and very important difference between competence and effectiveness. Second, it is important to understand both concepts in order to know if and when we and those around us are communicating effectively and competently. This concept is more difficult to grasp than some of the others. In fact, chapter 7 is devoted entirely to the subject of competence. Here, we have simplified the discussion of these two terms.

Larson, Backlund, Redmond, and Barbour (1978) define communication competence as "the ability of an individual to demonstrate knowledge of the appropriate communicative behavior in a given situation" (p. 16). It is our opinion that successful accomplishment of one's goal is "effectiveness." Thus, effective communicators are those who can stimulate in the mind of another person a meaning they intend to or want to stimulate. If the receiver gets a different meaning from that intended by the source, we can say that the source has ineffectively communicated, but he or she *still has communicated*. The distinction between effectiveness and competence is that a communicator may be effective without being competent (they get lucky, so to speak). Or he or she may be competent without being effective (even the best shot misses now and then).

Besides the definition of Larson and colleagues (1978), just what do we mean by communication competence? Communication effectiveness is neither a necessary nor sufficient condition for communication competence. Just as a very incompetent communicator may be effective in a given situation, an extremely competent communicator may be ineffective in a given situation. It's a condition, again, much like golf. Even the most competent golfer is ineffective on a given day at a given course. Oddly enough, it often happens that the most profoundly incompetent golfer is the one who makes the hole-in-one on the 200-yard fairway. In communication, just as in sports, communication competence does not equal communication effectiveness. *Competence has to do with understanding the way communication works. Effectiveness has to do with communicating successfully*.

One major problem underlying the misunderstanding of communication is that people have many misconceptions about what communication is or is not, and about how it functions. The purpose of this chapter was to point out and discuss ten such misconceptions and to explain a more appropriate and useful alternative to each misconception.

Notes

1 Many ideas in this section are based on similar ideas presented in J. C. McCroskey and L. R. Wheeless, *Introduction to Human Communication* (Boston: Allyn & Bacon, 1976), pp. 3–10, and in J. C. McCroskey, *An Introduction to Rhetorical Communication*, 6th ed. (Englewood Cliffs, NJ: Prentice-Hall, 1982), pp. 17–21.

2 Much of the material in this section is taken from the discussion presented in J. C. McCroskey, "Communication competence and performance: A research and pedagogical perspective," *Communication Education*, 1982, *31*, 1–8.

References

Allen, R. R., & Brown, K. L. (1976). *Developing communication competence in children*. Skokie, IL: National Textbook Company.

Larson, C. E., Backlund, P. M., Redmond, M. K., & Barbour, A. (1978). *Assessing communicative competence*. Falls Church, VA: Speech Communication Association and ERIC.

McCroskey, J. C. (1993). *An introduction to rhetorical communication* (6th ed.). Englewood Cliffs, NJ: Prentice-Hall.

_____. (1982). Communication competence and performance: A research and pedagogical perspective. *Communication Education, 31,* 1–8.

McCroskey, J. C., & Wheeless, L. R. (1976). *Introduction to human communication*. Boston: Allyn & Bacon.

Wiemann, J. M. (1977). Explication and test of a model of communication competence. *Human Communication Research, 3,* 195–213.

MEDIATED
COMMUNICATION

4

The previous chapters of this book have looked at human communication in its most common form—face-to-face, oral interaction. For much of the history of the human race, that was the only form of communication available. It remains the most used, and therefore, the most important form today; but it certainly no longer stands as the only form.

Today we also have "mediated communication." Mediated communication is similar to the more common form except that the source(s) and receiver(s) are not physically in the presence of each other at the same time. They may be separated by distance or time, or both, which makes live interaction either difficult or impossible. Some "medium," therefore, is necessary to link them together.

Evolution of Human Communication

We do not really know when humans started communicating with each other, but we are certain it was a very long time ago. That early communication most likely was little different from animal communication—monkeys, dogs, bears, birds, whales, and so on. It probably involved nothing more than grunting, squealing, smiling, pushing, and grabbing. While such communicative efforts certainly were not sophisticated, they did permit these early humans to relate to one another to some extent. This primitive behavior did allow the communication of some very basic emotions, such as anger and affection.

Nonverbal behavior, then, is the foundation on which human communication has evolved. Even today, nonverbal behaviors function as the primary means to communicate emotional, or affective, meanings between humans (McCroskey, 1992; Richmond, 1992; Richmond & McCroskey, 1995). Nonverbal behaviors remain essential to oral languages. Without them, oral languages cannot exist.

After many thousands of years, humans evolved the power of speech. Again, this probably was a very slow process, with a very few words being learned during the comparatively short lifespan of humans at the time. In due course, the few words grew into language with syntax and grammar, and the offspring of the adults with language competence were taught the language of their parents.

As these humans ventured forth to populate various parts of the world, more oral languages evolved. Today, approximately 5,000 oral languages exist on earth. No single one of these is spoken or understood by a majority of humans, although Mandarin is spoken by more people than any other language. Thus, even today, when people travel to various parts of the world, unless they can find someone who speaks their own language or another language they have learned, they must resort to nonverbal behaviors to communicate. Even if you were to become fluent in a dozen languages, a feat achieved by only rare individuals, you would be unable to communicate in the languages of the overwhelming majority of countries in the world.

Early Development of Mediated Communication

While it is difficult today for us to imagine a world without writing, writing is a very recent development in the history of human communication. If the history of human communication were represented by a typical 12-inch ruler, the history of writing would be included in *less than the last quarter of an inch*. Even today the overwhelming majority of the 5,000 languages in the world *have no written form*. In fact, only about 100 of them even have an alphabet. While writing is central to the educational system in the United States today, there are many who believe its time is running out. In the not-too-distant future, humans may have no further use for this very inefficient and imprecise tool!

Writing is believed to have evolved from humans' desire to record information for the use of people who came along after them. They recognized that history by hearsay is very imprecise and subject to each teller's biases and fantasies. They realized that as information passes through such a serial communication process (McCroskey, 1992), it is distorted severely and might not even remotely represent what actually happened. The remnants of such oral histories can be seen in the mythologies and religions of the various cultures of the world.

Writing was not the first ''medium'' developed for communicating with people who were not present. The earliest attempts at recording information for later humans were left as drawings by ancient cave dwellers. Obviously, this was neither an efficient nor particularly effective method of communicating anything but the most primitive of thoughts. Such drawings slowly evolved into more complex picture systems.

Today we have cultures that continue to use a *pictographic* system (albeit a more sophisticated one) for their written language, Chinese being one of the best examples. In these cultures, there is no pretense that the written language is the same as the oral language. It is recognized that both the oral and the written languages are symbolic representations of ideas the user is trying to communicate, but that they are very different systems.

In other cultures, an alphabet has been developed. In these ***orthographic*** systems the alphabetical symbols are put together to approximate the sounds of the oral language. Early on, that relationship may have been fairly close. However, as those of us who have grown up as English speakers are apt to recognize quickly, that approximation is extremely strained in contemporary societies.

The relationship between oral and written English is remote indeed. While each uses symbols to represent ideas, those symbols have little relationship to each other. People in the United States culture continue to consider these radically different language forms to be the same language. The problems this mythology creates for the users of the language, particularly children, are severe indeed (Richmond, McCroskey, & Thompson, 1992).

Very recently, within far less than one-sixteenth of an inch on our imaginary twelve-inch ruler, we humans have developed what many believe to be an incredibly improved system of recording the oral language, one that may make writing obsolete. The advances in electronic recording and transmission have been extremely rapid—radio, film, television, imaging, holography, and who knows what next.

Written descriptions of what your grandmother looked like, sounded like, and walked like can never compete with the holographic representation of your grandmother in your own living room talking to you. And that cannot compete with a virtual reality program designed to let humans communicate with their great, great, great grandfathers—an advance which many see as coming in the very near future. While only a dream a few years ago, these technologies now exist, and most are either already economically feasible or projected to be so in the near future. As much as we who take pride in being authors might wish it otherwise, the hand-held video camera and its relatives and descendants are making us as obsolete as Model-T Fords. While writing most likely will continue to exist for many more generations, particularly as an art form, its central role in passing information from one generation to another may soon end.

Viewing Communication Multi-Dimensionally

As we have described the evolution of communication above, you may have noticed that we proceeded from communication that is primarily dyadic to that which involves potentially millions of people. At the same time, we moved from live interaction to mediated communication. It is important to determine two elements in distinguishing types of communication. The first is concerned with the number of receivers, either real or potential. The second is concerned with live, face-to-face interaction as opposed to communication which is mediated through space and/or time.

An examination of figure 4.1 will help keep these two ideas distinct. As is illustrated in this figure, media are designed to overcome problems related to separation of source and receiver(s) by space and/or time. Examples of the types of media which might be used for the various combinations of potential receivers and level of mediation are included. The examples provided are *not* presumed to be exhaustive, only illustrative.

Figure 4.1
Communication Dimensions and Media Forms

| Potential Receivers | Level of Mediation | | | |
	None	Space Only	Time Only	Space & Time
Dyadic Interaction	Live conversation	Telephone Interactive computer Video phone C.B. radio	Memo/letter E-mail Voice Mail Art	Memo/Letter E-mail Voice mail Virtual reality
Small Group Interaction	Live group discussion	Teleconference Videoconference Interactive computer	E-mail with copies Letter with copies	E-mail with copies Letter with copies
Large Group Meeting	Formal meeting Speeches & questions	Interactive TV Interactive computer	Videotape Film	Videotape Film
Mass Audience	Public speech or series of speeches	Microphone Ham radio Live radio Live TV	Book Newspaper Magazine Film Videotape Billboard CD rom	Book Newspaper Magazine Film Videotape CD rom

In order to envision the place of media in communication, it is useful to focus first on the impact of the number of potential receivers available on communication. Most of our everyday communication is with one other individual at a time, what we have referred to in this book as "dyadic" communication. Our potential, however, includes communication with an infinite number of people if we are able to command the necessary media. It is not, however, necessary to involve either electronic or print media to engage in "mass communication." Before there was either electronic or print media, there was mass communication. It occurred in the form of public speeches to large (mass) audiences.

It is useful, therefore, to think of audience size on a continuum, moving from dyadic communication to public communication. As we do, our communication becomes more monological. That is, when more people are involved, those who speak tend to "make speeches" rather than interact with short comments made by one person after another. Public communication is primarily monological, although people in the audience are often invited to ask questions or to make comments after the formal speech is completed.

Even though public communication is monological, when no print or electronic media are involved, the source and receivers are "live" and feedback is possible. As we noted in chapter 2, feedback is one of the very important aspects of communication in increasing the likelihood of success. Feedback permits speakers to get some sense of how the receiver(s) is responding and to adapt to that response if necessary. Live interaction is instantaneous, therefore more likely to gain and maintain another person's attention and interest, and hence increase the effectiveness of the interaction. The same is true for interactive computer linkages.

To the extent that any form of communication is mediated, distancing of communication occurs. Not all media have the same effect on the interaction however. To examine the impact of media on human communication, we will first look at dyadic communication.

Media and Dyadic Communication

When most people think of mediated communication, they think of television or some other form of mass communication. Mediated dyadic communication, however, is something most of us have been involved with since we were children. One of the earliest forms of mediated dyadic communication was letter writing. Until the last fifty years or so, this was about the only method by which a person could keep in touch with someone who lived a long way away. Remember, at that time a couple of hundred miles was very distant for many people. Hence letter writing was very popular. However, it took several days to get a letter across a state, much less across the United States. Even if the person to whom we wrote answered immediately, there was quite a delay while the response worked its way back through the system to us.

Writing letters, while certainly better than nothing, is limited by the lack of instantaneous reactions. While interaction still occurs between members of the dyad, feedback and response are long delayed, and confusion and misunderstandings are likely to be troublesome since they cannot be cleared up immediately. The arrival of the telephone overcame much of the difficulty presented by letters. At least the time aspect became less of an issue. Telephone communicators are spatially apart, but temporally together. Unfortunately, only the vocal aspect of nonverbal communication is present. All of the other aspects of non-verbal behavior which increase the closeness of dyadic communication are lost. This is improved markedly by the use of videophones. Once cost issues are overcome, videophones will probably replace today's telephones in both offices and homes.

Two other forms of media also facilitate dyadic communication: CB radio and ham radio. Essentially these are the same thing as the telephone except they operate through the air rather than via telephone lines. They also are somewhat less private, since anyone with a receiver can tune into the radio messages.

Falling between writing letters and calling on the videophone are two electronic media systems which may be thought of as "telephonic letters." Facsimile transmission and E-mail speed the process of getting a letter to someone. But both FAX and E-mail are more like letters than videophone. They move complete messages over great distances very quickly (unlike letters), but allow for no feedback during the presentation of that message (unlike videophones). Feedback may come soon after transmission and reception, or it may be delayed for a substantial period because the receiver may not be present when the FAX or E-mail message is sent.

Media and Group Communication

Group communication is a difficult process when it is live; it becomes more difficult when it is mediated. As the size of a group becomes larger, more group members cease to be group participants and become group observers instead. Mediation of group communication encourages this transformation and, in the process, reduces the usefulness of group communication itself. As a result, most group communication today still is conducted in live, face-to-face encounters.

Group communication is possible, although very difficult, to conduct via written messages (copied to all group members) or audio- or videotaped messages similarly distributed. Of the three, the written form is the most distancing and usually the least effective, even if it is handled as E-mail rather than letter, while the videotape would be the most effective since it contains both visual and nonverbal elements. In all cases, however, since group communication thrives on feedback and immediate interaction, these mediated approaches are only better than nothing at all, and sometimes not even that.

Interactive computer conferencing, telephone conferencing, and video conferencing are all mediated approaches which have fewer drawbacks than written or taped message transmissions. The big advantage of these media approaches is that feedback and immediate response and adaptation are possible. Of course, the written (computer) mode has fewer advantages while the video mode is closest to the live. The big advantage of these modes over the live group meeting, of course, is cost if the people would otherwise need to travel to get together. It should be remembered, however, that there also is a cost paid in terms of interpersonal affect among group members when they are separated by great distance. It is much easier to be unpleasant or unresponsive with a person a long way off than it is to do so when sitting next to that person. Also, the social needs of the group members may be ignored in the attempt to save money.

Finally, holding mediated meetings for large groups is extremely difficult. About the only use for such an approach is a meeting that is intended to distribute information with little or no questioning or interaction. Essentially, this format takes on a public speaking mode rather than a group interaction mode. Virtually all the group members become observers rather than participants. If group participation is needed, a mediated meeting is not the approach to follow.

Mediated Public Communication

Public communication is sometimes referred to as person-to-group communication or one-to-many communication. It is primarily monological, although some questioning and response may be possible depending on the level of mediation involved. As soon as there are enough people in the audience to require a microphone for the speaker, we have moved into the realm of mediated communication, although the intrusion of the medium is minimal at this level.

When the potential receivers of the message are spread over a wide distance, electronic media are very likely to be involved in public communication. From the ham radio operator to the live radio and television stations and networks, to computer bulletin boards, the electronic media have the capacity to get the message live to large numbers of people. If the receivers are not all available at the same time, these same media can deliver the public communication, or parts of it, at various times. So too can the "less-instantaneous" print and electronic media—books, magazines, newspapers, films, audio or video tape rom, billboards, etc.

The industries we are concerned with at this level are what are co. monly referred to as the "mass media." That is, they serve as a mediu to take a message to a large mass of people. In this form of communica tion little feedback is expected, and very little normally is received. This, of course, means that the public communication can only be as effective as its original design will permit it to be. When there is no feedback, there is no adaptation. When the message is one of news or entertain- ment, the delayed feedback is in the count of how many people listened to or watched the message. If the message has a more direct goal, such as selling cars or political candidates, the feedback comes in terms of how many cars are sold or how many votes the candidate receives.

Future Considerations

New media will certainly be created and implemented in society, for our need to "reach out and touch someone," as the telephone company has told us, never ceases. We are likely always to seek to communicate farther and faster, although the speed level of our media today is already extremely high. Our goals in the future will likely focus more on the quality of the communication than on its quantity or speed.

As we noted above, introducing media to the communication process does not improve the quality of the communication, but it does what it is supposed to—namely it establishes the linkage between source and receiver. It does so imperfectly. It is never "just like being there." Important facets of the communication process are lost, particularly nonverbal and affective aspects. As a result, farther and faster are not enough. Let us draw on two phenomena which are virtually certain to get more attention in the future to illustrate our communication concerns: distance education and telecommuting.

"Distance education" is a term used to reference mediated instruction which is used to replace live instruction in a classroom. Ever since the advent of radio, and particularly in the early days of television, media buffs have argued that use of whatever new medium was available would be the savior of education—and would reduce its costs. A current fad is the use of satellite links to transmit video lectures from one campus or school to others, which enables students to see the instructor, and, in many cases, ask questions via the computer. Earlier forms of distance education included correspondence courses, televised lecture courses, telephone lecture courses, radio lecture courses, and the earliest of all— books. Other versions have included programmed instruction texts, tapes, films, and videos. More recently, interactive computer-mediated videos have been used with considerable success.

One should be very careful before jumping on this mediated bandwagon. The concern should be "What is being substituted for what?" Generally, a mediated instructor is being substituted for a live one—that is it. The question then is whether the amount of money saved is worth any amount of learning lost. In most cases, the satellite instruction, for example, is far more expensive than just sending the instructor to the student—or sending the student to the instructor. While basic content learning has been found to be quite achievable with well-programmed interactive video cassettes, development of higher levels of cognitive learning and shaping positive attitudes usually require an effective live teacher. Going to the wrong media, or inserting media where live instruction is necessary, will not advance education in this society.

"Telecommuting" is a new term for working at home—being connected to the office via computer link, fax machine, phone links, etc. This option is very attractive to people who have other reasons to be at home—young children, disabled person to care for, etc.—or simply want to avoid long commutes and still be able to live where they want to live or are constrained to live.

For some positions in organizations, this option may be very reasonable. If the work to be done is primarily solitary and not dependent on collaboration with others, it may be that this option is best for both the employee and the employer—who would not have to expend money to provide the employee expensive office space. It is also likely that many people who do not work for a single organization, "freelancers," can exercise this option.

Unfortunately, there are not very many jobs that fit this description in most organizations. Communication is central to most positions in organizations, particularly those above the entry level. People with higher positions often have supervisory responsibilities, and most people in organizations today function as part of teams that require frequent interpersonal communication.

Bottom line: The media make many positive contributions to our everyday lives. However, mediated communication as an alternative to live, face-to-face communication is not an equivalent substitute. It facilitates communication among numerous people in distant locations, but the communication is affected by the additional element of the medium by which it is transmitted.

We have discussed the additional channels provided by the mass media for communication, but we have not addressed the influence of messages received via those channels. You may have unconsciously thought about which interpersonal channels you prefer for certain kinds of communication. For example, would you rather explain to someone face-to-face that you will not be attending their tennis match, or would you prefer to explain your absence by telephoning? Does one channel make the task easier? Similarly, you may have decided that you would rather read about news events in the newspaper or a weekly magazine rather than rely on television newscasts—and you could probably give reasons to support your choice. Have you ever wondered whether your concept of family is influenced by the television programs you watch, by the films you see in the theater, or even by the compact discs you purchase? Are your opinions about older people formed by images you see on television? If you think minorities are portrayed fairly in films and on television, do the situations in which you see minorities on the evening newscast vary?

Although mass communication theories are beyond the scope of this text, it is crucial to think about all the information we receive—whether it is from a friend, a teacher, the newspaper, or television. Why was a particular idea, event, or individual selected for discussion? In the case of the media, how do we use each medium and why? Are we looking for information, entertainment, something to fill the silence, to escape, to relax, or to forget about problems? When do you most often choose a particular medium? While driving your car, do you listen to talk radio, novels on cassettes, or music on your compact disc? Do you watch David Letterman so you can discuss the show the next day with your friends?

An equally important consideration is from the other side of the coin. The subject matter presented by the various mass media are carefully chosen by people working for large organizations. Today, the same company frequently owns movie production companies, television and radio stations, and publishing houses. Their goal is to earn a profit. In order to succeed, they must persuade us to buy their product—whether a newspaper, book, television program, or the products of the advertisers who support those media. Do the people with the power to decide what is presented influence us? Do we influence their selections? Is it mutual? Clearly, by the time a particular message is presented on any medium, a number of people—often called gatekeepers—have influenced the presentation. This textbook is a good example. There are two authors who have discussed whether to include a particular topic and how to present it; the authors have been influenced by numerous students over years of teaching; the editorial staff at the publishing house read the manuscript and suggested changes. The final version thus passed through many filters before reaching you.

One final area of consideration is the effect a particular medium has on those who choose it. Do people who watch television regularly differ from those who rarely watch a program? Are radio listeners more likely to be persuaded by advertisements they hear rather than ones they read? Do you subconsciously compare your attitudes and beliefs to those of characters on the movie screen? There are a multitude of choices of media for communicating and receiving communication. The critical components of communication addressed in chapter 2 may be difficult to isolate as we move up the continuum from dyadic to mass communication, but identifying those components will help us determine what communication is effective in a specific situation and why.

References

McCroskey, J. C. (1992). *An introduction to communication in the classroom.* Edina, MN: Burgess.

Richmond, V. P. (1992). *Nonverbal communication in the classroom.* Edina, MN: Burgess.

Richmond, V. P., & McCroskey, J. C. (1995). *Nonverbal behavior in interpersonal relations* (3rd ed.). Boston, MA: Allyn & Bacon.

Richmond, V. P., McCroskey, J. C., & Thompson, C. A. (1992). *Communication problems of children.* Edina, MN: Burgess.

ORIENTATIONS TOWARD COMMUNICATION

Section 2

WILLINGNESS TO COMMUNICATE

5

Mary is the type of person who seldom has anything to say. When she's with other people, she seems to just go along with the crowd, seldom making any suggestions or having any complaints about what the group does. Her eyes tend to look everywhere except directly at the person with whom she is speaking. She usually sits or stands with her arms crossed, head facing downward, and shoulders and back slumped over. At school, Mary always selects a seat in the back or along the side of the room when she can. She never seems to get involved in class or school activities, and she is by herself most of the time.

Does the description of Mary remind you of anyone you know? A friend? A relative? Yourself? Chances are that you know many people who fit such a description. If you could think of one word to sum up Mary, what would it be? If *shy* is the word that comes to mind, it is probably because the term is the one most commonly used for describing the behavior of people like Mary. If someone close to you is a shy person, you know how difficult it can be to try to communicate with someone who is not willing to communicate with you. All else being equal, the tendency to be unwilling to initiate communication and/or respond to the initiatives of others may be the most important factor leading to ineffective communication between people.

This chapter discusses willingness to communicate. Our goal is to make you aware of and help you understand the nature and causes of people's tendencies to initiate or avoid communicating with others. To begin with, we want you to have some idea about your own level of willingness to communicate. Please complete the Willingness to Communicate (WTC) scale in figure 5.1. Be sure you follow closely the directions for the scale. Compute your scores on the WTC scale by following the directions in figure 5.2.

Figure 5.1
Willingness to Communicate Scale

DIRECTIONS: Below are twenty situations in which a person might choose to communicate or not to communicate. Presume you have **completely free choice.** Determine the percentage of times you would **choose to initiate communication** in each type of situation. Indicate in the space at the left what percent of the time you would choose to communicate. Choose any numbers between 0 and 100.

_____ 1. Talk with a service station attendant.

_____ 2. Talk with a physician.

_____ 3. Present a talk to a group of strangers.

_____ 4. Talk with an acquaintance while standing in line.

_____ 5. Talk with a salesperson in a store.

_____ 6. Talk in a large meeting of friends.

_____ 7. Talk with a police officer.

_____ 8. Talk in a small group of strangers.

_____ 9. Talk with a friend while standing in line.

_____ 10. Talk with a waiter/waitress in a restaurant.

_____ 11. Talk in a large meeting of acquaintances.

_____ 12. Talk with a stranger while standing in line.

_____ 13. Talk with a secretary.

_____ 14. Present a talk to a group of friends.

_____ 15. Talk in a small group of acquaintances.

_____ 16. Talk with a garbage collector.

_____ 17. Talk in a large meeting of strangers.

_____ 18. Talk with a spouse (or girl/boy friend).

_____ 19. Talk in a small group of friends.

_____ 20. Present a talk to a group of acquaintances.

Figure 5.2
Computing Scores on the Willingness to Communicate Scale

SCORING: The WTC permits computation of one total score and seven subscores. The range for all scores is 0–100. Follow the procedures outlined below.

---

1. Group discussion—add scores for items 8, 15, and 19; divide sum by 3. Scores above 89 = high WTC, scores below 57 = low WTC in this context.
2. Meetings—add scores for items 6, 11, & 17; divide sum by 3. Scores above 80 = high WTC, scores below 39 = low WTC in this context.
3. Interpersonal—add scores for items 4, 9, & 12; divide sum by 3. Scores above 94 = high WTC, scores below 64 = low WTC in this context.
4. Public speaking—add scores for items 3, 14, & 20; divide sum by 3. Scores above 78 = high WTC, scores below 33 = low WTC in this context.
5. Stranger—add scores for items 3, 8, 12, & 17; divide sum by 4. Scores above 63 = high WTC, scores below 18 = low WTC with these receivers.
6. Acquaintance—add scores for items 4, 11, 15, & 20; divide sum by 4. Scores above 92 = high WTC, scores below 57 = low WTC with these receivers.
7. Friend—add scores for items 6, 9, 14, & 19; divide sum by 4. Scores above 99 = high WTC, scores below 71 = low WTC with these receivers.

To compute the total score for the WTC, add the totals for stranger, friend, and acquaintance; then divide by 3. Scores above 82 = high WTC, below 52 = low WTC.

The Nature of Willingness to Communicate

We will begin our discussion of willingness to communicate by returning to the concept of shyness. We begin with two yes-no questions. Please mark your responses below:

1. Do you presently consider yourself a shy person?

   _____ Yes _____ No

2. If you answered "no" to the first question, was there ever a period in your life during which you considered yourself a shy person?

   _____ Yes _____ No

Zimbardo (1977) posed these same two questions to over 5,000 people in the western United States. His results were remarkable. More than 40 percent (2,000) of the people who responded answered "yes" to the first question, and over 80 percent (4,000) answered "yes" to one of the two questions. Generalizing these findings to the population as a whole, one can estimate that two out of every five people you meet consider themselves to be shy. And two more believe that they were shy at one time. Thus, only one person in five reports not being and never having been shy. To bring it a bit closer to home, if there are twenty-five people in your class, at least ten of them think of themselves as shy people.

The authors of this book replicated Zimbardo's study with twice as many respondents as he had. Our results were virtually identical to his, although our data were collected in over 50 universities across the United States (Berger, Baldwin, McCroskey, & Richmond, 1983). We also found the same results with a sample of approximately 2,500 adult nonstudents in a national study (Allen, Richmond, & McCroskey, 1984). Clearly, many people think they are, or used to be, shy.

Defining shyness has been a difficult task for scholars. Zimbardo said that "Shyness is a fuzzy concept," meaning that shyness as a concept is too vague to explain with a single definition. Pilkonis, another shyness researcher and a former student of Zimbardo, has offered a behavioral description of shy people. Pilkonis, Heape, and Klein (1980) suggest that shy people "are characterized by avoidance of social interaction, and when this is impossible, by inhibition and an inability to respond in an engaging way; they are reluctant to talk, to make eye contact, to gesture, and to smile" (Pilkonis, Heape, & Klein, 1980).

We, like Pilkonis, find it useful to refer to shyness as *the behavioral tendency to not initiate communication and/or respond to the initiatives of others.* Presumably, this behavior stems from a preference for noncommunication by the individual—a reduced willingness to communicate. There are a number of possible factors contributing to this preference (some controlled by the communicator and some not) which we will discuss later. At this point it may be useful to look at the scores you computed from your responses to the WTC scale. Compare your scores with the norms listed in figure 5.3. If your score on the general WTC measure is lower than the moderate range, you very likely are seen by others as a shy person. If your score on the overall measure is in the moderate or high range, but you are low in one or more contexts, you may prefer to behave like a shy person in some contexts but not in others.

Zimbardo, in terms less specific than those used by Pilkonis, thinks of shyness as simply a *discomfort* associated with many different communication situations. In other words, a shy person is one who is likely to feel uncomfortable when communicating one-on-one with another person, when interacting within a group of people, when called upon in class, when giving a talk, and when being introduced to a new

Figure 5.3
Norms for Willingness to Communicate Scale

Group Discussion	> 89 High WTC, < 57 Low WTC
Meetings	> 80 High WTC, < 39 Low WTC
Interpersonal Conversations	> 94 High WTC, < 64 Low WTC
Public Speaking	> 78 High WTC, < 33 Low WTC
Stranger	> 63 High WTC, < 18 Low WTC
Acquaintance	> 92 High WTC, < 57 Low WTC
Friend	> 99 High WTC, < 71 Low WTC
Total WTC	> 82 High Overall WTC
	< 52 Low Overall WTC

acquaintance by a friend. This notion of shyness is very similar to **communication apprehension**, which also refers to discomfort associated with communication. Communication apprehension is *the fear or anxiety associated with either real or anticipated communication with another person or persons*. The next chapter will deal solely with communication apprehension (CA). It is important to note that CA is but one factor associated with a person being less willing to communicate. Research on communication apprehension indicates that approximately two out of ten people (20 percent) experience such fear or anxiety. Communication apprehension is the most pervasive cause of communication avoidance.

So that there is no confusion, let's pause and distinguish carefully among the concepts of shyness, willingness to communicate, and communication apprehension.

1. "Shyness" refers to a person's behavioral tendency to not talk.
2. "Willingness to Communicate" refers to the person's general level of desire to initiate and respond to communication with others. WTC may be considered an attitude toward initiating and responding to communication, or as some prefer, the person's intent or disposition toward the behavior of initiating and responding to communication.
3. "Communication Apprehension" is the level of the person's fear or anxiety associated with either real or anticipated communication with another person or persons.

These concepts are interrelated in that it is presumed that if a person has high communication apprehension he or she will have a more negative attitude toward communication, and therefore will behave in ways that will be less likely to initiate communication with others. In contrast, if the person has low communication apprehension it is presumed that he/she will have a more positive predisposition toward communicating. The person will behave in ways that are more likely to instigate communication with others.

There are, of course, other possible causes of reduced willingness to communicate. Although each cause differs from the others in certain ways, one factor they all have in common is that each is believed to alter the individual's willingness to communicate. This is evidenced behaviorally by a reduced amount of talk. We devote the next section to a brief discussion of seven contributors to lowered willingness to communicate.

Factors Leading to Reduced WTC

The amount of communication in which people engage differs greatly from person to person. There are people who talk constantly no matter what the situation or with whom they are interacting (we will consider these compulsive communicators, or "talkaholics," later in this chapter). There are people who are constantly quiet from situation to situation, interaction to interaction. These are the people who are usually labeled shy. Although these people are much alike behaviorally in that they are low talkers, their reasons for being so may not be the same. There are at least seven reasons why people may prefer to communicate less: (1) hereditary factors, (2) childhood reinforcement, (3) skill deficiencies, (4) social introversion, (5) social alienation, (6) ethnic or cultural divergence, and (7) communication apprehension.

Hereditary Factors

You know that you have certain physical and emotional characteristics that you inherited from one or both of your natural parents. Perhaps you have your "mother's nose and your father's eyes." Maybe you share many of your father's physical traits but have a personality more similar to your mother's. That we do inherit certain personality traits from our parents is crucial to the notion that a predisposition for low talk can be hereditary. Although early researchers (including the authors of this book!) believed that heredity played little if any role in the development of communication behavior, contemporary studies of genetics involving twins have accumulated findings that suggest that a trait known as "sociability" probably is hereditary.

Sociability can be defined loosely as the degree to which people desire social contact with others. A person's level of sociability at a very early age appears to be associated with his or her sociability later in life. Much research in this area has compared the sociability levels of fraternal twins with those of identical twins (biologically identical). The general findings of this research show that identical twins are very similar in their sociability, but that fraternal twins are not as similar. These findings have important implications for the heredity notion because of how some studies were conducted. Some of the research was conducted on adult twins who had varied social experiences different from their siblings. The twins had often taken different life paths and developed relationships with different people in different environments. Although the identical twins had different social experiences, their predispositions for sociability remained similar. This suggests that environmental influences played less of a role in their sociability than did some hereditary trait.

This does not mean that heredity is the sole cause of sociability, much less of one's level of willingness to communicate. It can be concluded, however, that genetic predisposition probably is *one* contributing cause of individuals' general level of willingness to communicate. Research in this area is not yet extensive. Many questions remain to be answered before we have the full picture of exactly how genetic factors influence this aspect of one's personality. What is believed at this point is that genetic factors interact with a person's environment to determine that person's emotional and behavioral tendencies. Particularly important among environmental factors are the reinforcement patterns that an individual is exposed to, especially during childhood.

Childhood Reinforcement

You may be able to recall from your childhood instances when your parents praised you for talking in certain situations. You may recall when they ignored you or otherwise refused reinforcement for talking in other situations. What happened because of either of these instances? Chances are that if you were reinforced for talking, you talked more; if you were not reinforced for talking, you quit talking in some situations, or at least talked less. The latter very well may represent the experiences of many quiet adults when they were growing up. When you notice someone "acting shy" in a certain situation, it could be that as a child that individual received little or no reinforcement for talking in similar situations, or was punished for doing so. Moreover, it is even possible that the individual *was* reinforced for *not* talking. This occurs, for instance, when a younger sibling learns not to tell too much information about friends because an older, talkative brother was frequently prevented from visiting friends because he had told stories about behavior the parents found unacceptable.

Another type of reinforcement that might explain the development of shyness is *modeling*. The theory of modeling suggests that people observe the behavior of other people and then try to engage in that same behavior if they see the other person being rewarded for it. Many children observe their parents or other significant relatives engaging in low talk in certain situations, such as in church. The children too become low talkers in those situations, especially when the low talk is reinforced. Looking at it a different way, some children will model the talkative behavior of others, receive no reinforcement for such behavior, and because of that become less talkative.

Reinforcement offers a viable explanation for why many people are low talkers. However, like the heredity notion, research has not directly assessed the role of reinforcement in the development of this type of communicative behavior. We suggest, then, that reinforcement patterns in childhood likely contribute to one's level of willingness to communicate but are not the sole causal factor.

Skill Deficiencies

An interesting informal study was conducted at the University of Texas. In hypothetical situations, male college students were asked to act out the process they go through in telephoning a woman for a first date. Many men very easily picked up the phone, dialed a number, and portrayed a typical conversation. Others, however, had a very difficult time completing the task. Some could not even finish dialing the number before they gave up in total frustration. They were actually afraid to make the call. Their fear was not due to a lack of knowing the other party well, for there was no other party. Nor was it due to a fear of telephones, for the telephone used was a toy one. For the most part, the frustration and the fear experienced by these young men were due to a skill deficiency. They did not know how to ask a woman for a date!

Most of us have an inability to engage in certain activities. Some of us are poor singers. Some of us are unable to swim. Some of us could not dance if our lives depended on it. Many of us have no idea at all about how to drive a large truck or fly an airplane. Whenever we lack sufficient skills for performing a particular activity, we usually avoid situations that would require us to use those skills. Communicating is no different. As we noted earlier, communication is a learned process, a skill that is acquired through much practice and experience. Without that skill, many people become less willing to communicate and may be labeled "shy" by others with whom they come in contact.

Many problems of oral communication are considered skill deficiencies. Articulation problems, stuttering, voice impairments, and the like are just a few. In the United States, people who speak English as their first language often find communicating with Spanish-speaking people to be problematic. Whether the communication skills a person lacks are physical or linguistic, very often that individual is apt to be less willing to communicate in situations that demand use of those skills. Imagine taking a first course in conversational Cantonese (a Chinese dialect) in which the instructor presents all of the content to you in that language. Chances are quite high that you would withdraw from that course, to avoid failing it miserably. In short, some people become less willing to communicate not because they have no desire to communicate, but because they are inept in certain communication skills. If they can improve their skills, they would likely increase their attempts at communicating.

Social Introversion

Extroversion/introversion is a heavily researched area in the field of personality. It concerns the degree to which people desire to interact with others. Some people have a very strong need or desire to interact with others (social extroverts), and others prefer to be alone most of the time (social introverts). The people in the former group need frequent contact and communication with other people. Those in the latter group prefer their own company! It is people who fall in the latter group who are most likely to be less willing to communicate. This is not because they lack appropriate communication skills but because they perceive little need for interacting with others. People like this are quite apt to be labeled shy, but they usually are neither unskilled in communication nor apprehensive about it. They just do not have as much need for it as others do. Research suggests that extroversion/introversion is one of the central aspects of an individual's personality and that it probably is genetically linked.

Social Alienation

Most of us try to conform to the norms and values of our society. We complete some level of education because it is a norm in our society to do so. We make plans to be successful at our chosen careers, to raise a family, and to retire leisurely because these are high values for members of our society. People who conform to society's norms, whatever they may be, are said to be "well adjusted"—they do what society expects of them. People who do not conform to the norms and values of society, however, are said to be "alienated" from the society. They reject what society values and make few or no attempts to follow those values. Subsequently, they become *socially alienated*.

A norm of most societies, and especially of the general American society, is that of engaging in a moderate to high amount of communication with others. Although society values communication in its own right, it also deems communication necessary for the achievement of goals and other values. The socially alienated individual may reject the value of communication and become a low talker. This person simply does not see the value in communication to the extent that most of the rest of the people in society do. The individual's rejection of this value may be due to a lack of interest in attaining the goals and values that are sought by other members of society. Perhaps the individual dismisses the value of communication because he or she sees others using it in ways that are negative and inappropriate to the individual. When someone views communication in these ways, that person typically becomes much less willing to communicate.

Ethnic or Cultural Divergence

If someone were to ask you if people are the same in all parts of the country, how would you reply? Think about it for a moment. Are natives of Southern California any different from those born and raised in Indiana? Are the behaviors, customs, and values of Cornhuskers like those of people from Massachusetts? You probably don't have to think long to answer "no" to these questions. Within almost any large, well-developed culture like the general American culture, there are many subcultures and ethnic groups. Within the United States, we see cultural and ethnic divergence not only from one state to another but among different regions of a given state, and even among different neighborhoods within a given city. Communication norms in these various groupings are not alike; dialects are different; conversational rules are different; and some tend to value silence more than talk.

Even when people share a common language, sometimes it is difficult to adapt one's communicative behavior to the norms of a group with which one is unfamiliar. We may find that a common word is used with a different meaning or that a familiar gesture we use has no apparent meaning for others. The problem can arise whether it involves a person from a majority group entering a minority environment or a person from a minority group entering a majority environment. Moving across the country, to a different county in the same state, or just to a new neighborhood can present similar problems. In each situation, the outsider moving in may be unable to cope with the heavy demands of trying to communicate in a new environment and thus may become less willing to communicate. Consider a foreign student whom you know. You might think of the person as shy, but when that person is back home or with friends from her or his native culture he or she might be very talkative.

Communication Apprehension

The final cause of reduced willingness to communicate we want to discuss is, as we defined it earlier, *the fear or anxiety associated with either real or anticipated communication with another person or persons*. We will focus this discussion of communication apprehension on norms from the Personal Report of Communication Apprehension scale (figure 5.4). If you have not yet completed the PRCA scale, do so now so that you will know where you fall within the normative range of scores. To figure out your PRCA score, follow the steps noted in figure 5.5.

Although some people desire to communicate with others and see the importance of doing so, they may be impeded by their fear or anxiety. People who lack appropriate communication skills or whose communication is ethnically or culturally divergent may also develop communication apprehension. Most people who are communication apprehensive, however, are neither skill deficient nor different from others in the general culture. Typically, they are normal people who are simply afraid to communicate. Because it is natural for people to avoid things they fear, communication-apprehensive people tend to be less willing to communicate. Therefore, they may be labeled shy by others around them. It is important to note, also, that many communication-apprehensive people do not feel restricted by their feelings about communicating—they can be as happy and as productive as nonapprehensive communicators. Most of the social problems experienced by these individuals stem from how they are perceived by others and how others respond to them.

Your score on the PRCA scale should range between 24 and 120 (if it is below 24 or over 120, you have made a computational error). The PRCA scale is designed to measure a general trait of communication apprehension—how a person typically reacts to oral communication with others. The higher your score, the more apprehension you generally feel about communicating.

Between 60 percent and 70 percent of the people who have completed the PRCA scale have scores ranging from 50 to 80. This is called the "normal" range. If your score falls anywhere outside this range, the idea of communication apprehension may be especially relevant to you. If your score is between 24 and 50, you are among those in our society who experience the least communication apprehension. You are apt to

Figure 5.4
PRCA-24

DIRECTIONS: This instrument is composed of twenty-four statements concerning feelings about communicating with other people. Please indicate the degree to which each statement applies to you by marking whether you (1) strongly agree, (2) agree, (3) are undecided, (4) disagree, or (5) strongly disagree. Work quickly; record your first impression.

_____ 1. I dislike participating in group discussions.

_____ 2. Generally, I am comfortable while participating in group discussions.

_____ 3. I am tense and nervous while participating in group discussions.

_____ 4. I like to get involved in group discussions.

_____ 5. Engaging in a group discussion with new people makes me tense and nervous.

_____ 6. I am calm and relaxed while participating in group discussions.

_____ 7. Generally, I am nervous when I have to participate in a meeting.

_____ 8. Usually I am calm and relaxed while participating in meetings.

_____ 9. I am very calm and relaxed when I am called upon to express an opinion at a meeting.

_____ 10. I am afraid to express myself at meetings.

_____ 11. Communicating at meetings usually makes me uncomfortable.

_____ 12. I am very relaxed when answering questions at a meeting.

_____ 13. While participating in a conversation with a new acquaintance, I feel very nervous.

_____ 14. I have no fear of speaking up in conversations.

_____ 15. Ordinarily I am very tense and nervous in conversations.

_____ 16. While conversing with a new acquaintance, I feel very relaxed.

_____ 17. Ordinarily I am very calm and relaxed in conversations.

_____ 18. I'm afraid to speak up in conversations.

_____ 19. I have no fear of giving a speech.

_____ 20. Certain parts of my body feel very tense and rigid while I am giving a speech.

_____ 21. I feel relaxed while giving a speech.

_____ 22. My thoughts become confused and jumbled when I am giving a speech.

_____ 23. I face the prospect of giving a speech with confidence.

_____ 24. While giving a speech, I get so nervous I forget facts I really know.

Figure 5.5
Computing Score for PRCA-24

SCORING: To compute context subscores begin with a score of 18 for each context and follow the instructions below.

1. Group discussion—add scores for items 2, 4, & 6. Subtract scores for items 1, 3, & 5. Scores can range from 6 to 30.
2. Meetings—add scores for items 8, 9, & 12. Subtract scores for items 7, 10, & 11. Scores can range from 6 to 30.
3. Interpersonal—add scores for items 14, 16, & 17. Subtract scores for items 13, 15, & 18. Scores can range from 6 to 30.
4. Public speaking—add scores for items 19, 21, & 23. Subtract scores for items 20, 22, & 24. Scores can range from 6 to 30.

To compute the total score for the PRCA-24, add the four subscores. Total scores can range from 24 to 120. Scores above 80 = high CA; below 50 = low CA.

be a higher talker and may actively seek out opportunities to interact with others. Very few, if any, communication situations cause you to be fearful or anxious. If your score is somewhere between 50 and 60, you experience less communication apprehension than most people. However, you are likely to feel some fear or anxiety about a few situations. If your score falls between 60 and 70, your level of communication apprehension is similar to that of most people. There are some communication situations that may cause you to feel anxious or tense; in others you will feel quite comfortable. If your score is between 70 and 80, you experience more communication apprehension than most people. Probably many communication situations cause you to be fearful and tense, but some do not bother you. If your score falls between 80 and 120, you are among those who experience the most communication apprehension. You likely are a low talker, one who actively avoids many communication situations because you feel much anxiety and tension in those situations.

Let us examine a little more closely those who fall within the various score ranges on the PRCA scale. People in the "normal" range (50 to 80) tend to respond quite differently in different situations (for PRCA norms, see figure 5.6). They may be very tense in one situation (when giving a speech) but quite comfortable in another (when out on a date). Those who score in the "low" (below 50) and "high" (above 80) ranges tend to respond to most communication situations in the same way.

Researchers consider both extremes to be abnormal. The "low" communication-apprehensive person is considered abnormal because this person is unlikely to feel any fear or anxiety about communicating even in situations in which he or she *should* be anxious (for example, when entering his or her very first job interview). Although it is often an advantage not to be bothered by oral communication, it *is* also normal to feel some fear in response to a threatening situation. The person who experiences no fear in such situations usually makes poor decisions about when to communicate and when not to (therefore the expression, "insert foot in mouth"). The "high" communication apprehensive person is considered abnormal because this person usually experiences fear and anxiety about communicating—even in presumably non-threatening situations such as calling a friend on the phone. Such people are likely to avoid communication in many, even most, situations. This avoidance can be quite costly when communicating would be advantageous. A common example is the student who never participates in class discussion even when participation is a criterion for a higher grade.

In the next chapter, we discuss other aspects of communication apprehension, including the distinction between generalized communication apprehension and situation-specific communication apprehension. The causes and effects of communication apprehension will also be discussed.

Figure 5.6
Norms for the PRCA-24

	Mean	Standard Deviation
For Total Score	65.6	15.3
Group	15.4	4.8
Meeting	16.4	4.8
Dyad (Interpersonal)	14.5	4.2
Public	19.3	5.1

Talkaholics

Up to this point in this chapter we have primarily focused attention on one end of the willingness to communicate continuum. Despite brief references to the other end of the continuum, we may have created a dichotomy in your mind—an image of two kinds of people in the world—those who are "normal" and those who are "quiet." We do not want to go to the next chapter without modifying that image. Not all non-quiet people are "normal." Before we continue, please complete the scale in figure 5.7 and compute your score.

Figure 5.7
The Talkaholic Scale

DIRECTIONS: The questionnaire below includes sixteen statements about talking behavior. Please indicate the degree to which you believe each of these characteristics applies to you by marking, on the line before each item, whether you (5) strongly agree that it applies, (4) agree that it applies, (3) are undecided, (2) disagree that it applies, or (1) strongly disagree that it applies. There are no right or wrong answers. Work quickly; record your first impression.

_____ 1. Often I keep quiet when I know I should talk.
_____ 2. I talk more than I should sometimes.
_____ 3. Often, I talk when I know I should keep quiet.
_____ 4. Sometimes I keep quiet when I know it would be to my advantage to talk.
_____ 5. I am a "talkaholic."
_____ 6. Sometimes I feel compelled to keep quiet.
_____ 7. In general, I talk more than I should.
_____ 8. I am a compulsive talker.
_____ 9. I am not a talker; rarely do I talk in communication situations.
_____ 10. Quite a few people have said I talk too much.
_____ 11. I just can't stop talking too much.
_____ 12. In general, I talk less than I should.
_____ 13. I am *not* a "talkaholic."
_____ 14. Sometimes I talk when I know it would be to my advantage to keep quiet.
_____ 15. I talk less than I should sometimes.
_____ 16. I am *not* a compulsive talker.

SCORING: To determine your score on this scale, complete the following steps:

Step 1.   Add the scores for items 2, 3, 5, 7, 8, 10, 11, and 14.
Step 2.   Add the scores for items 13 and 16.
Step 3.   Complete the following formula:
            Talkaholic score = 12 + total from step 1 − total from step 2.

Have you ever known someone who talked too much? When we ask this question of groups to whom we talk, we find almost everyone will answer "yes" to this question. Our research, and that of others which stretches back for over a half-century, however, suggests that increased talking, up to a very high level, has nothing but positive outcomes. Thus, perceptions that someone talks too much must indicate a response to the quality of the talk of that person, not the quantity.

Does this mean there are no extremely high talkers out there? Of course not. We all know people who "never shut up." Someone in your family may fall into that category. We refer to these extremely high willing to communicate people as "talkaholics." They are compulsive communicators. They are driven to communicate. If you scored above 40 on the "Talkaholic Scale," welcome to the group! Our research suggests that about one person in twenty can be placed in this category.

Talkaholics generally recognize that they are compulsive communicators. They can't change, even if they want to—and very few, we have found, want to. In the general American culture, people are rewarded for being talkaholics much more often than they are punished. Talkaholics have told us repeatedly that their talking has gotten them in trouble. However, their solution to the problem has been to just keep on talking and get themselves out of that trouble!

Being a talkaholic can be detrimental for a person, as criminal talkaholics have found when they have been unable to keep quiet about their activities! It can also be an advantage to people in cultures which value communication highly (as the general American culture does). It can be particularly advantageous in occupations that require a great deal of contact with the public. Being able to maintain a constant stream of chatter can be highly profitable and rewarding in many occupations. We have found, for example, that the proportion of talkaholics in an audience of communication professors and graduate students at a national convention was almost five times as high as we have found in the general public! Could this be the reason why they were drawn to that profession?

Are these talkaholics the people we all recognize as the "people who talk too much?" The research in this area is still quite limited, so we cannot be certain. However, we think most talkaholics probably are not seen as excessive communicators, but some probably are. Some talkaholics are not skilled communicators, so they are more likely to engage in low quality communication behavior that would lead to negative perceptions. Also, to our surprise we found that there were almost the same proportion of talkaholics who are high communication apprehensives as there are who are low communication apprehensives. These apprehensive-but-compulsive communicators are trying to defeat their fear of communication by doing more of it. It is likely that many of them do not communicate all that well.

The range of willingness to communicate crosses a broad spectrum. It ranges from the excruciatingly quiet to the talkaholic, with most people being in the normal range in between. The level of an individual's willingness to communicate can have a major influence on that person's life. We will examine this impact in the next chapter.

References

Allen, J., Richmond, V. P., & McCroskey, J. C. (1984). Communication and the chiropractic profession III, *Journal of Chiropractic*, *21* (Nov.), 36–39.

Berger, B. A., Baldwin, H. J., McCroskey, J. C., & Richmond, V. P. (1983). Communication apprehension in pharmacy students: A national study. *American Journal of Pharmaceutical Education*, *47* (Summer), 95–102.

Buss, A. H. (1980). *Self-consciousness and social anxiety.* San Francisco: W. H. Freeman & Company Publishers.

McCroskey, J. C. (1984). The communication apprehension perspective. In J. A. Daly and J. C. McCroskey, *Avoiding communication: Shyness, reticence, and communication apprehension*, pp. 13–38. Beverly Hills: Sage.

_____. (1977). Oral communication apprehension: A summary of recent theory and research. *Human Communication Research*, *4*, 78–96.

_____. (1993). *An introduction to rhetorical communication* (6th ed.). Englewood Cliffs, NJ: Prentice-Hall.

McCroskey, J. C., & Richmond, V. P. (1982). Communication apprehension and shyness: Conceptual and operational distinctions. *Central States Speech Journal*, *33*, 458–468.

_____. (1987). Willingness to communicate. In J. C. McCroskey and J. A. Daly, *Personality and interpersonal communication*, pp. 129–156. Newbury Park, CA: Sage.

_____. (1993). Identifying compulsive communicators: The talkaholic scale. *Communication Research Reports*, *10*, 107–114.

_____. (November, 1994). *Correlates of compulsive communication: Quantitative and qualitative characterizations.* Paper presented at the annual convention of the Speech Communication Association, New Orleans, LA.

Pilkonis, P., Heape, C., & Klein, R. H. (1980). Treating shyness and other relationship difficulties in psychiatric outpatients. *Communication Education*, *29*, 250–255.

Richmond, V. P., & McCroskey, J. C. (1985). *Communication: Apprehension, avoidance, and effectiveness.* Scottsdale, AZ: Gorsuch Scarisbrick.

Zimbardo, P. G. (1977). *Shyness: What it is, what to do about it.* Reading, MA: Addison-Wesley.

COMMUNICATION APPREHENSION

6

It is most useful to think of communication apprehension (CA) as existing along a four-point continuum (see figure 6.1). Starting at one extreme end of the continuum and moving to the other extreme, the four points are communication apprehension: (1) as a trait, (2) in a generalized context, (3) with a given individual or group across contexts, and (4) with a given individual or group in a given situation. Each type of communication apprehension is examined below.

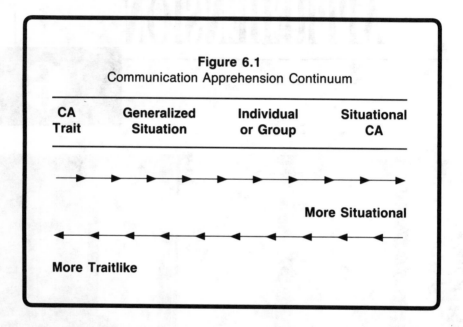

Figure 6.1
Communication Apprehension Continuum

CA Trait	Generalized Situation	Individual or Group	Situational CA

More Situational

More Traitlike

Communication Apprehension as a Trait

When we say "as a trait," we mean communication apprehension as a part of an individual's personality. Such a trait is most important for those people who have either very high or very low levels of communication apprehension. It is this trait that the total score on the PRCA scale was designed to measure. An extreme score on this measure suggests that your behavior is influenced as much, if not more, by your general fear or anxiety about communication as by any specifics of a communication situation in which you find yourself. At the extremes of the trait either you experience high degrees of anxiety in most communication situations, or you experience very little anxiety in most communication situations.

We should note at this point that from 15 percent to 20 percent of the population falls within each extreme category. Thus, if you score very low, or very high, on the PRCA scale, you are outside the normal range of scores where about two-thirds of the population score. At one end we have the people we call "high CAs" and at the other we have the "low CAs." Whenever we use these terms, or reference "moderate CA" (the normal range), we are referencing trait CA.

Communication Apprehension in Generalized Contexts

This view of communication apprehension recognizes those individuals who experience high levels of anxiety about communicating in a particular context or situation but who have much less or even no anxiety about communicating in other contexts. The PRCA scale, besides giving a measure of trait communication apprehension, can be broken down to yield measures of communication apprehension in four generalized contexts: talking within small groups, speaking in meetings or classroom situations, talking in dyadic interpersonal encounters, and presenting public speeches. To figure out your level of apprehension in each of these generalized contexts, compute the following formulas based on how you completed the PRCA:

Group CA = 18 + (Item 2 + Item 4 + Item 6 – Item 1 – Item 3 – Item 5)
Meeting CA = 18 + (Item 8 + Item 9 + Item 12 – Item 7 – Item 10 – Item 11)
Dyadic CA = 18 + (Item 14 + Item 16 + Item 17 – Item 13 – Item 15 – Item 18)
Public Speaking CA = 18 + (Item 19 + Item 21 + Item 23 – Item 20 – Item 22 – Item 24)

For these scales, a score above 18 is high, and a score above 23 shows an extremely high level of communication apprehension about that generalized context. It is quite possible for you to score very high in one context but relatively low in another or even all of the others. If this is the case, it indicates you are highly apprehensive about some but not all generalized contexts.

Perhaps you scored high on the measure for group communication but low on the others. Here, you feel apprehensive about communicating in situations in which you find yourself involved in a small group. Two types of groups are important here. One type is the task-oriented group. This type of group in which the participants get together for solving one or more problems (for example, a group of students who meet to study for an exam). The other type of small group is the social group, the type that is formed for enjoyment, amusement, and/or sharing friendship.

A person could feel apprehensive about communicating in either type of group for many reasons. Perhaps the person feels that other group members are too critical of her or his ideas or suggestions. Perhaps the person feels that her or his own contributions aren't important to the other members. Alternatively, the person's attitude could be: More than two people can't carry on a meaningful and effective oral exchange, so why get involved? For the person who is highly apprehensive in small-group contexts but not in others, there is simply some aspect of small-group situations that causes the individual much discomfort when participating in them.

You might have a higher level of communication apprehension in a meeting than in other situations. Meetings are similar to the group situation. Here the group is larger, and communication among participants is relatively formal and stylized. A good analogy is the typical college classroom. You may be very talkative when with your friends, when on a date, or even when meeting a new acquaintance. The formal structure of the classroom, combined with the pressure of having to display your knowledge orally, may cause you much anxiety in that context. Most people can communicate quite openly and easily when they feel free to say what they want when they want to say it. When they confront a context such as a classroom or committee meeting where communication is restricted by explicit rules, they can become very apprehensive.

If your level of communication apprehension is higher for dyadic interpersonal contexts than for the others, you experience anxiety when interacting with others on a one-on-one basis. There are several interpersonal contexts in which one might feel highly apprehensive about communicating. One context is when someone is interacting with a peer. The person may be so concerned with trying to make a good impression that it leads to much tension and anxiety. Another interpersonal context in which many people feel anxious is in interacting with a teacher. The individual may be very talkative in class. However when facing a teacher one-on-one, the person experiences anxiety because of uncertainty about how to react to the teacher or about how the teacher might respond. A third anxiety-producing dyadic context is that involving encounters with the opposite sex. Some people approach communication with the opposite sex with confidence. Others, however, because of past negative experiences or anticipated negative consequences, find communicating with the opposite sex to be quite traumatic. This is precisely the feeling experienced by the male college students in the telephone experiment mentioned in the previous chapter. Their lack of appropriate communicative skills had resulted in enough "failures" for them that even pretending to call a female for a date caused them much apprehension.

Have you ever interviewed for a job? How did you feel about it as the time grew nearer? If you have never had an interview, how does anticipating that time make you feel? Feeling some anxiety about such interpersonal situations puts you in the majority. A job interview, particularly the first one, is a very strange and novel experience, and few people really know how to deal with it. Communication is the key to a successful interview. Specifically, what kind of communication? Being uncertain and fearful about what to say in a job interview and how to respond to the interviewer can result in high levels of communication apprehension in those contexts. Many people feel apprehensive when communicating with their supervisors at work. This feeling may stem from a need to make a good impression on the supervisor. Perhaps it stems from a fear of having the ideas one puts forth to the supervisor explicitly rejected. Conversely, many supervisors have a high level of anxiety about communicating with subordinates. Their apprehension could stem from anticipating complaints about how matters involving subordinates are being handled. Their apprehension could stem from not having the information subordinates want or need to carry out their jobs in an effective way. Whether the situation is formal or informal, whether it involves friends or strangers or people of equal or different status, many individuals find dyadic interpersonal contexts to be very anxiety-producing.

Public speaking is the generalized context which causes the most problems for the most people. In fact, several national studies have indicated that the fear of public speaking is the number one fear of Americans. Public speaking places you in a conspicuous position in front of others who will be evaluating you and critically evaluating what you say. Many people have little experience and little or no training in effective speech making. Thus, it is not surprising that so many people find this context threatening.

Communication Apprehension with a Given Individual or Group across Contexts

Let us now examine communication apprehension experienced because of interacting with a specific individual or group in *any* context. Nearly 95 percent of the population reports having felt apprehension at least once in their lives when communicating with some specific person or group. It is not the communication context that triggers the problem, it is the other people!

Some people simply cause us to be apprehensive. It may be a parent, a teacher, a certain salesperson, the IRS agent, or the principal or the boss. This anxiety may be a function of how others behave toward us (for example, "Bring home an F, and you're on your own!"), or perhaps the role they play in our life (''Hello. I'm here to audit your tax returns for the past five years''). For most of us there is someone we know who makes us feel totally relaxed when interacting with her or him. It also is quite normal for us to find talking with some specific person or group to be anxiety-producing. Do you feel most comfortable talking with a friend? A relative? Do you feel least comfortable talking to a police officer? A doctor?

Communication Apprehension with a Given Individual or Group in a Given Situation

Virtually 100 percent of us experience communication apprehension with a given individual or group in a given situation. Most of the examples we can think of seem extreme. For example, you have to apologize to a friend for offending that person; you arrive home to find a message that tells you your date has had a last-minute change of heart; a teacher confronts you after class with the accusation that you have been cheating. What separates communication apprehension in these situations from the other forms of communication apprehension is that these situations are unique encounters with a specific individual. Thus, although we generally would not be apprehensive about communicating with the other person, the specific situation arouses anxiety. Most of us can communicate quite easily with our mothers, but forgetting Mom's birthday can lead to quite a hair-raising communicative event.

Communication apprehension, therefore, is a fear or anxiety about communicating that can stem from one's basic personality, the type of communication expected, the person or persons with whom we anticipate communicating, or from the unique circumstances surrounding a given interaction. No matter its source, communication apprehension causes us discomfort, may result in our avoiding communication, and can result in our being ineffective in our communication with others.

Causes of Communication Apprehension

Traitlike communication apprehension is thought to be a matter of personality. Thus, the causes of this type of communicative anxiety are much like those of any personality variable; namely, it is a function of either the environment or genetic factors, or most likely a combination of the two. The discussion that follows focuses on potential environmental causes of generalized apprehension. As for situational communication apprehension (the last three forms delineated in the previous section), many causes are possible. Some of these have to do with the nature of specific interactions, the relationships between the participants in the interaction, and past experience—all functions of the environment.

Generalized Communication Apprehension

Research has failed to find out with absolute certainty the causes of traitlike communication apprehension. The best that research has been able to do is show statistical correlations between communication apprehension and theoretically proposed ''causes.'' One particular theory, however, does permit a causal explanation of generalized communication apprehension because it takes into account both personality traits and situational constraints. The theory is *expectancy learning*, or, more specifically, a type of expectancy learning known as *learned helplessness*.

The underlying assumption of expectancy learning, as applied to communication apprehension, is that people develop expectations about other people and situations and about the probable outcomes of communication with those people and/or in those situations. A person develops confidence in his or her communication to the extent that such expectations are fulfilled. When expectations are not met, the individual develops a need to form new expectations. If expectations continually are not met, the person may develop a lack of confidence. Anxiety is produced when no appropriate expectations can be formed. Fear is produced when expectations lead to negative outcomes that are difficult or impossible to avoid. These two occurrences are the foundation of communication apprehension, according to expectancy learning theory.

An example will illustrate this point. Kelly has recently made a new acquaintance, Marty. At their first meeting, Kelly was quite attracted to Marty and felt the interest was reciprocal. After crossing paths a few more times, she was certain that Marty liked her and that he would soon call. At this point Kelly has formed two expectations: (1) Marty liked her, and (2) he was likely to ask her out. After many more meetings, Kelly begins to wonder why Marty has not called her. Later, at a dance, Kelly sees Marty with another woman and discovers that they have been dating for several weeks. At this point Kelly develops a lack of confidence in her predictions about Marty and his feelings for her. Having failed to form any appropriate expectations about their actual and potential relationship, Kelly becomes anxious about her interactions with the opposite sex. Were this to happen to Kelly with several different male acquaintances, she could very well develop a fear of interacting with them. Subsequently, we might estimate that Kelly will become apprehensive about communicating with males.

The example of Kelly is greatly oversimplified and perhaps overdramatized. The process portrayed would require a great amount of time and more than one relationship and situation. It does help to illustrate, however, how expectations can serve to heighten apprehension about communication. Regularity of appropriate expectations is the key. Our most general expectation is to have regularity in our environment. We expect to be reinforced for some behaviors and not reinforced for others. Reinforcement, or the lack of it, is the outcome we learn to expect by continually engaging in certain behaviors over time and across situations. From this process, three things can happen: (1) we develop new positive expectations; (2) we develop new negative expectations, or (3) we become helpless.

When we engage in communicative behaviors that work (that is, we receive reinforcement for them), we develop *positive expectations* for those behaviors. They become a regular part of our communicative "storehouse." Had Marty called Kelly for a date, she would have developed positive expectations for her communicative behavior that led to the date. She would have continued engaging in them since Marty reinforced them. Neither anxiety nor fear is associated with such positive expectations. *Negative expectations* are developed in much the same way as positive expectations. We discover that some communicative behaviors lead to punishment or lack of reinforcement, and we tend to reduce those behaviors. This is where we left Kelly. Marty offered no reinforcement for how Kelly communicated with him (at least as she saw it). Thus, she began to question the appropriateness of her behavior. The next time she meets a new potential date, having no other behaviors readily available from which to choose, Kelly's fear will be her natural response.

Learned helplessness results from irregular or inconsistent reward and punishment. Perhaps the last young man Kelly met was very responsive to her, and they had a good relationship for quite some time. Now Marty comes along and offers no reinforcement for her behaviors. If this inconsistency were to occur through several relationships for Kelly, and were she unable to determine the appropriate (reinforced) behaviors from the inappropriate, she would become literally "helpless" in her relationships with males. Learned helplessness and negative expectations are the primary components of communication apprehension. The more general the helplessness or negative expectations, the more traitlike the apprehension. In other words, if an individual constantly forms negative expectations about and becomes helpless in her or his communication with others, the more likely he or she is to have communication apprehension as a trait.

Situational Communication Apprehension

The causes of situational communication apprehension appear clear. Buss (1980) has provided a useful exposition of the major elements in the situation that he believes can lead to communication apprehension. They are novelty, formality, subordinate status, conspicuousness, unfamiliarity, dissimilarity, and excessive attention from others. Additionally, Daly and Hailey (1983) suggest that high evaluation and previous failure can cause situational communication apprehension. Each of these elements is discussed in the following paragraphs.

Recall your first day alone at college. Did you find it a difficult situation to deal with initially? If so, it was probably because college was a *novel*, or new, experience for you. Novel situations present us with increased uncertainty about how we should behave: the first date; a new job; meeting a dating partner's parents. Approaching each of these untested situations is very likely to increase communication apprehension.

We behave much differently than normal when we dress in formal attire and attend some auspicious occasion. *Formal situations* are associated with highly prescribed behaviors. In these situations, the prescribed behaviors are deemed ''appropriate,'' and there is little latitude for deviation from them. Because of the narrower restrictions placed on acceptable behavior in formal situations, communication apprehension is likely to increase in such situations. The same is true when we interact from a *subordinate position*. In these situations, the person holding higher status defines what is appropriate behavior. Examples are seen in teacher-student, employer-employee, parent-child interactions, and the like.

Have you attended a family reunion? You probably experienced having all your aunts and uncles, many of whom you do not even know, gawk and fuss over you. Were you embarrassed? Perhaps more than anything else, being *conspicuous* in one's environment sharply increases communication apprehension. This is precisely what causes your fear when you rise to give a speech or accept an award, stand to make a comment in a meeting or crowded classroom, or when you are introduced for the first time to a long line of distant relatives.

How do you feel when you attend a large party where you know perhaps only one or two people? Do you find yourself standing alone in a corner just waiting for someone to come over and begin a conversation? Many people feel much more comfortable when communicating with people they know than when communicating with people they do not know. Generally, the more *unfamiliar* the people around us, the more likely our communication apprehension will rise. In much the same way, *dissimilarity* of those around us causes communication apprehension to increase. For most of us, talking to people who are similar to us is easier than talking to people who are greatly different. If you are a social sciences major, try carrying on a conversation with a diehard engineering major. If you are a science major, try talking to an English major. You may find the conversation very difficult to maintain. There are exceptions, of course. Some people are less comfortable when talking to people like themselves than when talking to people who are very different, or even strangers. This is because the former is more likely to make evaluations about us that may prove threatening.

Most of us do not like to be stared at. Neither do we care to be ignored by others. A moderate degree of attention from others is usually the most comfortable situation. *Excessive attention*, such as staring or having someone probe into our private thoughts, can cause our level of communication apprehension to rise sharply.

Many students have little trouble conversing with their teachers, until the teacher begins *evaluating* the student's classroom performance. The same holds true for workers in relation to their supervisors. When we are evaluated, we tend to become more anxious than we would otherwise. As the intensity of the evaluation increases, so might the level of apprehension. Research done on apprehension associated with writing suggests an exception to this possibility, however. Daly and Hailey (1983) have found that high evaluation improves the performance of good writers but worsens the performance of poor writers. We can speculate that the same holds true for oral communication, but no research has substantiated that speculation yet.

Finally, of all the causal elements of communication apprehension discussed, the most important may be previous failure. When we fail at something once, we will probably fear failing again. It is a case of expectations. If we expect to fail and do so, the negative expectations are reinforced. If we are unable to decide the successful behavior to engage in, we are quite apt to develop apprehension. Of course, success causes confidence, which leads to more success—and thus reduces apprehension.

To summarize, many elements are tied to the communication situation that appear to increase communication apprehension. It is important to note, however, that the absence of these elements is presumed to *decrease* communication apprehension. Few if any of these elements are under our direct control. Situational communication apprehension is often controlled by others in our environment: a required class presentation, an interview to obtain a job, asking for time off. The only way to deter the unpleasant aspects of this form of communication apprehension is to avoid or withdraw from anxiety-producing communication situations. As we will see in the next section, avoidance and withdrawal from interaction are two of the many effects of communication apprehension.

While all of the above seems obvious and straightforward, more recent research has raised serious questions about how much impact these variables in the situation really have. Research by Beatty (1988; Beatty & Friedland, 1989) has shown that people's presumed responses to situations actually are more traitlike than situation-produced. People who tend to be sensitive to evaluation, for example, see all situations as more evaluative than people who do not have this trait. People who tend to be sensitive to conspicuousness report feeling more conspicuous than do other people, no matter how conspicuous they really are.

What is making these "obvious" causes of situational communication apprehension appear obvious is that both experts and normal people are susceptible to what is known as "basic attribution error." This phenomenon is discussed in more detail in chapter 10. Here it is sufficient to note that we prefer to attribute our negative feelings and behaviors to situational matters beyond our control than to our own traits and emotions. It is, therefore, not surprising that when we try to explain why we are fearful or anxious that we seek "obvious" and reasonable external factors to blame rather than admit to a failing of our own, small though it may be.

Effects of CA and WTC

In the previous chapter, we discussed the nature of willingness to communicate and the potential causes of WTC. In this chapter we have looked at communication apprehension as but one form or cause of shyness and considered its probable causes as well. Now we want to focus on the effects of communication apprehension and willingness to communicate. This is an important section. Although we have discussed some of the differences between low talkers and high talkers, here we want to emphasize the consequences of the specific individual and social behaviors of quiet and apprehensive people.

Communication Apprehension

The most obvious effects of communication apprehension are internal discomfort, avoidance or withdrawal from communication situations, and communication disruption. People experience communication apprehension internally. That is, the experience of communication apprehension is a mental one—it is felt psychologically. Thus, while some individuals may experience communication apprehension to greater or lesser degrees than other individuals, or only with certain people or in certain situations, the one thing people all share when anxious about communicating is an internally experienced feeling of discomfort. Typically, the lower our communication apprehension, the lower our discomfort.

People tend to differ in their individual responses to communication apprehension. Some handle it well and can communicate effectively despite their internal discomfort. For most people who experience communication apprehension, however, particularly high levels of it, communication is a problem. Three typical response patterns emerge when communication apprehension is experienced: communication avoidance, communication withdrawal, and communication disruption.

When people are confronted with a situation that they expect will make them uncomfortable and they have a choice of whether to enter the situation, they can decide to either confront the situation and make the best of it or avoid it and thus avoid the discomfort. An analogy is the student who receives poor midterm grades and decides not to go home for spring break. By not going home, the student avoids the discomfort of having to face Mom and Dad's wrath about the grades (this assumes, of course, that the student has a choice of whether to go home). Frequently, people with high communication apprehension will avoid situations that require them to communicate orally with others.

It is not always possible for a person to avoid communication. Sometimes there is no reason to expect a situation to cause discomfort, so a person may enter it with her or his psychological guard down. When situations such as these arise, withdrawal is the typical response for the person experiencing communication apprehension. The withdrawal may be total (such as absolute silence) or partial (such as talking only when absolutely necessary). An example of possible withdrawal is the student who speaks in class only when directly called upon by the teacher. Another is when a person in a one-on-one interaction only answers questions and gives responses but never initiates conversation. When unable to avoid a communication situation, the communication-apprehensive person usually will withdraw from interaction, if possible.

A third typical response to communication apprehension is communication disruption. This disruption can take two forms. One form is disturbed or nonfluent communication. Examples are stuttering, stammering, speaking too softly, increased pauses, use of inappropriate gestures and expressions, and poor choices of words and phrases. The other form of disruption is overcommunication. This is an over-compensation reflected in one's attempt to succeed in the situation despite the internal discomfort it causes. An example is the person who, in spite of her or his apprehension, attempts to dominate interactions with others, refuses to acknowledge cues that others want to leave, or tries to answer every question a teacher poses in a class. Thus, the highly communication-apprehensive individual is likely to use inappropriate behaviors in a discomforting communication situation. It is important to note, however, that disruption is also characteristic of people with inadequate communication skills and that overcommunication is often mistaken for low apprehension.

Willingness to Communicate

Willingness to communicate produces important effects only if the person's WTC impacts his or her behavior. People who have a low level of WTC are most likely to exhibit shy behavior. That is, they initiate fewer communicative interactions and respond less positively to others who attempt to initiate interaction with them. The effects of low WTC, then, can best be considered by first looking at the differences in behavior exhibited by people with low WTC versus high WTC and then, in the next section, reviewing perceptions other people have about people with low WTC.

We turn first to the quiet person's behavior in the classroom, in small groups, in dyads, in social situations, and in occupational choice. Again, when we refer to quiet people we are thinking of low talkers, people who exhibit a low level of WTC. Thus, the behaviors and perceptions discussed below apply equally to people who are low in WTC because they have high communication apprehension and to others who are low in WTC for different reasons.

The typical U.S. classroom environment demands a high level of communication. Much research has focused on how low and high talkers differ in their classroom behavior. Low talkers, particularly communication-apprehensive people, avoid small classes in which there are many opportunities for student-student and student-instructor interaction. They prefer large lecture-type classes in which most communication is the instructor talking to students, and the students remaining quiet and listening. Low talkers avoid classes that require oral reports or speeches and in which part of the grade is based on "class participation." When they must be in such a class, they almost never volunteer to participate, choosing to wait until they are called upon by the teacher. Low talkers often will drop a class that has high communication demands, even if it is a required course. Finally, low talkers differ from high talkers in their preference for seating in the classroom. When given a choice of where to sit, low talkers will choose to sit along the sides or in the rear of the classroom. This is because most interaction takes place in the front and down the middle of the room.

Although a small-group setting is not as threatening to most people as, say, a public speaking setting, it still places great communication demands on the participants. Typically, the low talker will avoid small-group interactions. When avoidance is not possible, withdrawal occurs in several forms. The low talker may withdraw from group discussion by remaining quiet. If required to speak, low talkers will often make irrelevant comments, apparently hoping that this will get other group members to stop asking them questions. When questioned in a group setting, the favored response of many low talkers is a simple "I don't know." Finally, as in the classroom, low takers will choose seats in a group setting that inhibit their interaction with other members. They will avoid seats at the head or foot of the table and choose inconspicuous seats along the side.

As in other settings, communication in dyads (one-on-one interactions) differs sharply for low and high talkers. In general, low talkers take on a submissive, follower role in dyadic encounters. They refrain from saying much about themselves to their partner, but they have a high concern that their partner understands or agrees with what they have to say. The latter is evidenced in the low talker's heavy use of "trailers" such as "you know?", "OK?", and "you see?"

High talkers tend to involve themselves in more social activities and situations than do low talkers. Low talkers tend to engage in much more steady dating than do high talkers. That is, low talkers are more likely to have an exclusive relationship than are high talkers. This tendency toward exclusive relationships is also seen in the marital behavior of low talkers. In one study, over 50 percent of the low talkers (here, communication apprehensives) married within one year after completing their undergraduate degrees. No similar pattern was found for high talkers. What these behavioral tendencies suggest is that low talkers find it difficult to establish social relationships, so they make very strong efforts to maintain ones they can establish. High talkers apparently find the establishment of relationships to be not so difficult. Thus, they are more apt to allow established ones to end and look forward to beginning new ones.

Finally, it is important to consider the differences between low talkers and high talkers in their choices of occupations. The choice of an occupation is one of the most significant decisions one can make. It determines whether the person will be successful, what the person's social and economic standing will be, and, to a large extent, whether the person will be happy in later life. Many factors influence one's selection of an occupation, but one important factor is the person's willingness to communicate. Low talkers tend to choose occupations with lower communication demands than those chosen by high talkers. Thus, low talkers are more likely to select occupations such as forest ranger, auto mechanic, accountant, and lab technician. High talkers may lean more toward salesperson, trial lawyer, telephone operator, and broadcast journalist. What about teaching as an occupation? Interestingly, research has found that teachers who are low talkers prefer the lower elementary grades and preschool to secondary and college teaching. This may be because teaching young children is less likely to garner direct social and professional evaluation from students than does teaching older children and adults.

In summary, the effects of willingness to communicate on communicative behavior are most apparent in the differences in the behaviors of low talkers compared with high talkers. Generally, low talkers will avoid any communication situation that they anticipate will result in discomfort. They will avoid taking classes that place high demands on communication. They will avoid small-group interactions whenever possible. They will avoid self-disclosure and disagreement in dyadic situations; they will avoid ending established relationships; and they will avoid occupations that require a high level of communication. When avoidance is impossible, low talkers typically will withdraw from the communication situation.

It is important to realize these are typical response tendencies of people with low willingness to communicate and particularly highly communication-apprehensive persons. However, some people who are highly willing to communicate will also engage in these behaviors on occasion. All people who have low levels of willingness to communicate do not engage in the same avoidance behaviors. We noted above that some will choose to confront rather than avoid the demands of a discomforting situation and try to overcome it. Therefore, we should exercise caution when observing the behavior of others. For instance, just because an individual is quiet in the classroom does not mean that person is highly apprehensive; he or she may be a heavy daydreamer or an uninterested student.

This brings us directly to a consideration of some perceptions others have of shy and communication-apprehensive people. We first look at people's general perceptions of low talkers in terms of their attractiveness, competence, anxiety, and leadership. Next we look at how low talkers are perceived in three specific settings—school, social, and work.

Perceptions about Quiet People

As we noted earlier, our society places a great deal of importance on communication. It is no surprise, then, that low talkers are usually perceived as unfriendly. Therefore, low talkers are viewed as less attractive than are talkative people. Moreover, even low talkers perceive other low talkers to be less attractive than talkative persons.

Low talkers are perceived as less competent than talkative people. Research has found people to have a stereotype of a quiet person as less competent and less intelligent. Fortunately, this is only a stereotype.

We say this is fortunate because stereotypes do not hold true for all members of a group. There are just as many intelligent low talkers as there are intelligent high talkers. Nevertheless, the general perception of low talkers is that they are less competent and less intelligent.

A frequently accurate perception of low talkers is that they are generally more anxious than talkative people. Although not all low talkers are apprehensive about communication, many are. Their tendency for apprehension is generalized to other low talkers. This leads to another stereotype: that low talkers are anxious people.

The role of leader in most situations requires at least a moderate degree of communication with other people. Thus, low talkers are perceived to be poor leaders. This perception is very often correct. There are, of course, instances in which quiet people provide leadership functions. For example, they might provide some necessary information that helps a group reach a decision. However, even in these situations the low talker is unlikely to be perceived as a leader.

Perceptions such as the ones just presented are important for several reasons. How we perceive people determines the nature of our relationship with them. In addition, how we perceive people will have a significant impact on our interactions with them in certain settings. Three of these settings—school, social, and work—are our final concern in this chapter.

School

The perception of low talkers as less competent and less intelligent than talkative people greatly affects how they are responded to in school. For example, since teachers tend to expect low talkers to do less well in school, they treat low talkers as if they were less intelligent. Low talkers are less likely to be called upon in class, receive less attention from teachers, and ask for help less frequently than do talkative people. Therefore, with so little interaction, the low talker has fewer opportunities to correct mistakes and to receive reinforcement. Does this affect their achievement? Research suggests that it does. Take for example the classroom in which much of the final grade depends on "participation." Because the low talker is less likely to participate in class activities, this student's grade is apt to be lower than that of talkative students. As this type of evaluation affects the low-talking student's achievement throughout school, it ultimately has an impact on the student's general learning. Lack of opportunity and even discrimination lead to less learning for the low talker in the long run, although the low talker is no less intelligent than the talkative person. In short, low talkers tend to fare poorly in school while talkative people tend to fare well.

Social

Social relationships require communication for their establishment and maintenance. Typically, when someone doesn't want to talk with us, we disregard that person and move on to someone else. As we noted earlier, low talkers are perceived as less friendly and less attractive than talkative people. Low talkers have fewer dating relationships than talkative people and, to some extent, they have fewer people whom they can call "friends." In one study that asked high communication apprehensives and low communication apprehensives to indicate how many people they knew that they could classify as "good friends," the high apprehensives indicated a range from 0 to 2, with more than one-third indicating none. More interesting was the finding that, when asked to list the names of their good friends, the high apprehensives most often named relatives while the low apprehensives seldom listed relatives. Just as in school, then, it seems that low talkers tend to fare less well in the general social environment than do talkative people.

Work

The many perceptions people have of low talkers are perhaps most felt in the work setting. Low talkers are less likely than talkative people to be given job interviews, especially when their qualifications are equal. Even when an interview is granted, the low talker will garner negative perceptions from the interviewer because of her or his likelihood of engaging in dysfunctional communication behaviors. This is not to suggest that low talkers never get job interviews or obtain employment. Most do. It is much harder for them than it is for talkative people. Similarly, low talkers and talkative people are not equally successful once employment is gained. Research in a variety of occupations has found low talkers to be less satisfied with their jobs than are more talkative people. The most dramatic work-related difference between low talkers and high talkers, however, appears at promotion time. Not only are low talkers less frequently promoted than more talkative persons, but they often report not anticipating or even wanting to be promoted. This is because promotions to higher positions typically require greater communicative responsibilities. In short, then, as in the school setting and social environments, life at work seems much more difficult for low talkers than it is for more talkative people.

To summarize this section, low talkers tend to be perceived by most people quite differently from the ways in which talkative people tend to be perceived. Generally, low talkers are seen as less attractive, less competent, more anxious, and less qualified for leadership roles. These perceptions carry over into various aspects of everyday life, where perceived differences between low and high talkers abound. The low talker is less successful in school, has difficulty forming interpersonal relationships, and has difficulty obtaining and retaining employment. The talkative person, on the other hand, tends to be successful in the school environment, to find it easy to establish relationships, and to be successful in the world of work.

People have perceptions about low talkers as incompetent and therefore in a highly undesirable condition. Is this necessarily true? Fortunately, it is not. As noted at the outset of this chapter, many quiet people are most happy and content with their lives. Many are successful at what they do. When offered help to overcome communication apprehension, many quiet people decline. Many have adjusted well to their lifestyle and have no desire to change. Nevertheless, people who are highly willing to communicate and happily engage in communication with others generally have a major advantage in this culture over those less willing to communicate.

This chapter's goal was to make you aware of and help you to understand not only the nature and causes of communication apprehension but also what effects CA and WTC have on communication behaviors and the resulting perceptions of others. Our focus has been mainly on the source in the communication process. Willingness to communicate can be a dominant force in a source's behavior. This is particularly true when a source's low willingness to communicate is generalized, or traitlike. In such cases, any communication situation may cause discomfort for a source. As a result, the person is likely to avoid the situation or withdraw from it if he or she cannot avoid it. Perhaps at worst, an inability to avoid or withdraw will lead the source to engage in dysfunctional communication. Essentially, if communication is dysfunctional for the source it will be dysfunctional for the receiver, resulting in an ineffective encounter.

We hope that this chapter and the previous one have communicated a sense of how important willingness to talk is to human communication. It is central to the **outcomes** of communication. Through talk we realize the fulfillment of our expectations for a given communication situation. Through talk we reduce the uncertainties we have about various situations, other people, and ourselves. Through talk we establish, maintain, and, when necessary, terminate relationships. Too little talk is usually an inappropriate form of communication. Too much talk can be too, but if the quality of that talk is high, it probably will not be perceived as too much. The effective source is one who knows when to talk, when to be silent, and what are appropriate responses to both from another person.

References

Beatty, M. J. (1988). Situational and predispositional correlates of public speaking anxiety. *Communication Education, 37,* 29–39.

Beatty, M. J., & Friedland, M. H. (1989). Public speaking state anxiety as a function of selected situational and predispositional variables. *Communication Education, 38,* 142–147.

Beatty, M. J., Balfantz, G. L., & Kuwabara, A. Y. (1989). Trait-like qualities of selected variables assumed to be transient causes of performance state anxiety. *Communication Education, 38,* 227–289.

Buss, A. H. (1980). *Self-consciousness and social anxiety.* San Francisco: W. H. Freeman & Company Publishers.

Daly, J. A., & Hailey, J. L. (1983). Putting the situation into writing research: Situational parameters of writing apprehension as disposition and state. In R. E. Beach & L. Bidwell (Eds.), *New directions in composition research.* New York: Guilford.

McCroskey, J. C. (1993). *An introduction to rhetorical communication* (6th ed.). Englewood Cliffs, NJ: Prentice-Hall.

_____. (1992). Reliability and validity of the willingness to communicate scale. *Communication Quarterly, 40,* 16–25.

_____. (1984). The communication apprehension perspective. In J. A. Daly and J. C. McCroskey (Eds.), *Avoiding communication: Shyness, reticence, and communication apprehension,* pp. 13–38. Beverly Hills: Sage Publications.

_____. (1977). Oral communication apprehension: A summary of recent theory and research. *Human Communication Research, 4,* 78–96.

_____. (1972). The implementation of a large-scale program of systematic desensitization for communication apprehension. *Speech Teacher, 21,* 255–264.

_____. (1970). Measures of communication-bound anxiety. *Speech Monographs, 37,* 269–277.

Phillips, G. M. (1981). *Help for shy people.* Englewood Cliffs, NJ: Prentice-Hall.

Pilkonis, P., Heape, C., & Klein, R. H. (1980). Treating shyness and other relationship difficulties in psychiatric outpatients. *Communication Education, 29,* 250–255.

Richmond, V. P., Beatty, M. J., & Dyba, P. (1985). Shyness and popularity: Children's views. *Western Journal of Speech Communication, 49,* 116–125.

Richmond, V. P., & McCroskey, J. C. (1985). *Communication: Apprehension, avoidance, and effectiveness.* Scottsdale, AZ: Gorsuch-Scarisbrick.

Zimbardo, P. G. (1977). *Shyness: What it is, what to do about it.* Reading, MA: Addison-Wesley.

COMMUNICATION COMPETENCE

7

When we refer to someone as "communicatively competent," we are suggesting that the person has "adequate ability to make ideas known to others by talking or writing" (McCroskey, 1984, p. 263). This is communication competence at its most basic level. It ignores feelings, attitudes, and behavior—focusing simply on being understood.

Basic communication competence depends on at least three elements: a cognitive understanding of the communication process, the psychomotor capacity to produce necessary communication behaviors, and a positive affective orientation toward communication. To put it more simply, to achieve basic communication competence, you must develop an understanding of what you need to do, develop the physical behaviors required to do it (learn to write, articulate words, and so forth), and want to do it.

If you are reading this book, you most likely have developed a sufficient repertoire of psychomotor behaviors for many kinds of oral communication, although you may lack skills for certain types of communication. You may or may not have a positive attitude toward communication. Thus, the greatest need you probably had when you began this book was the development of a greater cognitive understanding of the communication process. Many of the chapters in this book are directed primarily toward helping you meet that need.

Unfortunately, basic communication competence is not enough. Most of us do not simply want to be understood by others. We also want them to like us, we want to build relationships with them, and frequently we want to influence them. In short, we want to be *interpersonally* communicatively competent. Interpersonal communication competence rests on a foundation of general communication competence. In addition, the interpersonally competent communicator exhibits three critical elements in her or his communication: assertiveness, responsiveness, and versatility.

Before we go on, turn to figure 7.1 and complete the Socio-Communicative Orientation (SCO) scale by following the instructions included in the figure. Compute your scores as shown at the bottom of the figure.

Implicit in the concept of communication competence, as we are using it here, is the idea that a person's level of competence is very similar across many contexts. That is, an individual's level of communication competence is "traitlike." It is rooted firmly in the person's personality. The idea that personality has a major influence on communication behavior, of course, is not new. The impact of personality on communication behavior has been clearly demonstrated for decades (McCroskey & Daly, 1987) and we will consider personality in more detail in the next section of this book. Similarly, it has been established that individuals exhibit traitlike differences in their basic communication styles (Norton, 1983). These styles also have been examined under such labels as "personal style" (Merrill & Reid, 1981), "social style" (Lashbrook, 1974), and "psychological androgyny" (Bem, 1974; Wheeless & Dierks-Stewart, 1981). These approaches are rooted in Jungian psychology and are represented in the very popular Myers-Briggs personality inventory.

Figure 7.1
Socio-Communicative Orientation*

DIRECTIONS: The questionnaire below lists twenty personality characteristics. Please indicate the degree to which you believe each of these characteristics applies to YOU, as you normally communicate with others, by marking whether you (5) strongly agree that it applies, (4) agree that it applies, (3) are undecided, (2) disagree that it applies, or (1) strongly disagree that it applies. There are no right or wrong answers. Work quickly; record your first impression.

_____ 1. helpful
_____ 2. defends own beliefs
_____ 3. independent
_____ 4. responsive to others
_____ 5. forceful
_____ 6. has strong personality
_____ 7. sympathetic
_____ 8. compassionate
_____ 9. assertive
_____ 10. sensitive to the needs of others
_____ 11. dominant
_____ 12. sincere
_____ 13. gentle
_____ 14. willing to take a stand
_____ 15. warm
_____ 16. tender
_____ 17. friendly
_____ 18. acts as a leader
_____ 19. aggressive
_____ 20. competitive

*Items 2, 3, 5, 6, 9, 11, 14, 18, 19, and 20 measure assertiveness. Add the scores on these items to get your assertiveness score. Items 1, 4, 7, 8, 10, 12, 13, 15, 16, and 17 measure responsiveness. Add the scores on these items to get your responsiveness score.

These style-based approaches characteristically suggest two or more dimensions to the individual's style which are assumed to result in differential communication behaviors. These behaviors are presumed to communicate distinctive impressions of the individual to others. This set of behaviors is what we have chosen to refer to as the person's "Socio-Communicative Style."

It is presumed that observers can gain insight into the personality of individuals by taking note of their characteristic communication behaviors (Thomas, Richmond, & McCroskey, 1994). The two most commonly referenced dimensions are "assertiveness" (called masculinity by Bem) and "responsiveness" (called femininity by Bem). Assertiveness is characterized by descripters such as independent, dominant, aggressive, competitive, and forceful. Responsiveness is characterized by describers such as helpful, sympathetic, compassionate, sincere, and friendly. McCroskey, Richmond, and Stewart (1986) have drawn from this body of research to suggest that assertiveness and responsiveness are two of the three critical components of interpersonal communication competence, as mentioned above.

Assertiveness

Assertiveness is the capacity to make requests, actively disagree, express positive or negative personal rights and feelings, initiate, maintain or disengage from conversations, and stand up for oneself without attacking another. In the Bem-Wheeless research this aspect of communication is referred to as "masculinity." This, of course, does not suggest that only males are likely to exhibit this element of communication. However, in many societies the stereotype of appropriate male communication behavior is closely associated with this characteristic.

Terms that are commonly used to describe a person who engages in assertive communication behaviors include: willing to defend own beliefs, independent, forceful, strong of personality, dominant, willing to take a stand and act as a leader, and (of course) assertive. You will recognize these as items on the SCO and SCS scales. Such terms do describe the stereotypical male image in American society, but more importantly, they describe a person who is in control both of self and of the communication process.

It is important that we distinguish between assertiveness and something with which it often is confused—aggressiveness. Aggressiveness essentially is assertiveness *plus*. That is, the aggressive person not only stands up for his or her rights but also demands that others yield their rights. An assertive person, for example, makes **requests**; an aggressive person makes **demands**. Assertive individuals insist that others respect their rights; aggressive people do the same thing while ignoring the rights of others.

The effects of assertiveness and aggressiveness can be similar, yet essentially they are different. To clarify, either approach is likely to help people get their way. In the process, however, the assertive individual is likely to maintain good relationships with others, but the aggressive individual is likely to alienate others. The interpersonally competent communicator, of course, can influence others while maintaining good relationships with those others.

Our research indicates a major factor that inhibits individuals from behaving in an appropriately assertive manner in communication is shyness brought on by communication apprehension. Engaging in assertive behavior usually prompts others in an interaction to communicate more. Highly communication-apprehensive individuals, of course, tend to avoid communication. High apprehensives often yield their rights rather than assertively defend them, thus avoiding communication. Highly apprehensive individuals, therefore, are frequently not interpersonally competent communicators.

Responsiveness

Responsiveness is the capacity to be sensitive to the communication of others, to be a good listener, to make others comfortable in communicating, and to recognize the needs and desires of others. In the Bem-Wheeless research this aspect of communication is referred to as "femininity." This label does not suggest that only females can be responsive to others. It merely suggests that this is the American stereotype of appropriate female communication behavior.

Terms that are commonly used to describe a person who engages in responsive communication behaviors include: helpful, sympathetic, compassionate, sensitive to needs of others, sincere, gentle, warm, tender, friendly, understanding, and (of course) responsive to others. Again, you will recognize these as items from the SCO scales. Although such terms do describe the stereotypical female image in American society, in a broader sense they describe any person who is open to the communication of others and empathic with those others.

Empathy is the capacity of an individual to put himself or herself into the shoes of another, to see things from the other person's vantage point. This is communicated to the other person both verbally and nonverbally. When we state the other person's view correctly (in their mind) or say things like "I see your point," "I understand what you mean," or "I have had that experience too," we communicate empathy and responsiveness. We also communicate responsiveness when we look at other people when they are talking, when we smile at them, lean toward them, touch them, and so forth. In other words, we communicate responsively when we are *immediate* with others.

It is important to distinguish between responsiveness and submissiveness. The two are confused with each other. **Submissiveness** is the yielding of one's rights to another. Responsiveness is recognizing the needs and rights of another **without** yielding one's own rights. The responsive individual understands and acknowledges the feelings of the other person. The submissive individual does that also but goes on to yield to the requests of the other person even when that requires that the submissive person go against his or her own feelings, rights, or needs.

As with assertiveness and aggressiveness, the effects of responsiveness and submissiveness are similar yet essentially different. Either approach is likely to get at least momentary liking from the other person. That liking is produced at the cost of one's own well-being in the case of submissiveness but not for responsiveness. The interpersonally competent communicator, of course, can generate good relationships with others while maintaining a position of influence with them.

As we stated earlier, shyness brought on by communication apprehension is a major factor that inhibits individuals from behaving in an appropriately responsive manner in communication. Being responsive in interpersonal communication presents an invitation to others to talk more. As we have repeatedly noted, high communication apprehensives typically do not want to increase their communication with others. Thus, high apprehensives may be unresponsive to others' communication to avoid more communication. As a result, these individuals are likely to be seen as cold and unfriendly. Highly apprehensive individuals, therefore, are frequently not interpersonally competent communicators.

Competence and Androgyny

The elements of assertiveness and responsiveness are not necessarily correlated. That is, a person who is high on one SCO/SCS dimension may be either high or low, or somewhere between, on the other. Figure 7.2 shows categories that may exist as a function of high and low assertiveness and high and low responsiveness. As indicated in figure 7.2, we would expect a person who is highly assertive and highly responsive (quadrant 1) to be the most competent interpersonal communicator. On the other hand, the person who is characteristically

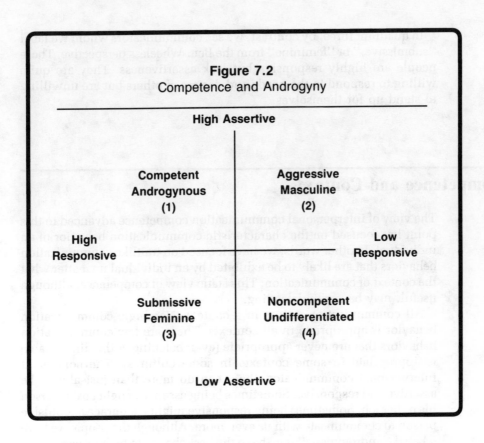

Figure 7.2
Competence and Androgyny

High Assertive

| Competent Androgynous (1) | Aggressive Masculine (2) |

High Responsive — Low Responsive

| Submissive Feminine (3) | Noncompetent Undifferentiated (4) |

Low Assertive

neither assertive nor responsive (quadrant 4) is the least likely to be interpersonally competent. Interestingly, research has shown that most people who are highly communicatively apprehensive fall in this latter category.

In the Bem-Wheeless research, those whom we consider most likely to be competent are called ''androgynous.'' This means that they characteristically display communication behaviors that are both masculine (assertive) and feminine (responsive). Those whom we consider least likely to be competent are referred to in the Bem-Wheeless research as ''undifferentiated.'' This means that they characteristically display neither assertive nor responsive behaviors.

In the other two quadrants in figure 7.2, we point to communicators who characteristically are either assertive or responsive but not both. We might refer to these individuals as ''partially competent.'' In quadrant two we find those individuals we label ''aggressive,'' or ''masculine'' from the Bem-Wheeless perspective. These are the people who are highly assertive but lack responsiveness. They are quite willing to stand up for themselves, but they do not exhibit a concern for others.

In quadrant three, by contrast, we see communicators whom we label "submissive," or "feminine" from the Bem-Wheeless perspective. These people are highly responsive but lack assertiveness. They are quite willing to respond to the needs and desires of others but are unwilling to stand up for themselves.

Competence and Context

The view of interpersonal communication competence advanced to this point has focused on the characteristic communication behavior of an individual. In other words, we have focused on traitlike communication behaviors that are likely to be exhibited by an individual no matter what the context of communication. This static view of competence, although useful, may be very misleading.

All communication occurs in a context. No single communication behavior is appropriate in all contexts. There are few communication behaviors that are never appropriate (even belching at the dinner table is appropriate in some contexts in some cultures). The competent interpersonal communicator, then, can do more than just always be assertive and responsive. Sometimes being assertive might cost a person his or her job. Sometimes being responsive might encourage a repulsive person to communicate with us even more. Although the people we have labeled "androgynous" may have the best chance to be interpersonally competent, there is no guarantee that they will be so in any given context. In fact, the "undifferentiated" person may behave more appropriately in some contexts.

Versatility

The critical element in interpersonal communication competence is versatility, the capacity to be *appropriately* assertive and *appropriately* responsive depending on the context. Terms that are used to describe individuals who are versatile communicators include: accommodating, adaptable, flexible, informal, compatible with others, versatile. Terms for individuals who lack this capacity include: rigid, inflexible, disliking of change, uncompromising, unyielding. As you can see, versatility appears to be related to how dogmatic, as opposed to open-minded, a person tends to be. While it is true that versatility is rooted in an individual's personality, that does not mean that even a dogmatic individual cannot learn to **communicate** in a versatile manner.

Individuals who are versatile in their interpersonal communication behavior are those whose basic personality permits them to be adaptable rather than rigidly consistent in communicating with different people or communicating with the same person at different times. In other words, versatile individuals are adapting their style of communication to the individuals with whom they are communicating and to the demands of the situation. While this is much more difficult for people with rigid personalities, it need not be impossible.

Consider, for example, a situation in which you are communicating with a highly aggressive individual. Should you be highly assertive in response? Should you be highly responsive? The former choice might lead to confrontation and conflict, the latter to submission. Neither would be seen as the "best" way to behave. The competent interpersonal communicator would be assertive when it was necessary to defend his or her own rights. He/she would remain responsive to the other's communication without submitting to unreasonable requests or demands. An outside observer would see the competent individual behaving differently at different points in the interaction.

As a very crude self-measure of your own versatility, go back to figure 7.2. Where would you put yourself generally? Where would you classify yourself when on a date? At work? Talking to your mother? Talking to a teacher? Returning an appliance you bought that does not work? Getting rid of a door-to-door salesperson? Talking to someone you know stole your book?

If you can easily classify yourself, and you place yourself in the same classification in most of the other contexts cited, you probably are not very versatile. On the other hand, if you had difficulty locating where you should be placed or found you moved all over the place depending on the other contexts, you may be quite versatile.

Another construct has appeared in the communication literature that is very similar to the construct of versatility. This is a personality-type trait that is called "rhetorical sensitivity" (Hart, Carlson, & Eadie, 1980). The rhetorically sensitive person has the ability and inclination to adapt messages to audiences; he or she falls midway between two extremes on a continuum. At one extreme are persons whom Darnell and Brockriede (1976) describe as seeing "any variation from their personal norms as hypocritical, as a denial of integrity, as a cardinal sin." These types are the stereotypically bullheaded, rigid dogmatics. At the other extreme are those persons Darnell and Brockriede describe as having "no Self to call their own. For each person and for each situation they present a new self" (Darnell & Brockriede, 1976). Such people are the "chameleons" of the world. They change their attitudes and feelings at the mere suggestion from another.

Not a great deal is yet known about why some people are highly versatile and others are not. There is a strong indication that versatility is associated with an individual's personality, as we noted previously. High communication apprehensives, for example, tend to be less versatile. In contrast, highly manipulative individuals, often called high Machiavellians, tend to talk in groups no more than the average but to participate at the time it counts most. These highly controlling individuals do exhibit versatility. Versatility clearly is more than just open-mindedness.

Personality is a contributing factor to a person's versatility, as is attitude. Training programs in both assertiveness and in nonverbal sensitivity (responsiveness) have proven effective in altering people's basic communication behavior. For some people who were deficient in either assertiveness or responsiveness skills, these programs have produced remarkable positive change; people have become more versatile communicators. For others, however, these programs produce behaviors better characterized as "obnoxiously aggressive" or "wimp-like." The key is the motivation of the individual who enters such training. If one's goal is to become more versatile, it appears that is the likely outcome. However, if one's goal is to "learn how to stop being pushed around" or to "learn how to make friends," other outcomes seem more likely.

Becoming a competent interpersonal communicator requires an understanding of the nature of effective interpersonal communication and acquisition of the necessary behavioral skills. These skills may be sufficient to make a person both assertive and responsive. To become versatile and truly interpersonally competent, the motivation to be an effective interpersonal communicator is critical.

Now that you've explored the relative merits of assertiveness and responsiveness and their variable applications depending on the context, it might be a good time to check your self-perception of your responsive and assertive behavior with the perception of those who know you.

Now turn to figure 7.3. This is a measure you should duplicate and give to a half-dozen people who know you well—not necessarily people who are good friends, just people who know you well. You will notice that this instrument is very much like the one in figure 7.1. However, it represents the perception of you by someone else rather than your perception of yourself. We call this a measure of "Socio-Communicative Style," or SCS. SCS is the way others see you, while SCO is the way you see yourself. If you have a clear and undistorted self-perception, the scores you report on your SCO and the scores you get on the SCS measure (on *average*, not every individual person's score) should be very similar. We developed these measures (Richmond & McCroskey, 1990) of assertiveness and responsiveness to help people gain insight into their probable level of communication competence.

Figure 7.3

Socio-Communicative Style*

DIRECTIONS: The questionnaire below lists twenty personality characteristics. Please indicate the degree to which you believe each of these characteristics applies to the person whose name appears above by marking whether you (5) strongly agree that it applies, (4) agree that it applies, (3) are undecided, (2) disagree that it applies, or (1) strongly disagree that it applies. There are no right or wrong answers. Work quickly; record your first impression.

_____ 1. helpful
_____ 2. defends own beliefs
_____ 3. independent
_____ 4. responsive to others
_____ 5. forceful
_____ 6. has strong personality
_____ 7. sympathetic
_____ 8. compassionate
_____ 9. assertive
_____ 10. sensitive to the needs of others
_____ 11. dominant
_____ 12. sincere
_____ 13. gentle
_____ 14. willing to take a stand
_____ 15. warm
_____ 16. tender
_____ 17. friendly
_____ 18. acts as a leader
_____ 19. aggressive
_____ 20. competitive

*Items 2, 3, 5, 6, 9, 11, 14, 18, 19, and 20 measure assertiveness. Add the scores on these items to get your assertiveness score. Items 1, 4, 7, 8, 10, 12, 13, 15, 16, and 17 measure responsiveness. Add the scores on these items to get your responsiveness score.

References

Bem, S. L. (1974). The measurement of psychological androgyny. *Journal of Consulting and Clinical Psychology, 42*, 155–162.

Darnell, D., & Brockriede, W. (1976). *Persons communicating.* Englewood Cliffs, NJ: Prentice-Hall.

Hart, R. P., Carlson, R. E., & Eadie, W. F. (1980). Attitudes toward communication and the assessment of rhetorical sensitivity. *Communication Monographs, 47*, 1–22.

Kearney, P., & McCroskey, J. C. (1980). Relationships among teacher communication style, trait and state communication apprehension, and teacher effectiveness. In D. Nimmo (Ed.), *Communication Yearbook 4.* New Brunswick, NJ: Transaction books.

Lashbrook, W. B. (1974). *Toward the measurement and processing of the social style profile.* Eden Prairie, MN: Wilson Learning Corporation.

Lashbrook, W. B., Knutson, P. K., Parsley, M. L., & Wenburg, J. R. (1976). *An empirical examination of versatility as a consequent of perceived social style.* Paper presented at the annual meeting of the Western States Speech Communication Association, Phoenix, November.

McCroskey, J. C. (1984). Communication competence: The elusive construct. In R. N. Bostrom (Ed.), *Competence in communication.* Beverly Hills: Sage Publications.

McCroskey, J. C., & Daly, J. A. (1987). *Personality and interpersonal communication.* Newbury Park, CA: Sage.

McCroskey, J. C., Richmond, V. P., & Stewart, R. A. (1986). *One on one: The foundations of interpersonal communication* (Ch. 16). Englewood Cliffs, NJ: Prentice-Hall.

Merrill, D. W., & Reid, R. (1981). *Personal styles and effective performance: Make your style work for you.* Radnor, PA: Chilton Book.

Norton, R. (1983). *Communicator style: Theory, applications, and measures.* Beverly Hills: Sage.

Richmond, V. P., & McCroskey, J. C. (1995). *Communication: Apprehension, avoidance and effectiveness,* 3rd edition. Scottsdale, AZ: Gorsuch-Scarisbrick.

————. (1990). Reliability and separation of factors on the assertiveness-responsiveness measure. *Psychological Reports, 67*, 449–450.

Thomas, C. E., Richmond, V. P., & McCroskey, J. C. (1994). Is immediacy anything more than just being nice? The association between immediacy and socio-communicative style. *Communication Research Reports, 11*, 107–115.

Wheeless, V. E., & Dierks-Stewart, K. (1981). The psychometric properties of the Bem sex-role inventory: Questions concerning reliability and validity. *Communication Quarterly, 29*, 173–186.

PSYCHOLOGY OF COMMUNICATION

Section 3

UNDERSTANDING INTERPERSONAL PERCEPTIONS

8

Receivers' perceptions of sources are critically important in the human communication process. The reason is this: ***Messages are interpreted through the receiver's impression of the source.*** Perceptions of the source, therefore, determine perceptions of the message. For example, take the message "I love you." Would this message be perceived any differently if it were stated by your mother rather than by your lover? Would it make a difference if the message were sent by a stranger as opposed to a close friend, or if it were sent by a same-sex friend as opposed to an opposite-sex friend? Consider the statement "Eating broccoli is very dangerous to your health." What would you think if a friend of yours said this to you? A stranger? The Surgeon General of the United States? Chances are that you would perceive and interpret the same message differently for each person who sends it. This is because we perceive a message according to the way we perceive its source. If you know your friend hates broccoli, you might interpret the statement as a humorous one. If you like broccoli, you may reject the stranger's view because you may doubt he or she has any expertise on that subject. If the Surgeon General says it, however, you might be very hesitant to eat broccoli in the future.

No message is interpreted by a receiver apart from its source. The source/message relationship is so strong it has been found that receivers will create a source in their minds if the real source is unknown (McCroskey & Dunham, 1966). There is an inherent realization in people that to understand and evaluate a message we need to know who was the source of the message. Almost 2,500 years ago the great philosophers and rhetoricians of the day were well aware that the image or "ethos" of a speaker had a major influence on the impact of the speaker's message. Aristotle, Cicero, Plato, and Quintilian all stressed this source/message relationship in their speaking and writing.

People will grasp at most anything to create the needed image of the unknown source. It has been found, for example, that when an unknown source is introduced by someone we know, we transfer much of the introducer's image to that unknown person. This has been called the "sponsorship effect" (Holtzman, 1966; McCroskey & Dunham, 1966). One place where use of this sponsorship effect is most obvious is in political campaigns, where unknown candidates make sure to have prominent local people introduce them to the audience. On the everyday level, most of us have asked someone, or have been asked by someone, to introduce us to someone we would like to know. We intuitively recognize that the introducer's "sponsorship" will create a positive initial image. This also is why we ask important and/or well-respected people to write letters of recommendation for us.

Contemporary social psychologists explain the role of the message source, and how a receiver responds to a message, in terms of several theories that collectively have generated what has come to be known as the "principle of consistency" (Brown, 1965; Heider, 1946; Festinger, 1957; Osgood & Tannenbaum, 1955). The essence of this principle is that if two attitudes (or perceptions, or beliefs, or values) are inconsistent with each other, change in one or both occurs because of the mind's efforts to establish and maintain consistency. This need for consistency is seen as a need of all people. While we can tolerate some inconsistency, the greater it becomes the more pressure there is on us to resolve it.

People of all cultures and backgrounds are also seen as having certain common beliefs. You most likely share these beliefs. This includes things like the following: "Good people agree with me." "Bad people disagree with me." "Good people tell the truth." "Bad people lie." When we hear someone we like say something we dislike, then we feel pressured to change our minds about the person, what he or she says, or both. The stronger our liking and respect for the person, the more difficult it is for us to disregard what he or she says or reject it as false or irrelevant.

The "image of the source" or "attitude toward the source" is a product of interpersonal perceptions. This chapter focuses primarily on the three main categories of interpersonal perceptions that have occupied the attention of communication scholars. These are source credibility, interpersonal attraction, and similarity. Four other types of interpersonal perceptions that influence communication, but do not fit within the three main categories, will also be considered. For most of these types of interpersonal perceptions, we will give you an example of an instrument which researchers have used to measure that perception. These should help you see applications for your everyday life.

Perceptions of Source Credibility

The effects of credibility have received more research interest than any other interpersonal perception variable. Credibility refers to how **believable** we perceive a source to be. It is a multidimensional construct, meaning that there are different dimensions or ways in which credibility is perceived by a receiver. The two dimensions of source credibility are "Competence" and "Trustworthiness" (McCroskey, 1966; McCroskey & Young, 1981). An example of an instrument used to measure these perceptions is presented in figure 8.1.

Competence

This dimension of credibility refers to the degree to which a source is perceived to be knowledgeable or expert in a given subject. This perception exists along a continuum ranging from completely incompetent

---

Figure 8.1

Measure of Source Credibility

DIRECTIONS: On the scales below, please indicate your feelings about "David Letterman." Circle the number between the adjectives which best represents your feelings about "David Letterman." Numbers "1" and "7" indicate a very strong feeling. Numbers "2" and "6" indicate a strong feeling. Numbers "3" and "5" indicate a fairly weak feeling. Number "4" indicates you are undecided or do not understand the adjectives themselves. There are no right or wrong answers.*

COMPETENCE   Reliable 7 6 5 4 3 2 1 Unreliable
Uninformed 1 2 3 4 5 6 7 Informed
Unqualified 1 2 3 4 5 6 7 Qualified
Intelligent 7 6 5 4 3 2 1 Unintelligent
Valuable 7 6 5 4 3 2 1 Worthless
Inexpert 1 2 3 4 5 6 7 Expert

CHARACTER   Virtuous 7 6 5 4 3 2 1 Sinful
Honest 7 6 5 4 3 2 1 Dishonest
Unfriendly 1 2 3 4 5 6 7 Friendly
Pleasant 7 6 5 4 3 2 1 Unpleasant
Selfish 1 2 3 4 5 6 7 Unselfish
Awful 1 2 3 4 5 6 7 Nice

---

* To compute your scores for competence and character, simply add up the numbers you circled for each measure separately. To measure the credibility of a different source, simply replace "David Letterman" with the other name.

Competence Total _____ Character Total _____

McCroskey (1966).

to extremely competent. The perception is mediated, however, by how competent receivers perceive themselves to be. On a scale of six to 42, if Lisa perceived Linda's competence in matters related to automobiles to be 38, and her own competence to be 24, then Linda is probably quite competent in Lisa's mind. On the other hand, if Lisa perceives her own competence to be 24, and that of Linda to be 18, then in Lisa's mind Linda is probably not very competent.

Our perception of a source's competence has an impact on our response to that source. If we perceive sources to be more competent than we are, we are likely to accept their opinions and to follow their advice. Of course, if we perceive a source to be less competent than ourselves on a subject, our opinions on the subject are unlikely to be influenced by that source.

Competence is usually the first judgment we make about a source's credibility. An equally important judgment follows—our perceptions of the source's character.

Character

We may perceive a source to be competent on a subject. However, if we feel that we cannot trust that person to be honest about what he or she knows, we are likely to perceive that person as having little credibility. For example, you may perceive an automobile salesperson to be very knowledgeable (a 42 on our scale) with regard to a particular car. If you believe that salesperson to be dishonest and untrustworthy in dealing with you, the salesperson probably has low credibility in your mind.

Perceptions of character exist along a continuum similar to that of competence; our judgments of a source range from being completely untrustworthy to totally trustworthy. This perception, however, is not mediated by our perception of our own trustworthiness. That is, how trustworthy we perceive ourselves to be likely has little impact on how trustworthy we perceive a source to be. Even a person who is totally dishonest will assign very little credibility to a source perceived to be dishonest also. Perceptions of a source's character, therefore, are important in communication, for we discount the validity and honesty of messages from a source we perceive to be untrustworthy. Moreover, we find little motivation to communicate with a source we perceive as untrustworthy because we cannot predict whether the person will be cooperative and straightforward with us. This occurs even when we perceive the source to be competent in a subject.

Perceptions of source credibility are critical in the human communication process. If we perceive a source as having low credibility, we are likely to misperceive the messages (from the source's vantage point) that the person gives us. The messages may "sound good," but because we question the source's credibility we also question the validity of the messages. Furthermore, we are less likely to expose ourselves to, learn from, and be influenced by a source who is not credible than by a source who is credible.

Credibility perceptions are but one set of perceptions that influences our responses to and attitudes about a source. Another equally important set of perceptions relates to the source's attraction.

Interpersonal Attraction of the Source

When people first think of interpersonal attractiveness, they usually think of physical attractiveness. However, physical attractiveness is not the only form of attraction that affects our reactions to another person. Like credibility, attraction is a multidimensional construct. Besides physical attractiveness, we also judge sources on their social attractiveness and task attractiveness. An instrument designed to measure each of these three dimensions of perceived interpersonal attractiveness is provided in figure 8.2. This measure was developed by McCroskey and McCain (1974).

Physical Attractiveness

A person's physical attractiveness is a perception, a perception which may not be shared by two people with different backgrounds or experiences, or who come from different cultures. That is why one person can think someone is attractive and a second person thinks that same someone is unattractive. Physical attractiveness relates directly to physical appearance. Research says that this perception is especially important in initial encounters with a source. Our earliest perceptions of a source's physical attractiveness will to some extent decide our affinity (liking) for that source. Negative physical attraction, therefore, means there is little likelihood that we will develop much affinity for the person. Physical attractiveness, thus, often is *the* critical perception. Often there will be no communication at all if we do not perceive physical attractiveness in the other person. Consider the last social affair you attended where there were many people with whom you were unacquainted. In making acquaintances with these people, whom were you more likely to approach first or be receptive to—those you perceived as physically attractive, or those you perceived as physically unattractive? Beauty may be only skin deep, but sometimes we decide not to try to go any deeper if we don't like the skin!

Although our culture places a heavy emphasis on appearance, fortunately the physical dimension of attractiveness becomes less important over time as we become more familiar with the other person. In short, as the relationship progresses, physical attractiveness loses much—but probably not all—of its impact. The other dimensions of attraction become more important the more we get to know another person (we get below the "skin" level). Nevertheless, our earliest encounters with that person are impacted most by how attractive we perceive his or her physical appearance to be. This is because in our initial interactions with the individual, the only information we have about that person is what we can see. Essentially, until we know the person better, our thinking is "what we see is what we get." We are more likely to initiate communication with a person whom we find physically attractive. Moreover, research suggests that, at least early, we are more likely to expose ourselves to and be influenced by a source

Figure 8.2
Measure of Interpersonal Attraction

DIRECTIONS: The scales below are designed to indicate how attractive you find another person to be. Please indicate your perceptions of the attractiveness of "David Letterman." Please circle the number which best indicates your feeling on each of these scales. Numbers "1" and "7" indicate a very strong feeling. Numbers "2" and "6" indicate a strong feeling. Numbers "3" and "5" indicate a fairly weak feeling. Number "4" indicates you are undecided. There are no right or wrong answers.*

Social Attraction	1.	I think he (she) could be a friend of mine.	Strongly Disagree	1 2 3 4 5 6 7	Strongly Agree
	2.	It would be difficult to meet and talk with him (her).	Strongly Disagree	7 6 5 4 3 2 1	Strongly Agree
	3.	He (she) just wouldn't fit into my circle of friends.	Strongly Disagree	7 6 5 4 3 2 1	Strongly Agree
	4.	We could never establish a personal friendship with each other.	Strongly Disagree	7 6 5 4 3 2 1	Strongly Agree
Physical Attraction	5.	I think he (she) is quite handsome (pretty).	Strongly Disagree	1 2 3 4 5 6 7	Strongly Agree
	6.	He (she) is very sexy looking.	Strongly Disagree	1 2 3 4 5 6 7	Strongly Agree
	7.	I find him (her) very attractive physically.	Strongly Disagree	1 2 3 4 5 6 7	Strongly Agree
	8.	I don't like the way he (she) looks.	Strongly Disagree	7 6 5 4 3 2 1	Strongly Agree
Task Attraction	9.	He (she) would be a typical goof-off when assigned a job to do.	Strongly Disagree	7 6 5 4 3 2 1	Strongly Agree
	10.	I have confidence in his (her) ability to get the job done.	Strongly Disagree	1 2 3 4 5 6 7	Strongly Agree
	11.	If I wanted to get things done I could probably depend on him (her).	Strongly Disagree	1 2 3 4 5 6 7	Strongly Agree
	12.	I couldn't get anything accomplished with him (her).	Strongly Disagree	7 6 5 4 3 2 1	Strongly Agree

* To compute your scores for the three dimensions of attraction, simply add up the numbers you circled for each measure separately. To measure the attractiveness of a different person, simply put in the other person's name in place of "David Letterman" above.

Social Total _____   Physical Total _____   Task Total _____ we perceive as physically attractive. Sometimes, particularly when we have little other information about the person, we are even likely to attribute more credibility to a physically attractive person.

Social Attractiveness

The dimension of social attractiveness refers to the degree to which we perceive a source to be someone with whom we would like to spend time on a social level. It is not based solely on the physical appearance of the source (although that aspect is *not* irrelevant). It is primarily based on how friendly and likable the source is perceived to be. Social attraction is particularly important when the potential outcome of communication with the person is affinity. Typically, no matter how physically attractive we perceive someone to be, over time our attraction and liking for that individual relies more on how friendly and likable we perceive the other person. If you have ever been dissatisfied with a "gorgeous" date, it is probably because you found the person's communication to be uninteresting, unamusing, and boring—you found it hard to develop affinity for the individual. He or she may have looked nice but was as socially stimulating as an attractive houseplant!

Social attractiveness of a source is more important after initial encounters. If we perceive the person to be attractive on a social level, we are likely to want future interactions with the individual. Conversely, if we perceive the source to be lacking in social attractiveness, we are inclined to expend our communicative energies on other acquaintances and friendships.

Task Attractiveness

The third dimension of interpersonal attractiveness refers to the degree to which we perceive the person to be a desirable one with whom to establish a work relationship. We perceive a source to be task attractive when he or she is viewed as one with whom it would be easy to work; one who probably would be productive in that work; and one who is motivated to achieve communication outcomes similar to the outcomes we want to achieve. Task attraction, therefore, is based on communication between source and receiver that is goal-directed and effective for achieving those goals. This dimension of attractiveness is also related to the competence dimension of credibility. When we perceive a source to be competent in a given task-related area, we will likely find that person to be an attractive one with whom to work in that area. An example of task attraction may be found in campus study groups. When cramming for a final exam in physics, if you desire to study with someone else, your choice of a study partner will be determined in large part by how competent you perceive that person to be in physics. If you know that person makes As in the subject, he or she will be more task attractive to you than will be a classmate who is doing poorly in the course.

It is important to realize that the three dimensions of source attractiveness are *independent* of one another. In other words, a source can be perceived as having high task attractiveness but little or no physical and social attractiveness. Take, for example, the stereotypical computer "nerd." This person is perceived by many to be a very task-attractive individual when they need information about computers, but not as attractive on a physical and social level. Source attractiveness is merely a matter of perception and not necessarily of reality. Simply put, a source is attractive only to the extent he or she is *perceived* as attractive. When sources are perceived as attractive, we are much more apt to expose ourselves to them, to learn from them, and to be influenced by them.

Similarity

Another set of perceptions affecting our attitudes about and responses to a source are based on our *similarity* to the source, technically known as "homophily." This loosely translates as "coming from the same category." There is a *principle of homophily* that holds that the more similar two communicators are, the more likely they are to interact with one another, the more likely their communication will be successful, and the more similar they are likely to become. The more similar we perceive a source to be to us, the more attracted to that person we are apt to be, the more influence he or she is likely to have over us, and the more we are likely to learn from that individual. Three dimensions of similarity are particularly important to our perceptions of sources. These are demographic similarity, background similarity, and attitude similarity. A measure of background and attitude similarity perceptions is presented in figure 8.3.

Demographic Similarity

Demographics are physical or social characteristics of an individual that are objectively identifiable: age, sex, height, socioeconomic status, educational level, religion, culture, and ethnicity. These are considered *real* characteristics because they are observable and knowable. They exist beyond the limitations of individual people's perceptions. Thus, demographic similarity refers to people's similarity on attributes such

Figure 8.3
Measure of Perceived Homophily

DIRECTIONS: On the scales below, please indicate your feelings about "David Letterman." Numbers "1" and "7" indicate a very strong feeling. Numbers "2" and "6" indicate a strong feeling. Numbers "3" and "5" indicate a fairly weak feeling. Number "4" indicates you are undecided or do not understand the adjectives themselves. There are no right or wrong answers.*

ATTITUDINAL HOMOPHILY		
Like me	7 6 5 4 3 2 1	Unlike me
Different from me	1 2 3 4 5 6 7	Similar to me
Thinks like me	7 6 5 4 3 2 1	Doesn't think like me
Doesn't behave like me	1 2 3 4 5 6 7	Behaves like me

BACKGROUND HOMOPHILY		
Status like mine	7 6 5 4 3 2 1	Status different from mine
From social class different from mine	1 2 3 4 5 6 7	From social class similar to mine
Culturally different	1 2 3 4 5 6 7	Culturally similar
Economic situation like mine	7 6 5 4 3 2 1	Economic situation different from mine

* To compute your scores for the two dimensions of homophily, simply add up the numbers you circled for each measure separately. To measure the perceived homophily of a different person, simply put in the other person's name in place of "David Letterman" above.

Attitude Total _____ Background Total _____

McCroskey, Richmond, & Daly (1966).

as those listed above. This type of similarity is more actual than it is perceived. In other words, if both you and the person sitting next to you are twenty years old, female, Hispanic, college sophomores, and Catholic, your demographic similarity is factual rather than perceptual. You may, of course, perceive yourselves to be similar (or dissimilar) on other dimensions. You also may over- or underestimate your similarity.

We can make certain predictions about the probable outcomes of communication between a source and receiver who have demographic similarities. For example, we can predict that a Native American who was raised on a reservation in South Dakota probably can return to that reservation after having obtained a teaching degree and be more successful in the reservation's school than a Caucasian teacher coming from Birmingham, Alabama. The reason is because, simply put, the Sioux teacher's basic demographic characteristics are more similar to those of the children than are the Alabamian's. As a result they can understand each other's messages better than they can an "outsider's" messages.

While demographic similarity is based primarily on actual characteristics, the other two dimensions of similarity are based on perceptions. Thus, they are akin to perceptions of credibility and attractiveness. We consider each below.

Background Similarity

As a college student, do you feel more similar to one of your classmates than you do to a Marine cadet? As an American, do you feel you have more in common with other Americans than you do with Japanese? If you are from a large city, do you consider yourself more similar to someone from a large city than to someone from a Midwestern dairy farm? Chances are, if these questions apply to you, that you answer yes to each one. We perceive people who have backgrounds similar to our own as more similar to us than people with different backgrounds. Perceptions of background similarity are different from demographic similarity, however, because the similarity in background need not be real. For instance, when a student from New Mexico began study in West Virginia, he met another student from Idaho. The student immediately perceived some background similarity between himself and his counterpart. Both were from "the West." However, Pocatello, Idaho, is nearly the same distance from Grants, New Mexico, as is Morgantown, West Virginia. Nevertheless, the fact that both individuals were from the West and had come together in the East led one of them to perceive they had some degree of similarity. That they were not the same age, were of different religions, and had lived most of their lives in very different kinds of families indicated they were demographically not very similar. Being "Westerners" still produced the background similarity perception.

An important feature of background similarity is that it may be generated before any actual communication between the two people takes place. For example, a particular college student may perceive a similarity with *any* college student, although the number of people in this category is enormous and encompasses very diverse backgrounds. Another example can be drawn from the similarity we feel with certain television or movie personalities. Although we have never met and interacted with Tom Hanks, based on what information we do have about him, we may perceive that we have some background factors that are similar. Perceptions such as these lead to increases in *perceived* similarity. The greater the perceived similarity, the greater the likelihood for wanting to interact with the other person. The greater the perceived similarity, the more frequent interactions become. Subsequently, because of these shared background experiences, the more effective communication will be.

Attitude Similarity

This type of similarity refers to the degree to which a receiver perceives her or his attitudes, beliefs, and values to be similar to those of a source. Like background similarity, it is based on perceived similarity in attitudes, not actual similarity. Unlike background similarity, however, perceptions of attitude similarity typically develop after the two people have become acquainted and have interacted with one another. Moreover, attitude similarity fluctuates over the span of a relationship. After interacting with a new acquaintance, for example, you may perceive that many of your attitudes are quite similar and thus develop perceptions of similarity with the person. Something may arise that causes you to discover that you and the other person differ greatly on an important issue. As a result, your perceptions of attitude similarity with that person may decrease or change sharply. This points out a critical restriction related to the principle of homophily described earlier.

Recall that the principle of homophily suggests that the more similarity two individuals perceive themselves to have, the more likely they are to engage in communication, the more likely their communication will be effective, and the more likely they actually will become similar. However, exceptions to this principle exist. Take the case of divorce (or any process that terminates a relationship, for that matter). Divorce appears to suggest a major flaw in the principle of similarity. Two people meet, develop similarity and affinity with each other, grow to love each other, then discover that what they once thought were similarities are big differences—or at least they are perceived to be. Over time, therefore, the perception of similarity can change to the point where two people no longer perceive themselves to be similar. Knapp (1978) refers to this process as "differentiation." At that point we would expect the relationship to begin deteriorating and eventually to terminate. It is important to realize, therefore, that the principle of homophily applies only if *real* similarity exists, or while perceived similarity is not thwarted by reality.

Similarity is important to human communication to the extent that, as we perceive ourselves to be similar to another person, we are likely to want to engage in interaction with that person. Relationships established by similarity perceptions usually enhance communication so that outcomes of affinity, information acquisition, and influence are more likely. Perceptions of credibility and attractiveness similarly influence the effects that people's messages have on each other. These three types of source perceptions are perhaps the most significant for most communication outcomes. However, other source perceptions often are very important.

Other Perceptions of Source

Our attitudes toward and responses to a source are affected by perceptions of that source's extroversion, composure, sociability, and power. The first three of these are particularly pertinent to the source's perceived credibility; the fourth is highly associated with a source's influence over us. Measures of each of these are presented in figure 8.4.

Figure 8.4
Measure of Other Perceptions

DIRECTIONS: On the scales below, please indicate your feelings about "David Letterman." Circle the number between the adjectives which best represents your feelings about "David Letterman." Numbers "1" and "7" indicate a very strong feeling. Numbers "2" and "6" indicate a strong feeling. Numbers "3" and "5" indicate a fairly weak feeling. Number "4" indicates you are undecided or do not understand the adjectives themselves. There are no right or wrong answers.*

COMPOSURE
Nervous 1 2 3 4 5 6 7 Poised
Tense 1 2 3 4 5 6 7 Relaxed
Calm 7 6 5 4 3 2 1 Anxious
Excitable 1 2 3 4 5 6 7 Composed

EXTROVERSION
Bold 7 6 5 4 3 2 1 Timid
Quiet 1 2 3 4 5 6 7 Verbal
Silent 1 2 3 4 5 6 7 Talkative
Aggressive 7 6 5 4 3 2 1 Meek

SOCIABILITY
Awful 1 2 3 4 5 6 7 Nice
Unpleasant 1 2 3 4 5 6 7 Pleasant
Irritable 1 2 3 4 5 6 7 Good Natured
Cheerful 7 6 5 4 3 2 1 Gloomy

* To compute your scores for the three other perceptions, simply add up the numbers you circled for each measure separately. To measure the other perception of a different person, simply replace "David Letterman" with the other name.

Composure Total _____ Extroversion Total _____ Sociability Total _____

McCroskey & Young (1981).

Extroversion

The term *extroversion* refers to the degree to which we perceive a source to be talkative, bold, dynamic, and outgoing. We suggested in chapter 6 how perceptions of a source's extroversion are affected by his or her level of shyness or communication apprehension. People in the general United States culture tend to have negative evaluations of people who are very introverted. Also, however, evaluations of people are apt to be negative if they are too extroverted. Thus, in terms of credibility, we are likely to perceive the extremely introverted (stereotyped as not competent) or the extremely extroverted (stereotyped as not trustworthy) person as not credible. We tend to doubt that a quiet person can be very credible. We may feel that the reason they do not talk is that they do not know anything worth saying. On the other hand, highly talkative people may be overbearing—we may wonder if perhaps they are trying to cover up their deceptiveness. A source perceived as credible, then, is more likely to be one who is more extroverted than introverted, but certainly not at the extreme end of the scale.

Composure

Perceptions of composure relate to the amount of emotional control we perceive a source to have. Composure is whether the source is poised, relaxed, and confident as opposed to nervous, tense, and uptight. A source perceived as credible is likely to be one who is also perceived as composed, but not *too* composed. Sources who are so much in control of their emotions as to be at the high end of the composure continuum are likely to be perceived as cold, unfriendly, and aloof. We like others to show some degree of emotion, whether positive or negative. We steer clear of "cold fish." Mass-media researchers have determined in recent years that one of the primary factors determining television viewers' respect for and acceptance of a broadcaster is the broadcaster's expression of emotion—not so much emotion that the broadcaster loses objectivity, but enough to show her or his humanity. Such a broadcaster is more likely to be considered "real" and trustworthy, and thus credible. Lack of composure also contributes to perceptions of a source as not credible. Nervous and uptight sources may be thought to be so because they lack competence, or perhaps because they fear that a receiver may not think them trustworthy. For whatever reason, a very unpoised individual normally will be perceived as having little credibility.

Sociability

Most of us seek to interact with people whom we perceive to be likable, friendly, and pleasant. Perceptions of a source's sociability relate to how likable and friendly we perceive the person to be. Typically, if we perceive a person to be unsociable, we will avoid contact with that person. This perception is important to affinity and credibility. We are more inclined to like a sociable person. When we like a source, we are more likely to perceive her or him to be competent and trustworthy. We are more likely to turn to that source for information. However, we are not apt to interact with people if we do not perceive them to be friendly, even if they are competent and trustworthy. This is because the perceived lack of friendliness carries with it expectations of an unpleasant interaction.

Power

The perception of power refers to the degree to which we believe a source can control our thoughts, feelings, or behavior. It is an important concept in human communication. We communicate differently with a person whom we view to have power over us than we do with a person whom we view not to have such power. The kind of power we are referring to is that which allows someone to control the rewards and punishments we may receive. A teacher, for example, has power over students to the extent that the teacher mediates (has control of) students' grades. When a student completes assignments to the teacher's satisfaction, the student receives higher grades (rewards); when the student fails to complete assignments satisfactorily, he or she receives lower grades (punishments). Power is like similarity in that it can be based on ''reality'' or on perception alone.

Perceptual power is that which we typically view teachers, parents, peers, and higher status persons to have over us. When power is perceived in such people, it is *legitimized*; that is, the source's power is her or his *right* because of the role that person has with the receiver. Referring to teachers again, students generally perceive a teacher to have the right to control their classroom behavior because of the teacher's role. The role is one given by the system to the teacher to reward appropriate classroom behavior and to punish inappropriate behavior. At a more interpersonal level, when you ask a member of the opposite sex for a date you give that person the right to accept or reject your invitation. Whether the person accepts the invitation or rejects it, to the extent that you give the person a choice in the matter, they control your dating behavior (you will either get the date or you won't).

The impact of perceived power on our communication with another person is quite strong. If we perceive a person to have legitimate power over us, we will usually follow that person's instructions and respond to their requests without much question. On the other hand, if we perceive a source to have illegitimate power (exercising rights the person does not actually have), we are likely to avoid influence from that person and question her or his instructions and requests.

Real power comes when a source has actual control over our behavior, despite whether the person's role is legitimized. Coercion is perhaps the most prominent form of real power. Take, for example, a mugging. When a mugger jabs a .44 magnum into a victim's back and demands "Your money or your life!", the victim who values life over money has little choice but to succumb to the mugger's demand. The source (mugger) has total control over the receiver's (victim's) choice of behavior; the source has exercised real power. Typically, we will avoid communicating with a source who has coercive power over us because we are likely to expect the interaction to be an unpleasant one; the person may have the power to punish us or to cause us to engage in behavior we find displeasing. Essentially, then, our communication with a source who has real power is likely to be negative because such power restricts our behavioral choices. Communication with a source who has perceived power, however, is more likely to be positive because it allows more behavioral freedom of choice. Even though your teacher can reward or punish your classroom behavior, if you find the teacher's particular rewards or punishments to be of little consequence to you, you can behave any way you please. Thus, the most influential source is the one who is *perceived* to have control over a receiver's behavior as a function of that source's role relative to the receiver. We consider power much more fully in chapter 16.

This chapter discussed a most critical aspect of the human communication process: how the source is perceived by the receiver. Source perceptions are important to the communication process because of their ability to affect the receiver's attitudes toward both the source and the source's message. Moreover, these attitudes affect the extent to which receivers will *expose* themselves to the source, *pay attention* to the source, *retain* and *learn from* the source's messages, and be *influenced by* the source. Perceptions of source credibility, attractiveness, and similarity seem to have the greatest influence on a receiver's responsiveness to a source. Generally, the more credible the receiver perceives the source to be, and the more attractive and similar he or she is to the receiver, the more likely it is that the receiver will turn to, learn from, and be influenced by the source. Additionally, perceptions of source credibility depend to some extent on the source's perceived level of extroversion, composure, and sociability. The source's influence over the receiver depends partly on how much power the source is perceived to have by the receiver.

The goal of this chapter was to make you aware of just how complex the role of source is during human communication. Not only do receivers adapt their behavior according to how they perceive the source, but the source must also adapt to receivers' responses. It is this reciprocation of behavior between source and receiver that makes interpersonal communication an interactional and transactional process. To the extent that people accurately perceive and appropriately respond to each other's behavior, their communication will be increasingly effective.

References

Brown, R. (1965). *Social psychology*. New York: The Free Press.

Festinger, L. (1957). *A theory of cognitive dissonance*. New York: Row, Peterson.

Heider, F. (1946). Attitudes and cognitive organization. *Journal of Psychology, 21*, 107–112.

Knapp, M. L. (1978). *Social intercourse: From greeting to good-bye*. Boston: Allyn & Bacon.

McCroskey, J. C. (1993). *An introduction to rhetorical communication* (6th ed.). Englewood Cliffs, NJ: Prentice-Hall.

_____. (1966). Scales for the measurement of ethos. *Speech Monographs, 33*, 65–72.

McCroskey, J. C., & Dunham, R. E. (1966). Ethos: A confounding element in communication research. *Speech Monographs, 33*, 456–463.

McCroskey, J. C., & McCain, T. A. (1974). The measurement of interpersonal attraction. *Speech Monographs, 41*, 261–266.

McCroskey, J. C., Richmond, V. P., & Daly, J. A. (1975). The measurement of perceived homophily in interpersonal communication. *Human Communication Research, 1*, 323–332.

McCroskey, J. C., & Young, T. J. (1981). Ethos and credibility: The construct and its measurement after three decades. *Central States Speech Journal, 32*, 24–34.

Osgood, C. E., & Tannenbaum, P. H. (1955). The principle of congruity in the prediction of attitude change. *Psychological Review, 62*, 42–55.

UNDERSTANDING ATTITUDES, BELIEFS, AND VALUES

9

Our attitudes, beliefs, and values—and those of the people with whom we communicate—are extremely important to the success of our communication. These orientations determine how we are likely to respond to one another and the extent to which our communication with each other will be effective and meaningful. Often such orientations are the actual subject of communication between us. At a minimum, these orientations serve as a filter through which we receive and decode the messages sent to us by others.

How we interpret other people's messages, therefore, is largely a function of our own attitudes, beliefs, and values. Likewise, the way others interpret our messages is largely a function of similar, or dissimilar, orientations that they have. To understand why communication efforts are often unsuccessful when they seem like they should be successful, we need to understand the orientations that incline us to accept or reject messages communicated to us.

We begin our discussion of these orientations by exploring their nature and structure. Next we consider how attitudes, beliefs, and values are developed, why they are subject to change, and finally how we respond to their change.

The Nature of Attitudes, Beliefs, and Values

If you are like most people, you use the terms *attitude*, *belief*, and *value* in many of your daily conversations without really knowing how they differ from one another. Many people use the terms interchangeably, and as a result never really understand this important aspect of the psychology of communication. This is unfortunate since such an understanding often is critical to being an effective communicator.

Attitudes

Coach to sports commentator: "That player's attitude has improved 100 percent this season."

Teacher to student: "You would get a lot more out of this class if you had a more positive attitude."

We hear and say expressions such as these almost every day. What are we talking about when we make a statement about someone else's attitude? What is an attitude? Well, attitude can mean whatever we choose to say it means, since it is just a word. It is very useful, however, for us to know what experts in communication and psychology mean when they use the term. An attitude is defined as *a predisposition to respond to people, ideas, or objects in an evaluative way*. Let's examine this definition a little more closely.

When we define an attitude as a predisposition, we mean a tendency to do something. Here, it is a tendency to **evaluate** people, ideas, or objects. The word "evaluate" in this definition means making judgments of good or bad, desirable or undesirable, likable or unlikable. Thus, an attitude is our tendency to judge a person, an idea, or an object as either good or bad.

It is important to note that our definition of attitude considers not only people but also ideas and objects. Take the examples above. The coach is probably referring to the player's attitude about the sport he or she plays. The teacher is referring to the student's attitude about the content of the course. Thus, our evaluative judgments about people are similar to our evaluative judgments about physical objects or entities, such as the game of basketball, and about abstract or concrete ideas, such as the information acquired in a particular course. Just as we evaluated objects and ideas as good or bad, so do we evaluate people around us as good or bad.

"Attitudes," like "beliefs" and "values," are what are known as "hypothetical constructs." We can't see them, touch them, or smell them. They are only presumed (thought) to exist in people's minds (as thoughts or constructs), therefore the technical term. It is critical, then, that we have a way of measuring these orientations. To do so we must have the cooperation of the person who has the attitude. That person must be willing to complete some sort of measure.

Figure 9.1 presents an instrument commonly used to measure attitudes. It was developed by McCroskey (1966) to measure attitudes in a study he was doing as a part of his doctoral dissertation. In the figure, the attitude being measured is the respondent's attitude toward capital punishment. The same bipolar scales used to measure attitude toward capital punishment can be used to measure thousands of other attitudes, since scales used are not topic (attitude) dependent. For example, you can replace "Capital Punishment" with "Gun Controls," "Abortion," or "Sex Education," or much less controversial topics such as "Broccoli," "Green Beans," or "Peanut Butter."

The attitude measure presented in figure 9.1 is a very direct measure. It asks for a series of **evaluations**, the essence of our definition of the term attitude. Figure 9.2, on the other hand, presents a different kind of attitude measure (known technically as a "Likert-type scale"—named after the person who developed this approach to measurement). This scale is more indirect in that it asks people to respond to beliefs that are thought to be related to the underlying attitude of interest. This measure also was developed for the dissertation mentioned above (McCroskey, 1966). This measure, unlike the previous one, is very attitude-specific. Obviously, it cannot be used to measure your attitude toward "Broccoli"! While these two types of attitude measure are very

Figure 9.1

Generalized Attitude Measure

DIRECTIONS: On the scales below, please indicate your feelings about "Capital Punishment." Numbers "1" and "7" indicate a very strong feeling. Numbers "2" and "6" indicate a strong feeling. Numbers "3" and "5" indicate a fairly weak feeling. Number "4" indicates you are undecided or do not understand the adjectives themselves. There are no right or wrong answers.*

Good	7	6	5	4	3	2	1	Bad
Wrong	1	2	3	4	5	6	7	Right
Harmful	1	2	3	4	5	6	7	Beneficial
Fair	7	6	5	4	3	2	1	Unfair
Wise	7	6	5	4	3	2	1	Foolish
Negative	1	2	3	4	5	6	7	Positive

---

* To compute your score, simply add up the numbers you circled. To measure attitude toward some other topic, simply insert that topic in place of "Capital Punishment" above.

different, they are capable of measuring the same attitude. If you are familiar with some basic statistics, the scores from the two measures correlate above $r = .90$ ($r = 1.00$ is perfect).

Attitudes are important to human communication for one major reason—it is through communication that we discover how similar our own attitudes are to those of other people. It is the way we establish attitudinal similarity with others. If your attitude about a particular course is similar to that of your teacher, you are more likely to accept the teacher's information than is someone whose attitude is very different from the teacher's.

Attitudes, then, are our evaluative responses to things around us, whether they are ideas, objects, or other people. It is assumed that our behavior is controlled, at least in part, by our attitudes. The way we evaluate something, in other words, helps us decide how we will behave toward it. Thus, many people prefer to define attitude *as an individual's predisposition to behave in a particular way in response to something in their environment*. While this is a reasonable view, we believe it is more useful to restrict our use of the term "attitude" to evaluative orientations. We use the term "predisposition to behave" to refer to behavioral dispositions or tendencies.

Figure 9.2
Likert-Type Attitude Scale—Capital Punishment

DIRECTIONS: This instrument is composed of 8 statements concerning your attitude toward capital punishment. Please indicate the degree to which you agree or disagree with each statement by marking whether you (1) Strongly Agree, (2) Agree, (3) Are Undecided, (4) Disagree, or (5) Strongly Disagree. There are no right or wrong answers. Just record your first impressions.

_____ 1. Capital punishment is nothing but legalized murder.

_____ 2. Capital punishment should be abolished in all states and territories.

_____ 3. There is no crime which justifies capital punishment.

_____ 4. In most cases when the death penalty is enforced, it is justified.

_____ 5. Capital punishment is a justifiable means for society to use to protect itself from certain types of criminals.

_____ 6. Capital punishment gives a murderer just what he/she deserves.

_____ 7. States which have abolished capital punishment should re-establish it.

_____ 8. Vicious criminals deserve capital punishment.

To compute your score, complete the following formula:

---

1. Add up your responses to items 1, 2, 3, and 6.
2. Add 24 to the total of step 1.
3. Add up your responses to items 4, 5, 7, and 8.
4. Subtract your total for step three from your total for step 2.

Possible scores range from 8 to 40. The higher the score, the more positive is the attitude toward capital punishment.

Beliefs

Two sentences above, we used the term "believe." We meant to imply that for us (not necessarily for everyone else) the differentiation between the terms "attitude" and "predisposition to behave" is a true, correct, appropriate, right way to look at things. We "believe" in the distinction. We also think the distinction is "good," so we have a positive attitude toward it. Belief has to do with our perceptions of reality, whereas attitude has to do with our evaluation of that reality.

With this distinction we hope that you can see that attitudes and beliefs are qualitatively different. Attitudes concern our *evaluation* of whether someone or something is good or bad. Beliefs concern our *perception of reality* about whether something is true or false. Consider the following belief statements:

1. Guns don't kill people—people kill people.
2. Abortion is killing a living human being.
3. Welfare subsidizes laziness and promiscuity.
4. The barometric pressure is 29.10—very low.
5. State and federal income taxes together are between 50 and 55 percent for many middle-income couples in some states. Counting social security taxes and local income taxes, the total is over 70 percent in only 12 states.

Now consider the following attitude statements and pick the one in each pair that goes with each belief statement:

1-A. I favor gun control.

1-B. I oppose gun control.

2-A. Abortion should be outlawed.

2-B. A woman has the right to control her own body.

3-A. The welfare system should be abolished.

3-B. The welfare system is very valuable for society.

4-A. Going on a picnic is a great idea.

4-B. Going on a picnic is a stupid idea.

5-A. Income taxes are good.

5-B. Income taxes are bad.

If you picked 1-B, 2-A, 3-A, 4-B, and 5-B you clearly understand the relationship between attitudes and beliefs. If you had trouble with number 4, it probably was because you did not know the relationship between barometric pressure and rain. The more the pressure is below 30.00, the more likely it will rain. As it approaches 29.00 it becomes virtually certain there is a major storm nearby—not the day to go on a picnic! If you picked 5-A, this probably indicates you have yet to pay income taxes.

Beliefs, like attitudes, are "hypothetical constructs." To deal with them we first need to measure them. Figure 9.3 presents an instrument we have used often to measure beliefs. Note that, like the attitude measure in figure 9.1, all you have to do is change the belief statement at the top to measure a different belief. This is a fairly sophisticated belief measure. As we noted, each item in the measure presented in figure 9.2 measures a single belief. Such individual item-measures tend to be less

DIRECTIONS: On the scales below, please indicate the degree to which you believe the following statement: "Federal Taxes Should Be Reduced." Circle the number between the adjectives which best represents your beliefs. Numbers "1" and "7" indicate a very strong feeling. Numbers "2" and "6" indicate a strong feeling. Numbers "3" and "5" indicate a fairly weak feeling. Number "4" indicates you are undecided or do not understand the adjectives themselves. There are no right or wrong answers.*

Agree	7	6	5	4	3	2	1	Disagree
False	1	2	3	4	5	6	7	True
Incorrect	1	2	3	4	5	6	7	Correct
Right	7	6	5	4	3	2	1	Wrong
Yes	7	6	5	4	3	2	1	No

* To compute your score, simply add up the numbers you circled. To measure beliefs about another topic, simply insert the new belief statement in place of the "Federal Taxes Should Be Reduced" statement.

valid and reliable than more sophisticated ones. Nevertheless, the single-item type of measure is the kind used by most polling groups and many marketing researchers, so they have some value.

Attitudes and beliefs tend to go together, as the above exercise demonstrates. This does not mean they always do. It is possible, for example, for two people to agree on the belief that capital punishment does not deter crime. Yet, one person could favor capital punishment and the other person oppose it. The one may oppose it because it is not a deterrent, the other may still favor it because it severely punishes the offender. The reason their attitudes are different although their beliefs are the same is that they are using different criteria for their evaluations. Often the criteria for evaluation boil down to the person's values.

Values

Values are more complex than are attitudes and beliefs. Values are *our enduring conceptions of the nature of right and wrong, good and bad.* The key to this definition is the term *enduring*. This is what forms the difference between values, on the one hand, and beliefs and attitudes on the other. Attitudes and beliefs are typically subject to change. We may find our attitudes about some things fluctuating daily, and perhaps some of our beliefs as well. Values are not so easily subject to change. They are highly resistant to change and tend to endure over very long periods of time, some of them a lifetime. Values are the foundation upon which we form our attitudes and beliefs about people, objects, and ideas.

People in a given culture tend to share similar values, and to some extent many values are shared by different cultures. Over 2,500 years ago Aristotle, in his work entitled **The Rhetoric,** listed values which he felt the people of his time used to distinguish between that which is good and that which is evil. The rough translation of the Aristotelian value list is: happiness, justice, courage, moderation, splendor, health, beauty, wealth, friendship, honor, reputation, power, wisdom, and life. Are these still major measures of "good" vs. "bad" in today's society? While not an exhaustive list, by any means, we think **most** of these are values held by **most** of us.

Many of us might agree that we hold most of these values. It is highly unlikely, however, that any two people would rank these values in the same order. The ordering of values in comparison with each other is critical. Most of the people who disagree with each other on the issue of abortion probably hold a positive value for the life of an embryo. They also hold a positive value for the right of a woman to make decisions about her own body. They do **not** have these two values in the same order in their hierarchy of values, therefore their very strong difference in attitude about the "goodness" or "badness" of abortion.

Consider some other values that many Americans would share: scientific research, attending church, treating children well, being kind to one's spouse, being loyal to one's community, being neat and clean, being efficient, having common sense, being educated, being financially well off, working hard, and being a good sport. Rank these for yourself, and then have someone whom you think is a lot like you rank them. Then compare your responses. You will probably find that you don't think as much alike as you had believed previously. But do not write this person off as a friend! You are only likely to have conflict when discussing an issue where competing values place one of you on one side and one on the other. The farther the two of you are apart in your ranking of those values, the more serious your disagreement will be.

Thus, attitudes and beliefs may be viewed as short-term expressions of our values. Values are long-term expressions of our judgments about good and bad, right and wrong, and they form the basis for our attitudes and beliefs. Our attitudes and beliefs about a given person, idea, or object may change quite easily. Our values regarding that person, idea, or thing are much more difficult to change. If you are an avid football fan, you value your favorite school, city, or state team very much. Although the team is having a losing season and your attitude about them is negative and you no longer believe they will make the play-offs, you still place much value on the team. Your attitude and beliefs about the team may change from season to season, but the value you place on the team endures relatively unchanged.

Dimensions of Attitudes, Beliefs, and Values

At this point you should have a general understanding of the nature of attitudes, beliefs, and values and of how they differ from one another. In this section we will elaborate on the multidimensional aspect of attitudes, beliefs, and values. When we say that a concept is multi-dimensional, we mean that it is composed of several critical characteristics, and we must understand each of them to fully understand the idea itself. A multidimensional concept is analogous to a multi-dimensional physical object, such as a desk. As you most likely remember from elementary school, physical objects have three dimensions—length, width, and depth. To understand the physical nature of a desk we have to be able to answer the following questions: How long is it? How wide is it? How deep (or high) is it?

Similarly, many psychological concepts have multiple dimensions. Attitudes, beliefs, and values are each composed of three dimensions—*direction*, *intensity*, and *salience*. Just as it is important to know the various dimensions of a physical object in order to fully understand it, it is also important to know something about the three dimensions of attitudes, beliefs, and values to more fully understand these orientations. We need to know its direction (positive vs. negative), its intensity (how extreme is it), and its salience (how important this orientation is compared to others).

Direction

We have already noted that attitudes range on a continuum from good to bad (or desirable to undesirable, favorable to unfavorable, and so on) and that beliefs range on a continuum from true to false. Values also range on a good-bad continuum. Within each of these ranges there also exists a neutral or undecided position. Thus, people may have a negative, positive, or neutral attitude about some person or thing; they may have a belief that something is true or false, or they may be undecided about it; and they may have a positive, negative, or neutral value toward something. These ranges represent the possible *directions* that attitudes, beliefs, and values may take.

To illustrate this dimension for each orientation, let's take the example of three directional orientations toward sports cars. Lee likes sports cars; Don doesn't think much about them one way or the other; and Jim dislikes them. The direction of Lee's attitude toward sports cars is positive, Jim's is negative, and Don's is neutral. Based solely on these different attitude directions, we would expect Lee to be likely to want to buy a sports car, read about sports cars, talk about sports cars, and so on. Don would not be likely to buy a sports car but might, from time to time, read an ad for sports cars or take notice of a particularly attractive one in a parking lot. Jim would not be likely to consider buying a sports car, read articles or advertisements about them, and might dismiss them curtly if the topic comes up in conversations.

Since we know that people's beliefs tend to be consistent with their attitudes, we would expect that Lee believed things like sports cars represent a good value for the price, are fun to drive, and make a positive impression on other people—all positive beliefs. Jim could be expected to believe that sports cars are overpriced, uncomfortable and/or dangerous to drive, and that people who are seen driving them are thought of as vain and/or frivolous—all negative beliefs. Don could be expected to agree with Lee on some things, but with Jim on others. He might think sports cars are fun to drive, for example, but too expensive. He might just not have any particular beliefs at all—he just doesn't spend time thinking about sports cars.

As we turn to considering the direction of values that these three people might have, it is important to remember that values are strong and enduring and, as a result, tend to shape our attitudes and beliefs. Our values lead us to form certain beliefs and attitudes. In the case of Lee, she may have positive values for status and impression making, or for excitement and danger. Jim may have positive values for frugality and safety or negative values for risk-taking or debt. Don's values may be ambiguous on the issue—positive for excitement but negative for debt, for example.

The direction dimension of attitude, belief, and value orientations references the polar-opposite orientations which people may have, *if they have a directional position at all*. It is important to recognize that we do not have attitudes, beliefs, and values about everything in our environment. We really don't know much about many things, and many we may know a little about, but not care at all. In such cases, if we think about that person, object, or whatever, we are most likely to be like Don—just plain neutral. No one could predict we would be forthcoming with any relevant behavior, not even ourselves! Direction, then, must develop for us to really have an orientation of any importance.

Intensity

The second dimension of personal orientations concerns the *strength* of attitudes, beliefs, or values about people, ideas, or objects. This strength is called *intensity*. Although the direction of two people's attitudes, beliefs, or values may be similar, the strength with which they feel those orientations may differ. This variation in strength of orientations is accounted for by the intensity dimension.

The predictions we made above concerning Lee, Don, and Jim's orientations and likelihoods of behavior were very simple ones. Their accuracy might be better than chance guessing, but not much better. Knowing direction of attitude, belief, or value is not enough. We must know how intense that orientation is. Does everyone who likes sports cars buy one? Of course not. Some like them a whole lot more than others, enough so that they might sacrifice going into serious debt or not going to college to get one. Others may like them a lot, but not that intensely. Intensity, then, has to do with extremity. Highly intense attitudes, beliefs, and values are extreme ones. They are the ones most likely to lead to behavior. They are the ones that are least likely to be changed through communication with others, for reasons we will discuss at length in the next chapter.

Let us refer you back to figures 9.1, 9.2, and 9.3. Each of these measures is designed to get an indication of both direction and intensity. The neutral point on each measure separates those who have positive attitudes or beliefs from those who have negative attitudes or beliefs. The more the person's score moves from the neutral position, either toward the positive extreme (highest possible score) or the negative extreme (lowest possible score) the more intense is the person's orientation.

While the scores on the instruments in the figures have finite ranges, of necessity, it may be easier for you to grasp the concept of intensity if you think of attitudes, beliefs, and values scoring on a range from zero intensity to infinity. The more of it you have, the more intense you are—and the more likely your behavior will be consistent with your orientations, but the less likely your orientations will be changed because of communication with others. Of course, the same may be said for other people's orientations and behaviors as well.

To visualize intensity concerning beliefs, it is useful to think of probability in terms of percentage, like commonly is done in weather reports—''There is 90% probability of rain for this afternoon.'' When we hear this forecast, if we believe the forecaster, we are likely to cancel our picnic plans. When the forecast is for a 20% probability of bad weather, of course, we are likely to behave in an opposite manner.

Salience

The third dimension comprising the multidimensional orientations of attitude, belief, and value is *salience*. Salience can be defined as *perceived importance of an attitude, a belief, or a value to the individual*. Two teenagers, Brian and Kristen, may have similar attitudes, beliefs, and values related to playing football. Often, those orientations probably are much more salient for Brian than for Kristen. Brian is more likely to be expected to play football than she is.

The essence of salience is involvement. The more involved we are with something, the more salient it is, and the more impact relevant attitudes, beliefs, and values about it will have on our behavior. This may best be illustrated by considering the salience of values. Returning to our income tax example, two people may have very intense attitudes and beliefs about the government's right to tax citizens, but if one is employed and the other is still supported by parents, income tax is more salient for the employed person. We hold many attitudes and beliefs on a theoretical basis; salience applies to actual participation in certain behaviors. As we noted before, our values tend to shape both our attitudes and our behaviors. The salience of those values tends to determine our behaviors.

Development of Attitudes, Beliefs, and Values

We are born without attitudes, beliefs, and values. These orientations are developed as we grow and mature; they are products of our life experiences. Thus, attitudes, beliefs, and values are *learned*. There is no one theory that best explains how these orientations are learned. However, *reinforcement theory* is a useful paradigm for describing the process by which attitudes, beliefs, and values are learned.

Reinforcement theory maintains that we respond to various stimuli according to whether these responses lead to rewarding or non-rewarding results for us. Responses that are rewarded become part of our habitual response pattern. Responses that are not rewarded or which result in punishment for us tend to decrease in frequency of occurrence, often to a point where they cease to be a part of our response pattern.

Take for example your own attitude toward communicating with others. If you were raised in a home in which you were reinforced (received reward) for communicating, you probably communicate more and may place much value on communication. In that environment you may have found that by communicating in certain ways—saying and doing certain things—you received very positive responses from those around you. Those positive responses served to reinforce your communication behavior so that eventually that behavior became habitual for you. On the other hand, if you were raised in a home in which communication was not reinforced or was punished, you probably communicate less, and your attitude toward and value for communication may be negative. Perhaps in that environment you were told ''don't speak unless you're spoken to'' or ''children are to be seen and not heard.'' Such responses from other people were non-rewarding or even punishing to your communication behavior. Thus, you may have decreased your use of that behavior. Consequently, you are likely to have developed quite negative attitudes and values about communication, even a belief that communication is not very important. Notice that this example of how negative orientations toward communication are developed is similar to the reinforcement explanation of communication apprehension. If our negative attitudes, beliefs, and values concerning communication are extreme, we may well develop deficiencies in our communicative behaviors—deficiencies such as communication apprehension and inadequate skills.

Many of our attitudes, beliefs, and values are formed through types of reinforcement that are less direct than exemplified above. A capacity we have as human beings is to generalize our responses to similar stimuli. For example, if in high school you had a very positive relationship with a teacher, you may have developed a positive attitude toward teachers in general. That we generalize our orientations in this way explains why we have many preferences in our lives: It explains why we prefer to go out with a certain type of person, why we choose to engage in a particular hobby, why we have our favorite style of music, why we like some foods over others, and why we are more comfortable in certain situations than in others. As long as our responses to these stimuli are reinforced, we are likely to maintain our favorable orientations toward them. When we experience no reinforcement for any given response, we are likely to make a different behavior choice.

Indirect reinforcement, as when we see someone else receive a reward for some specific behavior, is known as *vicarious reinforcement*. Vicarious reinforcement may also come from reading or watching movies or videos. As we learned earlier our communication with real people helps develop many of our attitudes, beliefs, and values. The orientations we have toward sex, careers, politics, religion, war, and the like develop in our youth, in large part from our interactions with others; many of the attitudes, beliefs, and values of other people tend to ''rub off'' on us. To some extent, therefore, we can predict a person's orientations based on the orientations held by the people with whom he or she associates.

The people who serve to shape an individual's orientations are that individual's *reference group*. A reference group, however, may be a group with whom the individual is not directly affiliated but whose opinions the individual values. When the individual's attitudes, beliefs, and values are similar to those of members of the reference group, the individual is likely to be accepted by the group and to be reinforced for her or his behavior. Conversely, if the individual's orientations differ from those of the reference group, the individual is apt to find their orientations unacceptable and may receive punishment from the group in the form of alienation. An example of this process can be drawn from your decision about whether to join a sorority or fraternity. If you have chosen not to be a "Greek," it may be because you do not share many attitudes, beliefs, and values generally held by such organizations. Of course, if you have chosen to join a sorority or fraternity, it is probably because you share the orientations of such groups. Moreover, attitudes, beliefs, and values vary from one fraternity or sorority to another. Therefore, your decision to join a particular organization is determined largely by how similar you perceive your own orientations to be to those of that group.

Attitudes, beliefs, and values are learned responses. These responses are learned from direct and vicarious everyday experiences. Other orientations are learned from generalizing to new or similar experiences. When we have no direct or vicarious experience on which to form our own orientations, we tend to rely on the attitudes, beliefs, and values of people around us. Our life experiences continue for as long as we live. Thus, there is always potential for our attitudes and beliefs to change from time to time as we encounter new experiences and develop new interpersonal relationships. Values, too, may change, although they endure much longer than attitudes and beliefs. Just how and why these orientations undergo change has been a major area of theory and research in social psychology and communication through the decades since World War II. Although most of this work has been labeled "attitude-change" theory and research, it applies equally well to beliefs and values as it does to attitudes. The theory that we believe has particular relevance to communication is consistency theory.

Consistency Theory

In chapter 8 we introduced you to the "principle of consistency" as it relates to perceptions of the source in human communication. In that brief discussion we explained that our perceptions of a source and its message are, to some extent, a function of how consistent we view our attitudes to be with those of the source. The attitudes we have or those held by the source may change (become inconsistent) at any time, thus affecting perceptions and ultimately communication behaviors. Let's look now at a particular consistency theory, the one known as **balance theory** (Heider, 1946; Newcomb, 1958).

Based on the principle of consistency, balance theory maintains that (1) a person needs consistency or "balance" among her or his attitudes, beliefs, and values; (2) when a person becomes aware of inconsistency or "imbalance" among attitudes, beliefs, and values, this leads to a state of tension; and (3) a person will seek to reduce this tension by altering one or more attitudes, beliefs, or values. As it applies to communication, the balance or consistency we are concerned with is that the attitudes, beliefs, and values held by two communicators for each other and for whatever it is they are communicating about correspond. These orientations can be illustrated in a model such as that in figure 9.4, where A represents one person, B represents the other person, and X represents something they are communicating about or may discuss.

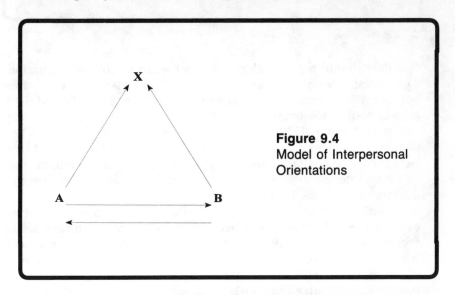

Figure 9.4
Model of Interpersonal Orientations

The theory holds that persons A and B have balanced orientations when their attitudes toward each other and toward X are consistent. That is, balance exists in any condition in which person A's attitudes toward B and X are consistent with person B's attitudes toward A and X. Two communicators—for example, Willie and Hank—can have balanced orientations in two ways as illustrated in figure 9.5. Willie and Hank are discussing the 1992 United States military intervention in Somalia to provide food for starving people in that country. In condition (a), Willie and Hank have positive attitudes toward each other and positive attitudes toward the Somalia intervention. This situation is balanced because when two people feel positively toward one another, it follows

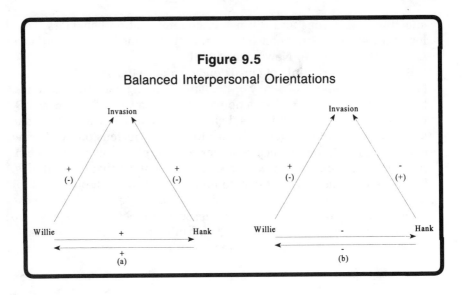

Figure 9.5

Balanced Interpersonal Orientations

that they should have similar attitudes toward a topic of discussion. Thus, balance would also exist when Willie and Hank like each other but look with disfavor on the invasion. In condition (b), Willie and Hank have opposing orientations toward the intervention in Somalia, and they dislike each other. This is also a balanced situation because when two people do not look favorably toward one another, it follows that they should have dissimilar attitudes toward a subject of discussion. In other words, we do not expect two people who feel negatively toward one another to agree with each other.

To put figure 9.5 into clearer terms, balance theory maintains that we expect people whom we like to favor things we approve of and to disfavor things we disapprove of—condition (a). Moreover, we expect people whom we dislike to disapprove of things we approve of and to approve of things we disapprove of—condition (b). Thus, balance theory holds that a communicative situation is balanced when our expectations about the similarity between our orientations and another person's orientations are consistent. When the other person shows an orientation different from what is consistent with our expectations, then we have an unbalanced situation. Figure 9.6 illustrates two possible situations in which orientations are unbalanced.

In condition (a) of figure 9.6, Willie and Hank both approve of the intervention in Somalia, but they dislike one another. This situation is unbalanced because we would not expect two people who look negatively toward each other to agree on a subject. Thus, imbalance also exists when Willie and Hank dislike each other but both look with disfavor on the Somalia intervention.

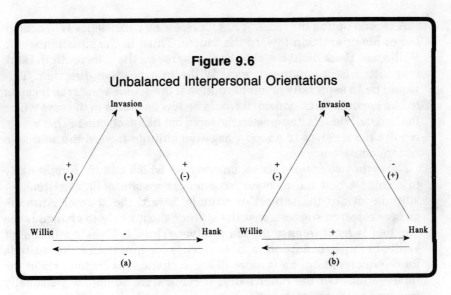

Figure 9.6
Unbalanced Interpersonal Orientations

Condition (b) illustrates the situation in which Willie and Hank like each other but disagree in their orientations about the invasion. This is an unbalanced situation because we would not expect that two people who like each other would have opposing viewpoints on a topic of discussion.

Consistency theory would predict that no change of orientations will occur in the balanced conditions depicted in figure 9.5. However, change in attitudes or beliefs would be predicted in the conditions illustrated in figure 9.6. As the theory states, tension is produced by inconsistency; reduction of tension requires some change in orientations. There are several ways that consistency can be restored in situations where orientations are unbalanced. Each is considered in the following section.

Restoring Consistency

Inconsistency is present in a communicative situation in which the receiver perceives that the source expresses attitudes different from what he or she expected the source would express. This inconsistency is likely to cause some tension in the receiver, tension that is potentially detrimental to communication outcomes. To alleviate this tension so that outcomes can be better achieved, the receiver must somehow resolve the inconsistency. One way that consistency can be restored is for the receiver to alter her or his attitude toward the subject of communication. This is what the source would want the receiver to do. In the case where Willie and Hank like each other and disagree on the topic, for example, to restore consistency Willie may attempt to get Hank to take a view of the intervention in Somalia that is similar to his own, so that both either approve or disapprove of the invasion.

A second option the receiver has for restoring consistency is to change her or his orientation toward the source. Thus, in the situation where Willie and Hank dislike each other but agree on the intervention, Hank may alter his orientation toward Willie in a positive direction. This would be an especially favorable option if the source wants the receiver to like her or him. Of course, it would be less favorable in the case where the two individuals disagree on the topic but like each other. That would require the receiver to adopt a negative attitude toward the source to restore consistency.

Given the two options above, one may ask which attitude is most likely to change when the receiver experiences a state of inconsistency—attitude toward the subject or attitude toward the source? Attitude-change research suggests that the attitude most likely to change is the one that is **least intense** for the receiver. Thus, if Hank's attitude for Willie in either condition is more intense for him than is his attitude for the intervention, he is more likely to change his attitude about the intervention. On the other hand, if Hank were somehow personally involved with the intervention—perhaps he had a brother serving with the troops—then he is more likely to alter his attitude about Willie. Sometimes, however, the receiver may choose not to change either of her or his attitudes and turn instead to another option for restoring consistency.

This third way of resolving inconsistency is called "leaving the field." This is a form of communication withdrawal that may take either a physical or a psychological form. In the physical sense, leaving the field assumes a literal dimension. Knowing that he and Willie disagree about Somalia, for example, Hank may simply remove himself from Willie's company when the topic arises. We all leave the field from time to time, particularly when a topic for which we have an intense attitude is brought up by someone whom we like very much but whose attitude toward the topic is quite different from our own. Recall a time in high school when your parents wanted to "discuss" with you your late school-night hours!

Psychological withdrawal from the communication situation occurs more often than physically leaving the field. Often it is simply inappropriate or impossible to remove ourselves from the other person's presence. If, for example, Hank knows that Willie disagrees with him on the topic of Somalia, Hank can avoid bringing up the subject when talking to him. If the topic does come up and if Hank values highly his friendship with Willie, he may selectively interpret what Willie is saying about the subject, a topic we consider in more detail in the next chapter. He may unconsciously misinterpret what Willie is saying to be the exact opposite of what was stated; he may perceive a reason other than the real reason for why Willie is saying what he is; or he may just tune out and not pay attention to Willie.

Perhaps the most often employed means for restoring consistency through psychologically leaving the field is "forgetting." Hank realizes that his and Willie's attitudes are inconsistent, but he finds it very difficult or undesirable to alter his own; so he may just try to forget the entire transaction concerning the intervention.

Thus several options are available for restoring consistency in those communicative situations where two people's attitudes toward each other and the subject of discussion do not fit one or the other person's expectations. When we partition the communication process into separate source and receiver processes and variables, the whole matter of interpersonal orientations and consistency among them perhaps has greater import for the receiver than for the source. This is because—as we have emphasized throughout this and the previous two chapters—how the receiver perceives and responds to the source has significant impact on communication outcomes. Central to those perceptions are the receiver's attitudes, beliefs, and values, and how similarly the receiver perceives these to be to the attitudes, beliefs, and values of the source. When the receiver perceives inconsistency between her or his own orientations and those of the source, tension results; the need to alleviate that tension leads to the receiver making some choice for restoring consistency. Whatever option the receiver selects to employ, some change in orientations and/or perceptions and behavior occur, and ultimately some change in communication also occurs. Depending on the nature of the transaction, these changes can either enhance the achievement of communication outcomes or inhibit their achievement.

An important concern of the receiver in communication is attempting to explain why the source behaves in a particular way. Such explanations rest largely with the receiver's orientations toward the source. These orientations affect the receiver's perceptions of what causes the source to say and do certain things. This process of explaining causes of another's behavior is called *attribution*, the subject of the next chapter.

References

Heider, F. (1946). Attitudes and cognitive organization. *Journal of Psychology*, 21, 107–112.

McCroskey, J. C. (1993). *An introduction to rhetorical communication* (6th ed.). Englewood Cliffs, NJ: Prentice-Hall.

Newcomb, T. M. (1958). Attitude development as a function of reference groups: The Bennington study. In E. E. Maccoby, T. M. Newcomb, & E. L. Hartley (Eds.), *Readings in social psychology*. New York: Holt, Rhinehart & Winston.

SELECTIVITY AND ATTRIBUTION
WHY OUR MESSAGES DON'T GET THROUGH

10

Getting through to people is not an easy task under the best of circumstances. Even if another person is highly motivated to communicate effectively with us, the odds are still against success unless we can overcome the selectivity and attribution barriers. The *noise in the receiver*, noted in our model of the rhetorical communication process (figure 1.1), is not there because someone wants it to be; it is there because of the basic psychology of human beings.

Human beings are *information processors*. That is, messages do not simply go directly from their source to the mind of the receiver. They go through a reception and processing system. Most messages do not get through that system at all. Those that do may be modified greatly before the meaning they generate is stored in the receiver's mind. That meaning may be only remotely related to the meaning the source was attempting to communicate with the message.

Selectivity Processes

Actually, trying to get our messages through to produce our intended meaning is like trying to make our way through an obstacle course. The obstacles are the various types of selectivity, as illustrated in figure 10.1. We must overcome each obstacle in turn, for at any point our message may be blocked from stimulating the meaning we want to communicate. If we fail to recognize an obstacle, or to deal with that obstacle, our communicative goals will be missed.

As indicated in figure 10.1, there are four types of selectivity that can directly interfere with initial reception of messages: selective exposure, selective attention, selective perception, and selective retention (McCroskey & Wheeless, 1976). A fifth type of selectivity may occur even after initial reception has occurred: selective recall (McCroskey, 1993). We will look at each of these in turn.

Selective Exposure

"Selective exposure" refers to a person's conscious or unconscious decision to place herself or himself in a position to receive messages from a particular source. We all engage in this type of behavior every day. When we choose a television channel, we have selectively exposed ourselves. Even if we just turn on the TV and watch whatever is on the channel to which it was turned by someone else, we have selectively exposed ourselves, for we choose not to change the channel.

Whether we are interested in influencing someone's behavior or building a better relationship with that person, we cannot do so unless

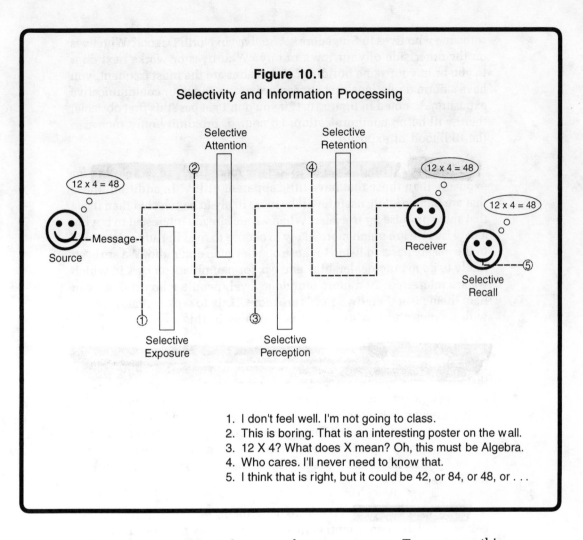

Figure 10.1

Selectivity and Information Processing

1. I don't feel well. I'm not going to class.
2. This is boring. That is an interesting poster on the wall.
3. 12 X 4? What does X mean? Oh, this must be Algebra.
4. Who cares. I'll never need to know that.
5. I think that is right, but it could be 42, or 84, or 48, or . . .

that person is willing to be exposed to our messages. To overcome this first barrier to our effectiveness, then, we need to understand what factors lead to exposure decisions. We will consider four.

Proximity. That which is immediately available is most likely to be chosen. If we want to communicate with someone, obviously we must make ourselves available for communication with that person when he or she is likely to wish to communicate. That is not necessarily the same time *we* want to communicate! Proximity is such an important factor in determining selective exposure it has even been found the single best predictor of whom a person chooses to marry (Katz & Hill, 1958). Since proximity is such an obvious factor, it often is overlooked; but that does not decrease its importance. How often have you talked with someone who lives in Singapore? Who lives in North Dakota? Who lives on the other side of your town or city? Who lives or works next door to you or in your same building? If the latter are the most frequent, you have a normal relationship between proximity and your communicative exposure. As noted in figure 10.1, if you don't get past this first obstacle, there will be no communication. Of course, proximity only increases the liklihood of exposure.

Utility. Things seen as useful are more likely to be selected for exposure than those that have little apparent utility. In addition, those that are ***immediately*** useful, will be more likely to be selected than those that show promise for use later. When we are already interested in buying a new car, we are much more likely to choose to read the advertisements in the magazines and listen to those on television and radio. We are even likely to go to auto dealerships and ask for pamphlets on cars in which we are interested. At a more mundane level, people who think we can help them meet their own needs are more likely to seek communication with us than those who do not perceive us in this way.

Involvement. The more important a topic is to a person, the more the person is likely to expose herself or himself to messages on that topic. Avid sports fans seek to communicate about sports. Politically active people want to talk about politics and public policy. As we noted in the previous chapter, the more salient an attitude, belief, or value is, the more involving it is. Communication on topics that relate to salient orientations of people is more likely to get them to expose themselves to us, particularly if it seems likely the communication will be reinforcing.

Reinforcement. People expose themselves to messages they believe will be consistent with their own beliefs. Democrats go to Democratic Party rallies. Republicans go to Republican Party rallies. When we attend athletic events, we sit on ''our'' side, not ''their'' side of the field or floor. Pro-choice people listen to and read messages that support a woman's right to an abortion. Anti-abortion people listen to and read messages that advocate abolition of abortion. In short, we all want to hear others present messages that agree with our own views. Only infrequently do we choose in advance to expose ourselves to messages that we believe will take positions with which we disagree. We seek advice from people whom we believe see the world the way we do, and we avoid communicating with those who see things differently. It is not surprising, then, that often when people get into conflict with each other they want little or no communication with each other. Some people, of course, are reinforced by getting into arguments with others rather than avoiding them. These people will actively seek to communicate with people who disagree with them.

Whatever the reason people engage in selective exposure, the bottom line remains the same—no exposure, no effective communication. Getting other people to make themselves available to receive messages from us will not guarantee that we can communicate with them effectively. But failing to expose our messages to them guarantees that we will *not* be effective. Exposure is a necessary, but not sufficient, condition for effective communication.

Selective Attention

There is an old saying which suggests you can bring a horse to water (selective exposure), but can't make it drink (selective attention). We cannot always control the types of messages to which we are exposed. Thus, when we are exposed to messages we would rather avoid, we may simply select to pay attention to something else.

In one sense, *all* attention is selective. Everything in our perceptual world makes some demand upon our attention, but we cannot attend to everything at once. Therefore, we may choose to pay attention to something other than a given message, or we may pay more attention to some messages and less to others. In any environment there are many things competing for our attention—sights, sounds, and odors abound. In a classroom, for example, there are other students, things on the wall, things going on outside windows, what the teacher is wearing, what the person next to you is wearing, a clock, what the person next to you smells like, what he or she says, what the teacher says, and so on. Many factors contribute to determining which of these things you will pay attention to at any given time. We will consider five of these.

Attention Span. No matter what we choose to pay attention to, that attention can continue only so long. The amount of time a person can spend attending to one thing before having to shift to something else is called one's "attention span." How long that span is depends in part on developmental factors. Young children typically have very brief attention spans while adult attention spans are longer. Even for adults, however, attention spans usually are measured in seconds, not minutes. People's attention, of necessity, will move from one thing to another continuously. Even in an important conversation, we are not able to maintain completely undivided attention to what our conversational partner is saying. Thus, if it is vitally important that we communicate a specific idea, we need to be redundant. That is, we need to use more than one message designed to communicate that idea. This will greatly enhance the probability that at least one message will capture the necessary attention to get through.

Novelty. Things that are unusual attract attention. The routine tends to be ignored. New Yorkers pay little attention to tall buildings, but visitors stare at them. People who live in Hawaii pay little attention to banyan trees and orchids, but tourists pay great attention to both of them. We get used to things in our environment, no matter how unusual those things are to people who are not used to them. Routine memos look like other routine memos, so one on bright green paper catches our attention. If all our memos come on bright green paper, none will be very attention-getting. If we want someone to pay attention to our message, we need to make that message stand out from all the other stimuli in the environment.

Concreteness. Since they are hard to understand, highly abstract messages bore most people. Consequently, people direct their attention away from such messages to others that are more concrete and interesting. Concrete things or ideas, those that relate to the life or experience of the receiver, attract attention. If we want our receiver to pay attention to our message, we should be certain the message relates to what our receiver understands and/or has experienced.

Size. As a rule, bigger things draw more attention than smaller ones. Big maps, big pictures, big graphs, even big people, will grab attention. Sometimes, of course, things that are unusually small will attract attention because of their novelty. Nevertheless, we tend to notice the bigger things first.

Duration. Attention is directed toward messages that are moderate in length (written) or duration (time). Very brief messages may be missed—they are over before attention turns to them. Long messages are likely to exceed the receiver's attention span. If we must communicate a large amount of information, it is best that we do so with messages that are devoted to smaller chunks of that information.

Whatever the reason for a receiver's use of selective attention, as we said with selective exposure, the bottom line is the same: no attention, no effective communication. While attention from our receiver is not sufficient to guarantee effective communication, the absence of attention will guarantee effective communication will **not** occur. Attention is a necessary, but not sufficient, condition for effective communication.

Selective Perception

Perception is the process of attributing meaning to messages. Messages do not "carry" meaning, as we have noted in previous chapters. They **stimulate** meaning in people's minds. The precise meaning that is stimulated depends on both the message and the receiver. Thus, in a sense, all perception is selective. That is, the receiver must select, from all the possible meanings that could be attributed to a message, the particular meaning which the source intended. It is most likely that different receivers of the same message, since they have different backgrounds and experiences, will attribute different meanings to that message. The problem for the source is to stimulate the meaning intended rather than another meaning. This outcome is more likely when factors which lead to other perceptions are controlled—although it is not usually possible to control, or even to recognize, all of the possibilities.

Even if we succeed in exposing our messages to our potential receiver and having him or her pay attention to those messages, the desired meaning may not be communicated because the receiver may perceive the messages to mean something different than what we intended. Many factors influence such perceptions or, at least from the source's view, **misperceptions**. We should also recognize that misperception is not only a problem for the source. In fact, it may be much more important to the receiver that he/she perceives the correct meaning in many cases. Students, for example, will be evaluated on how much of the ''correct'' meaning they learn—correct as defined by the teacher. Whenever we try to obtain information from someone else, it usually is more important to us, as receivers, to perceive messages the way the source intends them than it is to the source. Let us consider several factors that may cause a receiver to select perceptions different than those intended by the source.

Ambiguity of Messages.   Sometimes messages are very imprecise and open to misunderstanding. Words that people use in different ways can lead a receiver, even one who is trying hard to get the source's intended meaning, to select a meaning other than the one intended. Since language is inherently imprecise, careful choice of wording is very important if one hopes to avoid misunderstanding or being misunderstood. Use of abstract rather than concrete words and phrases is particularly problematic. In general, the more abstract a series of messages is, the more ambiguous those messages are. The more concrete and specific a message is, the less likely it will be misperceived. As receivers we should always remember that if we are not certain we understand a message, we should whenever possible ask the source for additional clarification.

Lack of Message Redundancy.   To the extent a series of messages lacks redundancy, those messages invite misperception. Redundancy permits a second (or third, fourth, and so on) chance for the receiver to capture the intended meaning. Single messages are far more likely to be misunderstood than multiple messages directed toward stimulating the same meaning. Again, receivers should never hesitate to ask for clarification when there is not sufficient redundancy in a source's messages to be assured of the intended meaning.

Lack of Receiver Schema. People learn by placing information into categories with information that is similar. Category systems of this kind are known as "schema." Imagine, please, you are in a post office that has mail boxes. The postal clerk invites you to walk around back so you can see the boxes from the back side. What you see is row after row of boxes, all connected to one another. In a small town, these boxes may have people's names marked on them. In a larger city, the boxes are more likely to have just numbers. The postal clerk sorts through the mail and puts various pieces in the various boxes, and has some mail left over that does not go in any of the boxes. That mail must be returned or another method must be employed to find the person for whom it is intended.

People's schema systems are somewhat like the mail boxes. As a message is received, we place it in one of our mental boxes if we believe we have one for it. If no box can be found for it, it must be shunted aside to be considered later, or simply ignored (in one ear and out the other!). If people do not have appropriate schema for the ideas included in our messages, they may not be able to cope with those ideas. We must avoid "talking over someone's head."

Missing schema, of course, are not only problems for sources. They have their most direct effect on us as receivers. When we hear a message and find no place for it, the idea the source was trying to communicate most likely will just pass on through our perceptual system and not really be perceived at all. Possibly even worse, we may find a place we think is appropriate, although it is not, and perceive that message as if it really did belong there. The child perceives an "invisible nation" rather than an "indivisible nation" in the Pledge of Allegiance. This occurs because the child is too young to have a schema system that can cope with the concept of "indivisible."

Previous Experiences. We know the world through our experiences. The experiences of a person who was a child in the 1950s are different from the experiences of a person who was a child in the 1980s. The former has a breadth of experience with cold-war politics, black and white television (and no television at all), and has fond memories of entertainers unknown to the latter. However, the 1950s child may have to ask the 1980s child how to set her or his VCR or operate a personal computer, things the 1980s child can't believe anyone doesn't already know. Just as generations have different experiences, so do people in the same age group who live in different cultures, or even different subcultures within a broader culture. Whenever people do not have similar backgrounds and experiences, they are highly likely to perceive messages differently.

Expectancies and Biases.   An expectancy is anticipation of a future occurrence. A bias is an unjustified evaluation. All people have both expectancies and biases. Whenever the receiver has either an expectancy or a bias related to a source's message, it is probable that the message will be perceived in a way that is consistent with that expectancy or bias. Unfortunately, this is more the norm than the exception. People tend to perceive what they expect to see or hear and are most likely to interpret messages in such a manner that they conform to their biases.

Selective perception is a difficult problem for us to control, as either a source or a receiver, because it will always occur to some extent. Even after overcoming selective exposure and attention, communication can fail to be effective due to misperception of messages. One positive thing is that even if misperception occurs, it can be corrected—if the misperception can be identified. Thus, we should seek as much feedback and questioning from our potential receivers as possible and provide such feedback and questions to other sources. Only by practicing such safeguards can we prevent misconceptions from causing ineffective communication.

Selective Retention

Selective retention may be the problem that is the most frustrating. People interact with one another, they pay attention to one another, and they even perceive one another's messages correctly. However, a few days (or sometimes minutes) later, it is as if the conversation never existed. Nothing is retained. Selective retention refers to the decision to store or not store information in long-term memory. As with the other selectivity factors, this process also occurs primarily at the non-conscious level, but the selection sometimes is made consciously. Several factors are known to influence selective retention.

Lack of Highlighting.   Although not restricted to instructional settings, this factor has a major impact in those settings. When important ideas are not highlighted by teachers, students often do not realize they are important. This is one of the reasons why providing students with learning objectives is such a good idea. While this is only one of many means of highlighting, it represents a clear message to the student about what the teacher expects will be retained. Have you ever gone through your notes after a test and found something that was the answer to a test question? Possibly something you did not even remember writing down? If you had been told that was important to learn—if it had been highlighted—you would have been much more likely to have learned it.

Lack of Redundancy. In general, the more we hear something, the more important we think it is, and the more likely we are to remember it. Redundancy capitalizes on this premise. Sometimes people simply do not think something is important until they hear about it several times. For children this idea is particularly important. In contrast to adults, children are exposed to vastly more "new" things each day. They cannot be expected to retain everything new they initially learn. Thus, if we expect a child to learn something and retain it more than a short time, it is important that the child hear it several times. It is only slightly less important for adults.

Lack of Schema. While schema are very important to initial learning, they are absolutely critical for retention. If there is no system for storage (schema) available, the outcome of communication is simple to predict. There will be no storage. It is like trying to store information on a computer that has no disk. You turn it off and the information is gone. The receiver's schema is the disk. If it is missing, or if it is defective, retention will not occur.

Lack of Concrete Application. Retention often depends on applying new ideas or information to real, concrete concerns. Retaining information for use at some indefinite time in the future is particularly difficult. The old saying, "Use it or loose it" is particularly appropriate in this instance. That which is used is retained.

Principles of Primacy and Recency. In the 1940s and 1950s, social scientists were very interested in persuasion. They sought to find out whether topics covered first in a message (the primacy principle) or topics covered last (the recency principle) were most remembered (Hovland, Janis, & Kelley, 1953). After many studies, clearly neither primacy nor recency had a universally stronger effect than the other. However, information presented near either the beginning or the ending of the message was more effective than information presented in the middle. What is said first and what is said last are most likely to be remembered.

The conclusion concerning selective retention is that you are not likely to get someone to retain much from your communication unless you take steps to increase the probability of retention. As we have noted previously, telling is not communicating. Simply presenting messages will not assure retention. You must design your message to produce retention if you expect it to do so.

Selective Recall

Selective retention and selective recall are often confused and sometimes thought to be the same thing. It is important to distinguish between these two forms of selectivity because they are quite different, although related.

Selective retention has to do with the *storage* of information, while selective recall has to do with the *retrieval* of information. Of course, if information is not stored (retained) in the first place, it cannot be retrieved (recalled) later. However, just because something is retained does not necessarily mean it will be recalled at any given point in time. Have you ever had a hard time recalling something at one time, but had it come back to you at another? It was stored away in your brain both times, but it was only retrieved once.

All of us have many things stored away in our long-term memories. Many of these things do not come back to us with ease. We need something to trigger the recall response. Things are learned in a context, and part of what is stored is information related to that context. When we try to recall the information in another context, it may not come back quickly, or even come back at all unless we can find an appropriate trigger. Sometimes we may not even want to recall something, particularly something that was unpleasant. We all repress some memories.

Effective communication is not easy. There are major barriers in the way, and these selectivity processes number among those most problematic. If one is not aware of these processes and/or does not take appropriate steps to overcome selectivity, effective communication can only be expected to occur by chance. That is a remote chance!

Causal Attribution

Our nature as human beings is such that we perceive events and circumstances to have causes. It is not enough for us simply to know that something happens; it is human nature to want to know why it happens. Even when we are uncertain about the actual causes of events, we tend to assign causes to them. We may pass the scene of an automobile accident during a thunder storm, for example, and attribute the cause to bad weather. In terms of interpersonal behavior, we may observe a friend being rude or short-tempered with another person and attribute our friend's behavior to the fact that he or she has the flu and is feeling a bit testy.

Attribution Defined

Attribution of causality is **the perception process by which we make sense out of the behavior of others**. We see people behave in certain ways, verbally or nonverbally, and attempt to make sense out of their behavior by assigning some probable cause to it. If, for instance, your mother has suddenly begun sending you extra money, you might attribute it to the fact that she has received a raise. If your dating partner has recently been treating you unusually nicely, you may attribute it to the possibility that he or she is jealous of your "new friend."

Generally we engage in this process of causal attribution because we want to know why a behavior occurs and what it might mean. In this sense, causal attribution is a process of uncertainty reduction. If we can pin down the probable cause of another person's behavior, we gain a better understanding of that behavior and become more certain of its implications for ourselves, the other person, and our relationship with that person.

Attribution Sources

The causes we may attribute to another person's behavior stem from one of two sources: **internal factors** or **external factors**. When we attribute a person's behavior to internal causes, we are attributing the person's behavior to her or his personality. For example, when someone asks you why you think another person has done something in particular and you reply with "I guess that is just the way she is," you are attributing the person's behavior to internal causes. The words "the way she is" suggest that the person has some predisposition or trait that makes her engage in certain behavior.

Similarly, when you suggest to a classmate that your high test scores are due to the instructor being "a really nice person," you are explaining the instructor's personality as the cause for giving students good grades. Attributing people's behavior to external factors, however, explains their behavior as caused by certain situational influences, which may include other people with whom they are associated. For example, when your roommate arrives home one evening in an angry mood and you think to yourself, "Snowy weather always makes him act this way," you are attributing his behavior to situational causes. It is not his personality or general emotional state that makes him act that way, but rather the weather, an external cause. Also, when a friend credits your good cooking to well-written recipes and a finely tuned microwave oven, he or she is attributing its cause to certain aspects of the environment rather than to your culinary talent (which would be internal).

Whenever we attribute a person's behavior to other people, we are also making external attributions. For instance, when parents explain that their child's poor conduct is due to "that crowd" he or she associates with, they are attributing the child's behavior to factors external to the child rather than to internal factors such as personality.

Attribution Conditions. Our explanations of a person's behavior at any given time as caused by either internal or external factors are typically based on one of three conditions (see figure 10.1).

Consensus. The first of these is **consensus**, or whether the individual acts in a way similar to the way other people act in a given situation. If consensus is high—that is, the person does act in a way similar to others—we tend to attribute the person's actions to external causes because he or she is responding to the particular situation and perhaps is conforming to how others in the situation are acting. However, if consensus is low—the person is not acting like others in the situation—then we are likely to attribute his or her behavior to internal causes because we will perceive that the individual is acting out of his or her own initiative and not necessarily out of response to others or the situation. An example of this might be the individual who sits in the corner at parties and ignores what is happening, keeping to himself or herself while others mingle and converse.

Consistency. The second condition on which we base attributions is consistency, or whether the individual behaves the same way in the same situation at different times. When consistency is high— that is, the person does always act the same way in the same situation— we tend to attribute his or her behavior to external causes. This is because it is most likely that some aspect of the situation is causing the person to behave in a particular way. Situational-bound communication apprehension is an example of high consistency. Although most of us tend to remain comfortable in face-to-face interactions, we become quite apprehensive in public-speaking situations. Low consistency occurs when the individual behaves differently in the same situation at different times, in which case we are likely to attribute the person's behavior to internal causes. If you are quite nervous about giving a speech on one occasion but rather calm about it on another, then we probably will attribute your reactions to your mood. You are not necessarily free of anxiety on the second occasion, but perhaps you just feel more enthusiastic and better prepared at the time.

Distinctiveness. The third condition that determines the causes to which we attribute a person's behavior is **distinctiveness**, or whether the individual behaves the same way in different situations. When distinctiveness is high—that is, the person acts differently in response to different situations—we are likely to attribute the individual's behavior to external causes. For example, if your mother curses when she bumps her toe on a table leg but generally does not curse on other occasions, we would tend to attribute her exclamation to the pain and frustration that come with hurting one's toe and not to her personality. If distinctiveness is low—the person acts the same way in different situations—then we attribute causality to internal factors. Your mother may curse when she hurts her toe, is late for work, welcomes you home, and sees a picture of Elvis. Observing her in these varied situations may lead one to attribute her cursing to her personality or her "earthy" vocabulary.

Given the three conditions on which we base attributions of causality, we can see that our judgments about a person's behavior are simply our perceptions. That is, we perceive the person either as having control over the situation in which we observe him or her, or as under the influence of situational constraints. How accurate these perceptions are, and thus the accuracy of our attributions, depends greatly on how well we know the other person. The better we know the other individual, the more accurate our causal attributions will be. For example, you likely can explain with much greater precision why your parents would be disappointed with your bad test score than you can explain why a new acquaintance would be upset. Simply put, the more information we have about a situation and the people in it with whom we interact, the more precise our judgments will be.

Basic Attribution Error

Closely linked with this information-attribution relationship is interpersonal orientations. The better we know someone, the more likely we are to share the person's attitudes. The greater our knowledge and understanding of the person's attitudes, the more likely we are to judge their behavior and its causes accurately. We can attribute the individual's behavior to the person or to the environment. If we know the person well, we may be able to deduce that he or she is acting based on some attitude, belief, or value; if we do not know the person well, the best we can do is to speculate as to the cause of his or her behavior. Such attributions usually are inaccurate and derive from "the basic attribution error."

The *basic attribution error* occurs when we attribute the causes of our own behavior to external factors and the causes of another person's behavior to internal causes. The "error" is that we more often perceive our behavior as due to situational matters beyond our control and other people's behavior as due to their personality or emotional state. In actuality, neither may be the case. For example, when your boyfriend or girlfriend is late for a date or fails to answer the phone, it is *his* or *her* fault. When you find yourself in these circumstances, however, you are likely to blame a late-running class or being in the shower. The likelihood of this error occurring can partly be determined by the attitudes, beliefs, and values held by us and the other person. Consider the following example.

Assume that you have borrowed a friend's new car for an evening on the town. You and your companion enjoy an exceptionally good time at several popular establishments and become rowdy. As your rowdiness heightens, so does your bravado. You challenge a driver who seems determined to prove his car's superiority to a drag race. Without going into the gory details, let's suppose that you crash the car into a cow pasture. Fortunately, no one is injured. It is understood your friend is a bit displeased about the incident. You try to reason things out anyway. Your friend is irate and has promised not to forgive you. You offer to pay for the damages, but your friend is not satisfied, claiming that your money cannot account for the emotional anguish resulting from the car's loss. Finally, you decide to wait until your friend has had a chance to calm down before you finish discussing how to settle the situation. You understand well the predicament your friend is in and the frustration it is causing. You share your friend's attitude about the incident ("it was stupid") and the value held for the car. With this knowledge, you can attribute your friend's hostile behavior to the situation. Generally your friend is a good-natured, easygoing person, but most anyone would get upset about his or her new car being totaled. Suppose now that you invite your friend to your parents' home for dinner, a sort of peace offering you think might help soothe the situation. The invitation is accepted, but your friend's attitude and behavior have not changed much since the accident—there is still much animosity. This animosity is detected by your parents at the dinner table, but they do not know your friend well at all and are unaware of the incident. Having had no previous interactions with your friend and having no knowledge of why the person behaves so coldly toward you, they attribute the cause to personality and general disposition. Have your parents made an error in judgment? Essentially, yes. They have made an attribution error—attributing your friend's behavior and attitude to personality factors when they are a function of situational factors. Their perceptions are quite different from yours and result from a difference in knowledge of the person and situation.

Thus, we do make errors in our perceptions of others. Typically, this error occurs from a lack of knowledge of the other person and/or the situation in which we observe them. The better we know the individual, however, and the more we share that person's orientations (directions, intensity, salience, and consistency) about the situation, the less likely we are to make attribution errors.

The process of causal attribution is very important in the total process of human communication. People behave in a certain fashion and others observe and interpret that behavior. In turn, the latter's behavior is observed and interpreted by the former. Thus, the attribution process follows directly the transactional process of interpersonal communication. The process is identical. The accuracy of the perceptions depends on which messages are selected for exposure, attention, retention and recall and whether our judgments about the causes of the behavior of others are based on sufficient knowledge about both the individuals and the context in which they are observed. That is, the communication process succeeds or fails in large part depending on both the selection and attribution of information.

References

Hovland, C. I., Janis, I. L., & Kelley, H. H. (1953). *Communication and persuasion*. New Haven: Yale University Press.

Katz, A. M., & Hill, R. (1958). Residential propinquity and marital selection: A review of theory, method, and fact. *Marriage and Family Living, 20,* 27–35.

Kelley, H. H. (1973). The process of causal attribution. *American Psychologist, 28,* 107–128.

McCroskey, J. C. (1993). *An introduction to communication in the classroom,* Ch. 6, pp. 81–95. Edina, MN: Burgess International.

McCroskey, J. C., Larson, C. E., & Knapp, M. L. (1971). *An introduction to interpersonal communication,* Ch. 4, pp. 54–76. Englewood Cliffs, NJ: Prentice-Hall.

McCroskey, J. C., Richmond, V. P., & Stewart, R. A. (1986). *One on one: The foundations of interpersonal communication,* Ch. 5, pp. 68–84. Englewood Cliffs, NJ: Prentice-Hall.

McCroskey, J. C., & Wheeless, L. R. (1976). *Introduction to human communication,* Ch. 14, pp. 264–289. Boston: Allyn & Bacon.

PERSONALITY AND COMMUNICATION

11

No two people communicate in exactly the same way. This is true whether their primary role in an interaction is that of source or of receiver. The effectiveness of a source's message is ultimately determined by the receiver's interpretation and understanding of that message. It is with the receiving process—perceiving, decoding, processing, and responding—that individual differences among people have their greatest impact on communication. For example, Lisa may state the same message to Tom that she states to Linda, but Tom responds much differently to Lisa's message than does Linda. Much of the reason for their different responses rests with the possible differences among their attitudes, beliefs, and values. Tom may respond in one way to Lisa's message because he is a middle-aged male from Oregon, while Linda responds in another way because she is a teen-aged female from Mexico. Personal orientations and general characteristics such as age, gender, and culture have major effects on human communication. Also important are the specific characteristics of the individual that make her or him unique from other individuals. This chapter focuses on these *personality variables*.

Personality is the total psychological makeup of an individual—a composite profile reflecting experiences, motivations, attitudes, beliefs, values, and behaviors. Moreover, a person's personality is derived from the interaction of these elements with the environment external to the individual. Thus, personality can be defined as *the sum of an individual's characteristics that make him or her unique* (Hollander, 1976). If all people had the same personality, they would all communicate in pretty much the same way in any given context and in similar situations across contexts. Obviously, they do not. Differences in personality among people result in differences in their characteristic communicative behavior that we can observe.

Although an in-depth examination of personality is beyond the scope of this textbook, there are certain aspects of personality that tend to remain fixed over time and from one situation to another. These identifiable aspects of personality affect both the composition of the message and the response to it. Remember that we discussed the symbolic aspects of language. It can only stimulate meaning in a receiver if that receiver has experience with a particular symbol. Similarly, we have discussed the importance of exposure and selection. If certain personality traits affect (limit or enhance, for example) one's ability to experience certain sensations and/or one's tendency to select particular types of messages, communication will be affected. Psychological dispositions can affect perception—which is a key element in the reception of messages (see chapter 8). Since all messages must be decoded by the receiver, knowing something about the receiver's personality should help the source encode a message with a greater likelihood of effective reception. Similarly, general knowledge of the possible effects of personality on communication may help the receiver interpret the source's message. As we note below, all receivers make inferences. If those inferences are better informed, effective communication is more likely to result.

More than 100 personality variables have been isolated by personality psychologists, but most of these have not been studied to determine their influence on communication behavior. Later in the chapter we examine several personality variables known to have an effect on communication. First, however, we will briefly review the interrelationship of personality and human communication.

Personality Traits and Communication Behavior

Hollander (1976) discusses two important features that help clarify what personality is. The first feature distinguishes the *external* level of personality from the *internal* level. The external level consists of observable characteristics of an individual and is represented primarily by her or his typical behavior. The internal level includes the individual's attitudes, values, and beliefs, interests and aspirations, and motivations. In interpersonal encounters, we tend to infer a person's internal level of personality from her or his external behavior. For example, we might observe Ron behaving in a loud, animated way in several situations. From Ron's behavior we might infer that he is fun-loving and needs much attention from others.

We generally expect that the internal and external levels of personality will operate in unison with one another. That is, we expect people to behave according to the way they think and feel. In reality, however, this state of unison typically doesn't exist. An example can be taken from many communication studies done a few years ago. These studies hypothesized that a person's level of communication apprehension could be inferred from certain physiological behaviors. It is thought that a person reporting a high level of communication apprehension would show, among other responses, a faster heart rate than would someone reporting a low level of apprehension. The research does not consistently support this assumption. The heart rates of many high apprehensives are no greater than those of low apprehensives.

In our daily interactions with others we infer that, because an individual is exhibiting a particular behavior, he or she is "that kind of person." Such inferences are attributable to the expectations we have about another person's consistent behavior, expectations that are established through interactions with that person over time. Experience with your significant other, for example, may lead you to expect that if you don't arrive on time, he or she will become irritated. Eventually you tend to regard the behavior from which this expectancy develops as characteristic of that person's personality. Then we say things like, "Oh, being punctual is an obsession." As Hollander (1976) notes, it's only a short time until you begin to view this characteristic of others as a *trait*, or the way he or she "typically" behaves.

In the psychology of personality, traits refer to individual characteristics that are not found in all people. Recall that earlier we referred to trait theories as portraying people as predictable. Traits are an individual's *predispositions* for responding in a certain way to various situations. That is, a given trait will exhibit itself in most any situation responded to by the individual. Recall our discussion in chapter 6.

For the individual who experiences communication apprehension in most all social situations, communication apprehension is a *personality trait*. Although other people may have this trait, it is the combination of this trait with many other specific personality traits that make the individual unique. This person's experiences, lifestyle, attitudes, interests, motivations, values, ethnic origin, ideals, aspirations, and even hereditary characteristics meld and operate together to form his or her personality. When we interact with a particular person, we begin to develop expectancies about her or his individual behavior. Based on these expectancies, our communication with the individual will not be exactly like our communication with other people. This is because we tend to adapt our communicative behavior to the differences among people.

Let us go back to the example involving Lisa, Tom, and Linda. If Tom and Linda's different responses to Lisa are problematic for her, she will have to take into consideration some of the characteristic differences between Tom and Linda. Lisa will have to adapt any subsequent messages to those differences. One way Lisa could do this would be to alter her expectancies of either person's behavior. If initially Lisa expected Linda's response to be similar to Tom's but then inferred that Linda is more apprehensive than Tom and this apprehension caused Linda to act differently, Lisa might change the way she communicates with Linda. This illustrates the basic way that personality traits influence interpersonal communication. In short, differences in personality manifest themselves in variations in the communication behavior among people.

Hollander's second feature of personality distinguishes its *dynamic* aspects from its *consistent* aspects. By dynamic we mean that personality undergoes some degree of change as an individual learns from new experiences. Getting married, moving to another part of the country, living through some tragedy, losing a job, and even becoming involved in a new relationship are just some experiences that can change how a person looks at life (internal level) and how he or she behaves (external level). There are, however, many aspects of personality that remain consistent. Elements of the internal level of personality that are least likely to undergo change—such as values—are those that comprise the consistent aspect of personality. It is also these elements that account for consistency in an individual's behavior. The consistency seen in the behavior of someone who never misses a class, for example, could be attributed to that individual's belief that the best way to get the most out of a course is to always be present. It is this sense of consistency in our personalities, then, that causes others to remark to us, "You haven't changed one bit, even after all this time." We turn now to the consideration of several specific personality traits that appear to have a marked impact on human communication.

Personality Variables in Communication

The number of ways people can differ from one another is probably infinite. However, one of the more meaningful ways, if not the *most* meaningful, involves patterns of communication behavior. Many everyday references show our awareness of such differences. Perhaps you've heard or even used comments such as these: "She never says much." "He surely has a strange way of dealing with people." "She's the most abrasive person I've ever met." Because of certain communication patterns and behaviors engaged in by an individual, we infer that he or she has a particular kind of personality. Although such inferences are sometimes incorrect, very often they are accurate. Some of these personality traits and how they affect communication behavior are the focus of this section.

Adventurousness

The person whose personality is characterized by a high level of *adventurousness* is always ready to try new things. He or she is sociable and tends to show an abundance of emotional responses (for example, excitability). The person with a low level of adventurousness, however, tends to be cautious, withdrawn, and to have feelings of inferiority. Highly adventurous people tend to show more interest in their communication with other people. They engage in discussions more openly and with more relevant contributions to the topic; they have a fairly high task orientation. In many circumstances, adventurous people tend to be more talkative than people who are less adventurous.

Authoritarianism

Authoritarianism refers to one's orientation toward power in social relationships. The authoritarian person seeks to be dominant over those seen as weaker and to be submissive toward those seen as stronger. This person tends to be more suspicious and less trusting than a non-authoritarian individual. Because they are suspicious of others, they tend to confide in or seek important information from others more than non-authoritarian people do. The person with a low authoritarian trait is more trusting of others and less inclined to strive for dominance in social situations.

Dogmatism

Dogmatic individuals are rigid in their thinking and can best be described as "close-minded." Individuals with highly dogmatic personalities are sometimes equated with authoritarian personalities because they hold an unusually high respect for persons in authority. Such people are also characterized by a high degree of anxiety and insecurity. They feel threatened by people with views opposing their own. Moreover, the dogmatic personality tends to conform to group influence more than to individual influence, unless the individual influence comes from an authority figure. Dogmatic people are very inflexible in their communication behavior and are intolerant of others who hold contrary views. Moreover, the dogmatic person's communication is more likely to be irrelevant to the topic of discussion and based more on emotions than on rational thinking.

Emotional Maturity

Emotional maturity distinguishes between people who are changeable, dissatisfied, and easily annoyed and those who are stable, calm, and well-balanced. People who are more emotionally mature exhibit much greater flexibility in their communication behavior and are less oriented toward irrelevant social information and issues. Those who are less mature tend to be more likely to get into conflict with others and to engage in very hostile communicative behaviors.

Extroversion-Introversion

We mentioned extroverted individuals in contrast to introverted individuals in chapter 5. The person with an *introverted* personality tends to be shy and withdrawn and to prefer being alone most of the time. These people generally find others to have a very limited appeal and thus are happier when they are alone. Introverts may or may not be communicatively apprehensive. Many withdraw from communication not because of anxiety or fear but simply because they prefer to; they just do not care much for being with other people. At the other extreme are *extroverts*. People with this type of personality are bold, aggressive, and talkative. They are much happier when they are with other people. Some extroverts are apprehensive about communicating, but they are so people-oriented that they force themselves to communicate despite their fears. Most of the people we label as friendly, outgoing, and fun to be with are probably extroverts. Conversely, many people we label as shy, aloof, and unfriendly are probably introverts.

General Anxiety

This personality trait distinguishes between those who tend to be tense, restless, and impatient most of the time and those who generally tend to be calm, relaxed, and composed. It is important that *general anxiety* as a trait not be confused with communication apprehension. Although the person with high general anxiety is more likely to be communication apprehensive than the person who is low in general anxiety, there is not a high correlation between these two characteristics. People with high general anxiety are likely to show more tension in communication with others. They are less likely to talk, and evidence less interest in most topics of discussion than do people with low general anxiety. Those with general anxiety frequently express fears about all types of potential (and often unlikely) problems.

Locus of Control

The concept of *locus of control* refers to an individual's orientation toward the source of rewards for his or her actions. Two orientations are considered by this concept. Individuals who perceive that reward for actions follows from their own behavior are said to have an *internal* locus of control. They believe that they are the primary source of control for their behavior, and they take full responsibility for the outcomes of their behavior. Individuals who perceive that reward for actions stems from outside forces are said to have an *external* locus of control. These people believe that luck, chance, or other people have the primary control over their behavior and that there is little they can do to affect their lives. At the communication level, people with an internal orientation differ in important ways from those with an external orientation. Internals are more independent and more resistant to influence attempts than are externals. In competitive situations, internals rely more on their own knowledge and less on others' information;

externals look to good luck or help from others to succeed in a competition. Although externals are not consistently given to being influenced more than internals, they are less resistant. Externals are more likely to be influenced by a highly credible source than are internals. Finally, when attempting to influence others, externals tend to use more aggressive and impersonal messages; internals use more passive and personal messages.

Machiavellianism

A person with a **Machiavellian** personality views other people as objects to be manipulated for her or his own purposes. The Machiavellian (or "high Mach") tends to show little concern for conventional morality and has little emotional involvement in the communication encounters in which he or she is engaged. The high Mach uses willful intent to influence people and does so with glee—very successfully. Conversely, the high Mach is less likely to be influenced by others. High Machs tend to distrust everyone, so much so that they seem not to form perceptions of other people on the criterion of character. Generally, in interpersonal communication, the Machiavellian personality displays a low regard for others, treats them as objects, and is unconcerned with the humanness of other people.

Self-Control

Self-control is a personality variable that separates people who have much control over their emotions from those who have little control over their emotions. People who are high in self-control tend to be calmer, more composed, more in control, and to have less fear of communicating. This personality variable is negatively related to communication apprehension: As self-control decreases, the level of communication apprehension increases. Thus, people low in self-control are more likely to be communication apprehensive. Their feelings of insecurity and lack of control lead them to be afraid of talking; they may withdraw from communication so that they do not lose control over their emotions and say things they do not mean.

Self-Esteem

Self-esteem refers to the view people have of themselves in terms of total worth compared to others. People with low self-esteem tend to lack confidence in their abilities and to evaluate their competence negatively. They expect failure in whatever they attempt, including their interactions with others. As you might guess, low self-esteem is positively related to communication apprehension, external locus of control, and low self-control. Therefore, those with low self-esteem tend to be followers in most interpersonal encounters; they are likely to accept other people's views because they consider their own views to be of less value. People with high self-esteem, on the other hand, are generally leaders in communication interactions. They are confident, expect to succeed, and expect to communicate well. If we place a person with high self-esteem in a dyad with a person with low self-esteem, the person with high self-esteem is most likely to dominate the interaction.

People with low self-esteem tend to see themselves as inadequate and believe others see them that way also. Innocuous comments of others are often taken as criticism by people with low self-esteem, and they sometimes respond very defensively.

Tolerance for Ambiguity

Much communication is aimed at reducing uncertainty. *Tolerance for ambiguity* is a personality variable that distinguishes people who can operate effectively in communication situations in which there is a great deal of uncertainty from those who cannot operate effectively in such situations. People with low tolerance for ambiguity have a need to identify all questions or issues as either good or bad, right or wrong. They are in constant search for correctness and closure. Thus, this type of person would rather make a decision today than seek information for a better decision tomorrow. Conversely, the person with high tolerance for ambiguity has less need for having things resolved. This person can continue communication over an extended period without needing to reach a resolution. People with low tolerance for ambiguity are likely to become impatient in group meetings when decisions are not reached quickly. The result may be intemperate criticism of the group or individual members, which can lead to harmful interpersonal relationships.

Even in almost identical circumstances, no two people can be expected to communicate in the same way. Personality is the sum of characteristics that make an individual unique. In summary, personality traits can predispose individuals to act in a certain manner; communication behavior often reveals certain traits. Understanding psychological characteristics of communication is valuable to both the source and the receiver. If the source understands that certain personalities might lean toward specific perspectives or attitudes about a particular subject, he or she may reflect more carefully on his or her position before presenting it. Thinking about possible responses to communication emphasizes empathic understanding and the transactional nature of communication. We all want others to understand us. One of the more effective means of ensuring understanding is to imagine how our message will be interpreted by someone whose personality differs from ours. The more reflection about the content of the message, our own psychological make-up and that of others involved in the transaction, the greater the chances that we will accurately represent our thoughts and feelings in the messages—and that they will be perceived as we intended.

References

Hollander, E. P. (1976). *Principles and methods of social psychology* (3rd ed.). New York: Oxford University Press.

McCroskey, J. C., & Daly, J. A. (1986). *Personality and interpersonal communication*. Beverly Hills: Sage Publications.

Richmond, V. P., & McCroskey, J. C. (1992). *Communication: Apprehension, avoidance, and effectiveness* (3rd ed.). Scottsdale, AZ: Gorsuch-Scarisbrick.

———. (1992). *Organizational communication for survival*. Englewood Cliffs, NJ: Prentice-Hall.

MESSAGES IN COMMUNICATION

Section 4

MESSAGES AND MEANINGS

12

Meanings are in people, not in words. When we want to get others to share our thoughts or feelings, the symbols we usually use are words. When we are concerned with verbal messages, our primary focus must be on words. However, verbal messages are not always words.

Verbal messages involve coded language. English, Spanish, French, Chinese, and Russian are but a few of the thousands of languages from which people create verbal messages. It is important to realize that there are other forms of coded language as well. The smoke signals of Native American tribes, a whistling system in the Canary Islands, drumbeats in parts of Africa, and gestures used by the deaf in North America (American Sign Language) are all symbols used to create messages.

The critical element in language—verbal messages—is the sharing of a common code between two communicators. Lacking a shared language, communication by means of verbal messages is literally impossible. In such circumstances, communication must be achieved entirely through nonverbal messages. It is important that we distinguish between these two primary forms of messages.

Distinctions between Verbal and Nonverbal Messages

Distinguishing between verbal and nonverbal messages is no simple task, although the differences seem obvious on the surface. People think of communicating "with words" as verbal and communicating "without words" as nonverbal. "Words" suggests a linguistic code. As we noted above, some languages do not have "words" as we commonly use that term. In addition, some nonverbal gestures (called *emblems*) are word-substitutes. Examples of these include head-shaking to show yes or no, the "OK" gesture, the peace gesture, counting gestures, and "throwing a kiss." Clearly there is a gray area between verbal and nonverbal messages that permits reasonable people to disagree about how a particular message should be classified. However, that gray area is restricted.

Compared to nonverbal messages, verbal messages are more *explicit* and *precise*, and are framed in a *linguistic* code. Verbal messages primarily convey information or content in communication. In other words, verbal messages are the *cognitive* component of the communication process. When a mother tells a young child to "sit," she is attempting to convey the information to the child that he or she is to be seated. The content may be clear in verbal messages, or it may be ambiguous. For example, if the mother were to say to the child, "repose on a seat," the child might not understand the language.

Therefore the child could not understand the message that presumably tells her or him what to do.

The verbal message component of the communication process is the provider of content and information, and it generally is used to clarify. However, we must be careful in assuming that the verbal message always is clear. For example, when a young child doesn't understand a particular word, someone may tell the child to look up the word in the dictionary. Of course, often children cannot spell words, so they cannot possibly "look up the word." If they are lucky enough to spell the word, they might find several definitions for the word. All the definitions have different connotations based upon the context in which the word is used. For example, the word "bag" has several different common definitions. It can be used to refer to a sack, a valise, a purse, a brown sack, a poke, or a receptacle of leather or cloth. As we can see, the verbal component of communication can convey the content or cognitive aspect of the message. However, we still need to understand the context in which the verbal message is being used to understand the content satisfactorily.

Compared to verbal messages, nonverbal messages tend to be more *implicit*, often *imprecise*, and usually *nonlinguistic* by nature. They represent such things as the attitudes and emotions of the source. In other words, the nonverbal message component of the human communication process is the *affective* component. Based upon such things as the source's body movements, vocal qualities, and facial expressions, the receiver can get an idea about how the source feels. Nonverbal messages can help clarify the verbal message and often can even be used in place of the verbal. However, we must be as cautious in interpreting nonverbal messages as we are when interpreting verbal ones. Much of our accidental and expressive communication is produced by nonverbal messages. A nonverbal message in one culture (particularly an emblem) might not mean the same thing in another culture. For example, the "OK" sign in American society is perceived as an obscene gesture in another culture. Similarly, shaking one's head from side to side conveys "no" in many cultures, but it conveys "yes" in Bulgaria. Touching someone in one context may be taken as an indication of warmth and intimacy. In another context the same touch may lead to a charge of attempted assault or sexual harassment.

In sum, verbal messages typically represent the cognitive component in communication while nonverbal messages represent the *affective* component. Communicating one component without the other is virtually impossible, for they usually accompany one another. Meanings can be stimulated in the minds of others by verbal or nonverbal messages individually, but most meaning is produced by a combination of verbal and nonverbal messages working together. As important as it is to distinguish between verbal and nonverbal messages, it is at least as important to understand how they function together.

Relationships between Verbal and Nonverbal Messages

Several years ago researchers tried to figure out how much of the meaning in communication is stimulated by nonverbal messages as compared to verbal messages. Estimates of the portion attributable to the nonverbal messages ran from 65 to 93 percent in the various studies. Such figures are often used to illustrate how important it is to study nonverbal communication. However, these findings are completely meaningless in terms of their generalizability to everyday communication situations. These estimates are artifacts of contrived experiments in artificial laboratory settings and have no necessary relationship to the way real human beings communicate.

Consider the following examples: (1) Someone walks by your room and sees you intently reading a textbook. That person concludes you are studying and goes on without interrupting you. (2) You type a letter to your friend describing what you did during spring break. Your friend reads your letter and decides that you had a good time. In the first example we believe that 100 percent of the meaning was stimulated nonverbally—you did not speak or write at all. In the second example, we believe that virtually 100 percent of the meaning was stimulated verbally. Although if you spilled coffee on the letter before you sent it, the resulting spot might have generated a conclusion that you were sloppy! What is the point? The relative importance of verbal and nonverbal messages depends entirely on the context of a given communicative event. Often, unlike the above examples, both types of messages are present, and they work together to produce meaning in the receiver's mind. To understand this relationship better, let us consider the six major functions of nonverbal messages in relationship to verbal messages.

Functions of Nonverbal Messages

Accenting

In this function the primary role of nonverbal messages is to **accentuate** or emphasize a particular point in the verbal message. For example, a skilled speaker knows when to raise or lower the voice when making a dramatic point. Although nonverbal messages are important in accenting or emphasizing a verbal point, the timing needs to be precise or the messages will seem "out of sync" with the verbal. For example, the public speaker who says "I want to make three major points" and raises three fingers while beginning to discuss the first point is "out of sync."

Nonverbal accenting can use many aspects of nonverbal communication, including gestures, touch, and vocal cues. This is the way people indicate which of their verbal messages are most important (in their own mind, at least) and which are of lesser concern. Teachers, for example, need to be very effective in using nonverbal messages in this way. If teachers are not effective, their students are very likely not to know what to put into their notes to study and remember for tests later. Teachers who are ineffective in accenting, either with nonverbal behaviors or with other methods (such as providing written objectives), often are criticized for playing the game students hate most: Guess what's in my mind! Injunctions such as "Study everything!" are most likely to result in students studying things that are unimportant and complaining that "The test is unfair."

Complementing

The function of **complementing** is to reinforce or enhance the verbal message. For example, when telling someone you love them, you may be hugging and holding that person. This is different from accenting. Here nonverbal complementing has to accompany the verbal message in order for the meaning of the verbal to be stimulated the way it should be. As we noted above, nonverbal messages are best at stimulating *affective* meaning. Therefore, when verbal messages address affective matters (e.g., feelings, emotions, liking, disliking), it is particularly important that appropriate nonverbal messages complement those verbal messages.

Contradicting

Sometimes nonverbal messages **contradict** the verbal. For example, when we tell someone in a sarcastic tone that he or she is "wearing a lovely outfit" our nonverbal message has contradicted the verbal message. Sometimes we mean to contradict; other times we don't.

Generally, when verbal and nonverbal messages are in conflict, people tend to lean most heavily on the nonverbal to make sense of what is going on. That is, we tend to believe the nonverbal more than the verbal. This may be because most people think it is easier to lie verbally than it is nonverbally, although this generally held belief is not always true. We must be particularly careful in this regard when we are communicating with children. Most children understand and adopt the adult norms by the time they reach their teenage years, and many do so several years earlier. However, all young children, many older children, and even some adults are not sensitive to the importance of nonverbal messages that are inconsistent with verbal messages. Therefore, these individuals respond to the verbal message. Sarcasm and satire are lost on them. They are particularly unresponsive to humor in which the nonverbal messages suggest that one should discount the serious tone of the verbal message.

Repeating

A repetition of the verbal message in a nonverbal manner is termed *repeating*. For example, after shouting to a crowd that things are "OK" we might also give a "thumbs up" sign, and our meaning will be more likely to be understood.

Redundancy is a critical factor in facilitating communication of information and understanding. Redundancy can be created by presenting more than one verbal message designed to stimulate the same meaning (a very good method). However, the use of nonverbal messages often is much simpler and frequently is more effective.

Regulating

The *regulation* function serves to coordinate the flow of speech. This can be done by vocal inflection, movement of the body, facial expressions, eye behavior, or several nonverbal cues in combination. In other words, the regulation function lets one person know when it is her or his time to speak in a conversation.

Conversations involve different individuals taking turns speaking. The rules for these interchanges are complex and usually learned through trial and error—therefore many people do not learn them well. We can indicate verbally to someone it is their turn to talk (such as a teacher might do in a class discussion). However, many conventional interactions are regulated by nonverbal messages. These messages operate at a barely conscious level. If they are working well, the interaction flows smoothly without awkward silences or "talkovers."

Substituting

When the nonverbal is used in place of the verbal, this is termed *substituting*. For example, when you dislike something that someone says to you, all you may have to do is to stare hard at that person to get your meaning across.

Substitution is used often when barriers to verbal communication exist. When you are trying to say goodbye to someone at a crowded airport, you simply throw the person a kiss or wave goodbye to them.

This is different than repeating. Substituting occurs when the nonverbal is used in place of the verbal whereas repeating is when the nonverbal is used immediately following the verbal.

In summary, both verbal and nonverbal messages have the potential to stimulate meaning in the minds of others. In ongoing interpersonal communication, however, most meaning is stimulated by a combination of the verbal and nonverbal. Although words and the sequencing of words account for the bulk of what we refer to as *verbal* messages, the variety of *nonverbal* messages in interpersonal communication is much greater. It is the interplay of these two types of messages that make human communication the vital and fascinating process it is.

References

Andersen, P. A., Garrison, J. P., & Andersen, J. F. (1976). Defining nonverbal communication: A neurophysiological explanation of nonverbal information processing. *Human Communication Research, 6,* 74–89.

Donaghy, W. C. (1980). *Our silent language: An introduction to nonverbal communication.* Dubuque, IA: Gorsuch Scarisbrick.

Hall, E. T. (1969). *The hidden dimension.* Garden City, NJ: Anchor Press/ Doubleday.

Hall, E. T. (1969). *The silent language.* Garden City, NJ: Anchor Press/Doubleday.

Harrison, R. P. (1974). *Beyond words: An introduction to nonverbal communication.* Englewood Cliffs, NJ: Prentice-Hall.

Henley, N. M. (1977). *Body politics: Power, sex, and nonverbal communication.* Englewood Cliffs, NJ: Prentice-Hall.

Hickson, M. L., III, & Stacks, D. W. (1993). *Nonverbal communication: Studies and applications.* Dubuque, IA: Brown & Benchmark.

Knapp, M. L., & Hall, J. A. (1992). *Nonverbal communication in human interaction* (3rd ed.). Fort Worth, TX: Holt, Rinehart & Winston.

Mehrabian, A. (1981). *Silent messages: Implicit communication of emotions and attitudes* (2nd ed.). Belmont, CA: Wadsworth.

Richmond, V. P. (1992). *Nonverbal communication in the classroom.* Edina, MN: Burgess International Group.

Richmond, V. P., & McCroskey, J. C. (1995). *Nonverbal behavior in interpersonal relations* (3rd ed.). Boston: Allyn & Bacon.

NONVERBAL MESSAGES

13

The previous chapters have directed much attention to verbal messages, and chapters 15 and 16 place primary emphasis on those messages. This chapter and the one following center primarily on nonverbal messages. In this chapter our focus will be on the categories of nonverbal messages. Nonverbal communication stems from the complex interplay of a variety of nonverbal messages being processed simultaneously (or nearly so). Before we look at that larger picture, we will take the process apart and look at the individual parts. Chapter 14 is designed to put the parts all back together and examine how the various verbal and nonverbal messages function together in communicative relationships. We have chosen to break nonverbal messages into ten categories. We will begin with the category that many people call "body language." While that label is not accurate, since these behaviors do not form a language, the category does include all those elements that encompass body movements and gestures.

Body Movements and Gestures

Body movements and gestures are commonly referred to as *kinesics*. Kinesics refers to any movement of the head, arms, legs, hands, and so on. Some authors have suggested that there are approximately 700,000 possible physical signs that can be transmitted by body movements. One author has suggested that there are twenty-three distinct eyebrow movements and that each communicates different meanings to receivers. Like most nonverbal messages, body movements and gestures are both learned and innate. However, we adopt the movements that are acceptable in our culture for communication. For the purpose of clarification we will examine the six main areas of kinesics: emblems, illustrators, regulators, affect displays, adaptors, and courtship readiness cues.

Emblems

This type of gesture has a specific meaning for those sending and receiving the message. Emblems, as we noted in the previous chapter, have a direct verbal translation, and the gesture(s) can be used in place of a verbal message. Emblems are behaviors that could be considered equivalent to verbal messages because of the coded, linguistic translation that is typical of such messages. Common emblems are the "OK" sign, nodding your head in agreement or disagreement, the hitchhiking sign, the wave for greeting, and so on. All these emblems are common in the North American culture. They can be used for verbal messages, and the meaning stimulated will probably be the same. Like many of our verbal messages, emblems represent very precise meanings. Emblems are excellent sources of nonverbal communication in interpersonal relationships. Emblems often express much more of what we mean than do verbal messages. For example, if you are caught in a traffic jam and someone behind you keeps honking the horn, you can always give them a gesture. You can give them an emblem such that the person will know exactly what you are saying. But others may not take too kindly to this and will return an emblem of their own. For example, they might raise their arm, clench their fist, and touch their other hand to the upper arm of their raised hand. You will know exactly what they are saying to you. Emblems are a very effective nonverbal means of communicating, without ever saying a word. Most emblems are not as offensive as these!

Illustrators

In this instance, the body movement and gestures are used to illustrate or add meaning to the verbal message. Illustrators help to clarify the verbal message. Illustrators are primarily made by using our hands, but not exclusively.

Small children will learn what illustrators to use with their words, and as they get older their gestures become more refined but fewer. The young child, for example, cannot say "water." However, the child probably can say something like "wawa" while pointing to a faucet, thus communicating her or his desire to a parent. As the child's language skills expand, such gestures will disappear because they are no longer needed. Small children, until about the age of seven, rely heavily upon illustrators to convey meaning, but after seven they start adopting the adult verbal norms. They use less illustration; it is more refined and adapted to the verbal dialogue.

Illustrators are also used to help in the synchronization of verbal and nonverbal message flow (remember the function of accenting in the previous chapter). The use of illustrators in interpersonal communication will help punctuate or synchronize the communication. For example, when we are excited, we use gestures that exhibit enthusiasm.

Regulators

As we discussed in chapter 12, these nonverbal gestures help us figure out the beginning and ending of turns in interpersonal communication. They assist us in regulating spoken language. This has been described by some as the "turn-taking system" in conversation. There are four major turn-taking situations (turn-yielding, turn-maintaining, turn-requesting, and turn-denying) that can take place in interpersonal communication. All of the turn-taking cues help in the flow of interpersonal communication. Regulators tell us when it is time to talk, cease talking, listen, and how to refuse our turn to talk.

Affect Displays

These are nonverbal behaviors, both voluntary and involuntary, that reflect one's emotional state. Affect displays could be facial expressions, body posture, or a combination of these. Think of a person who always looks sad, tired, and has a slumped posture. What is your perception of that person? You probably think of that person as unhappy or maybe lazy. You may even avoid communication with such individuals because their affect displays are so depressing. You infer that an interaction with them would be about some illness or problem that is bothering them. Therefore, how we display our feelings and emotions through our body movements and gestures will determine to a large extent whether others want to communicate with us and the type of communication that takes place.

Adaptors

Adaptors are movements that are usually exhibited unconsciously and are associated with tension or anxiety. As anxiety increases, the adaptors tend to increase. For example, in the initial acquaintance stage of a relationship, adaptor behaviors of each individual may be quite common. As the relationship becomes more secure, the adaptors will decrease. Typical adaptors include playing with hair, smoothing clothes, toying with an object, scratching. Some adaptors can even be something as extreme as touching another's hair or removing lint from the other person's clothing.

Certain people use more adaptors than others. For example, the generally anxious personality types might bite their nails, scratch their heads, smooth their clothing, and pick at your clothing within one interaction. Anxious persons often are not even aware of what they are doing or of the impact it has on interaction. Using lots of adaptors can make receivers nervous and uncomfortable, and they might even wish to end the conversation.

Courtship Readiness Cues

Another area of kinesics that has received extensive consideration is courtship. Here we are concerned with the behaviors exhibited in the courtship situation. *Courtship readiness* is shown when someone tries to display muscle tone, sucks in the stomach, and stands straight to impress another. **Preening behavior** is revealed in such actions as stroking the hair, fixing the collar on a dress or shirt, touching up one's makeup, and adjusting clothing such as socks and ties. Such behavior usually accompanies courtship readiness cues. **Positional cues** refer to how we arrange our bodies either to adapt to or to reject others. We sit with an open body position when we want to let others know we are willing to talk with them. On the other hand, we sit with a closed body position to show that we are not interested in conversation. **Actions of appeal or invitation** include flirtatious glances, batting one's eyelashes, seductive body movements, flexing the muscles, and thrusting out the chest. Both male and female heterosexuals engage in these behaviors when meeting or becoming acquainted with a person of the opposite sex whom they find attractive.

Research has unearthed some behaviors that are typical of both male and female heterosexuals who find someone of the opposite sex attractive. Females may lower their eyes, smile more, tilt their head, yield space to the male, cuddle, yield talking time to the male, bat their eyelashes, and generally exhibit less dominant nonverbal behaviors. In comparison, males when conversing with females will stare more, point, take more space, initiate touch, keep their head erect, have a straighter posture, and generally appear to be more dominant. One might ask, isn't this a bit sexist? No, it is simply a fact of communication between heterosexual males and females in the general American culture. The above behaviors tend to be present in many female/male interactions. There are exceptions: in the work environment where the boss is female and the subordinate is male and in the student-teacher relationship, where the teacher is female and the student male. However, in most male/female interpersonal communication, when the participants like each other, some behaviors listed above tend to be present. In some other cultures, the presence of these behaviors is even more pronounced than in the United States, and in others it is less pronounced.

Our body movements and gestures help to control the flow of speech, coordinate interactions, define relationships, and establish meaning in the mind of the receiver. They also suggest our emotional state and the type of person we are.

Physical Appearance and Attractiveness

As discussed in chapter 8, physical appearance and general attractiveness often will determine whether another person wants to interact with us. This level of desire for contact will decide whether the person will initiate a conversation with us and/or respond positively if we try to initiate the conversation. Once the conversation is initiated, general physical attractiveness may not be of such vital concern, for people are then more concerned with social or task attraction. However, physically attractive people are given higher grades and receive more attention in school, and are perceived by others as more likable, more socially skilled, and more sociable. Evidence shows they are even given lighter prison sentences than their unattractive counterparts when convicted of a crime. Indeed, physical appearance is a powerful nonverbal message.

The type of body structure a person has will also influence how others react to them. The **endomorphic** body type is rounded or heavy, with a large abdomen. This person tends to be perceived by others as sociable, slow, lazy, calm, soft-hearted, and kind. The **mesomorphic** body type is the triangular or athletic body shape, which is muscular, firm, and has good posture. The person with this body type tends to be perceived as intelligent, outgoing, confident, energetic, dominant, and determined. The **ectomorphic** body type is very thin, fragile, flat, and has poor muscle tone. Such types look much like a light pole. They tend to be perceived as tense, awkward, high-strung, detached, anxious, tactful, and withdrawn. As we can see from the above descriptions, the mesomorph is the preferred body type in terms of positive perceptions; however, not all of us are mesomorphs, so we should be aware of how others view us. Our body type will determine, to a major extent, how we will be perceived and reacted to in interpersonal interactions. The thin female is perceived as unstable, anxious and high-strung, and the thin male is perceived in a similar manner. The short, rounded heavy female is seen as unattractive in our society. However, the round, heavy male is more accepted, particularly if he is the class clown. The problem arises when people think they know how others should communicate based on their body type and then see their expectations violated. For example, a mesomorphic male who is extremely anxious, nervous, and quiet is counter to the stereotype of the mesomorph. Therefore, we should realize we cannot judge how to communicate with that person based solely on physique.

Our physical appearance and general attractiveness determine both whether others will communicate with us and the type of interaction that takes place. Other physical factors frequently contribute to initial impressions. Skin tone, hair, the amount of skin exposed, height and weight can determine how others will react to us. Generally, our society believes that having a tan is good, that hair should be clean and an appropriate length and that tactful exposure of the skin is acceptable. We also believe that being tall is positive for men, average height is positive for women, and that neither sex should be overweight, although it is more acceptable for men than for women.

In summary, our general body appearance and attractiveness predict how others will respond to us and how we respond to others. As stated earlier, we should remember that often people don't get past our general appearance to communicate with us and find what lies beneath. Our appearance sends a volley of nonverbal messages to others whenever we come anywhere near them. Maybe that is why most of us are so sensitive to making ourselves look better through our use of dress and artifacts.

Dress and Artifacts

Clothing communicates status, attitudes, values, professional goals, cultural background, occupation, sex, and age. The way we dress influences how others communicate with us on a daily basis.

We've heard the expression "you are what you eat." Well, "you are what you wear," at least in the eyes of the receiver. If you dress as if you work for IBM, you will normally be treated accordingly. If you dress like a coal miner, you will probably be treated accordingly. Try dressing in a sloppy, careless, unclean manner, then go to your local bank and try to cash a check. The people there are likely to scrutinize your appearance, decide you look like a bad risk, ask for identification, check your account, and then cash your check. If you dressed in a neat, clean, businesslike manner and asked to have a check cashed, the people at the bank would probably comply with minimal hassle because your appearance says you are reliable.

Clothing has three main functions: comfort and protection (to keep us warm and safe from objects in the environment), modesty (to keep from view those parts of our anatomy which our culture says shouldn't be visible), and cultural display. The cultural display we make with our clothing is a primary basis which others use to judge our attitudes, values, and background.

Years ago, cultures would decide what attire one could wear based on one's social standing in that culture. Therefore, it was easy to distinguish one social class from another. Fortunately, that is not so today in North America. We are fairly free of restraints in terms of what we can or cannot wear. We do have to wear clothing to cover our private areas. However, how much or how little we bare beyond that is primarily up to us. We should realize that if we want to deviate from the general norm, we usually will be stereotyped in a *negative* manner. However, there are groups of people who are allowed idiosyncratic behaviors in dress. For example, rock groups can dress in a very bizarre manner and still be accepted. In addition, many entertainers can dress in unusual fashions and still be accepted. In fact, their attire is part of their celebrity status. However, most of us must dress according to the culture in which we live and work. If we don't, we run the risk of being alienated from peers and not being able to establish effective interpersonal relationships with others.

Artifacts are items such as jewelry, briefcases, makeup, hats and so on, that contribute to how others judge us. While eyeglasses are sometimes a mandatory artifact, they also reveal or are perceived to indicate certain qualities.

Some research indicates that people who wear glasses are perceived as more intelligent, industrious, and dependable. Indeed, how a person uses her or his glasses often determines how that person is perceived. When someone in a meeting removes glasses, folds them, and relaxes, this is sometimes a signal that the meeting has ended. When someone throws glasses across the table, this usually signals extreme displeasure. When people remove their glasses and rub their eyes, they might be signaling they are tired, bored, or confused. People who wear tinted glasses indoors may be doing so because they wish to mask their feelings or are insecure. Of course, some people wear tinted glasses because their eyes are highly sensitive to light.

In summary, the type of clothing and the kinds of artifacts we use give others cues to our socioeconomic status, our attitudes, even our jobs. These enhancements of physical appearance have a significant impact on interpersonal relationships.

Facial Expressions and Eye Behavior

Someone once observed, "Our faces are our windows to the world." Our facial appearance provides others with information about our race, gender, nationality, emotional state, age, and even the type of person we are. The face is the most expressive part of our body. From isolated pictures of only eyes and eyebrows we can often predict the emotional state of an individual. We frequently can tell if a person is sad or happy, disgusted or pleased.

Research suggests that some of our facial expressions are innate. Blind children have facial expressions similar to those of sighted children. Since they are blind, they did not learn the expressions by watching and imitating. Many facial expressions are inborn. The smile is the universal facial expression of happiness or friendliness. It is a natural, easy response. This is one of only a very limited number of "pancultural" nonverbal behaviors. That is, one of only a few nonverbal behaviors which are used and responded to in the same way across many or all cultures.

Researchers suggest that we use four facial management techniques when controlling our facial expressions. We *intensify* or exaggerate our facial expressions (for example, our wedding day or birthday might cause us to intensify our positive facial expressions). We *deintensify* when we learn to control or subdue an expression (for example, we might be excited that we got an A on an exam, but if we find out our best friend got a D, we might suppress our happiness around our friend). We *neutralize* when we avoid showing any facial expression. For example, in the general American culture when a young man is being punished by a teacher, he must remain stoic. Lastly, we *mask* when we conceal our real emotions (for example, not letting our best friend know we cannot tolerate his or her girlfriend or boyfriend). We manipulate our facial expressions to fit the situation and to develop more effective interpersonal relationships with others. We learn to conceal or mask our real emotions and to express according to the norms of our society. A classic example of this is people who serve as emcees on television game shows. After introducing several thousand people, he or she probably has little real enthusiasm about new guests. However, the emcee has to mask the real emotions and carry on with the show. He or she keeps smiling, nodding, kissing, hand-shaking, hugging—and being employed.

Seven basic emotions can be identified fairly consistently by facial expression. Research indicates that people can readily, and with considerable accuracy, identify the following emotions based solely on facial and eye expression: sadness, happiness, anger, fear, surprise, disgust or contempt, and interest.

As with most of the nonverbal areas, eye behavior has several functions, in this case seven. The first, and some believe most important, function of eye behavior is to control the flow of interaction. It is the prime method we have of controlling turn-taking in conversations. The second function of eye behavior is to establish a relationship. We look more and longer at people with whom we want to interact. The third function of eye behavior is to help in maintaining a relationship. We maintain a person's eye contact if we like that person. The fourth function of eye behavior is to express our feelings about a person or a situation. The fifth function of eye behavior is to show respect to another (looking down or away when speaking to someone of higher status). The final function is to communicate our attention to and interest in what the other person is saying during a conversation.

Our face and eyes provide others with an impression of how we feel about them. As a result, these nonverbal messages are very important in the maintenance and development of relationships.

Use of the Voice

Vocalics refers to the use of, and the characteristics and qualities of, the human voice. This category of nonverbal messages is sometimes called "paralanguage." While it is not in any sense *language*, it most frequently occurs simultaneously with verbal messages. Vocalic inflections are potent nonverbal messages that aid in stimulating intended meaning in the mind of the receiver beyond that which could be stimulated by the verbal message alone. For example, people who use sarcasm are really intending to communicate a meaning the opposite of what their words are saying.

Vocalic cues affect how others see you. When you open your mouth, you have either confirmed the image your dress and body give to another, or you have negated that image. In addition, in oral communication at least, an old adage is true: "It's not what you say; it's how you say it." Oral verbal messages do not exist without vocalic messages, although some vocalic messages can exist without verbal messages (sighing, laughing, groaning, moaning, etc.).

The main failing of written verbal communication is the absence of vocalic cues to tell a reader how to interpret the verbal message. Written communication is a pitifully poor substitute for oral communication. It is thus ironic that our schools spend years trying to teach us to read and write and frequently ignore oral communication completely.

The use of your voice serves six important functions: 1) it communicates an image of you to another, 2) it communicates your emotional state, 3) it indicates your socioeconomic level and status, 4) it can serve to indicate your background and culture, 5) it can be used to regulate the flow of conversation, and 6) it can be used to show interest or disinterest in another.

Paralinguistic cues are usually divided into two major categories: (1) vocal quality, such as pitch range, articulation, rhythm control, and lip control, and (2) vocalizations, such as vocal characterizers (laughing, crying, yawning); vocal qualifiers (pitch height, intensity, loudness/softness); and vocal segregates ("Hum," "Huh," "Shh"). These qualities suggest an individual's emotional state to others.

Finally, vocalic cues—or lack of them in the case of silence—can display someone's age, sex, socioeconomic status, background, weight, height, and educational level. In fact, research suggests that vocal cues help more in stimulating meaning for content than the actual words themselves. The type of voice contributes to how a person will be perceived by others. For example, the breathy-voiced female is perceived as attractive and likable, whereas the breathy-voiced male is stereotyped as being weak and ineffective.

In summary, much meaning can be gleaned by listening not to what a person is saying, but to how the person is saying it. Vocalic cues are one of the best means of determining exactly what someone means by their verbal messages, but they are not infallible. If they were, we would never need to misunderstand one another again!

Personal Space and Territoriality

Proxemics refers to the way space is used in communication. Research suggests that the way a person uses space is determined by one's age, gender, status, and cultural orientation. The use of space, as with other nonverbal areas, differs dramatically from one culture to another.

Personal space is the movable, portable space that goes wherever we go. Personal space is like an "invisible bubble" we carry around with us. It expands and contracts based upon our response to the person with whom we are communicating. For example, if we like someone, we are more likely to let that person into our bubble than a person we don't like.

Research has shown that the space needs of males and females vary, but the differences are dependent upon the facial expression and eye behavior of the other person. For example, males will stand closer to someone who is not looking at them. Research also indicates that young children, up to the age of seven or so, are much more likely to violate spatial norms of adults. After age seven they start acquiring adult spatial norms.

People from some Latin American countries, Italians, people from the Middle East, and Puerto Ricans tend to maintain closer distances when talking to each other. On the other hand, Germans, Chinese, Japanese, and Americans generally prefer greater distance when communicating. However, these general patterns are subject to substantial variation within each of the major groups. For example, people with higher status in most cultural groups stand closer to, or even tower over, people with lower status.

One researcher identified four distinct categories of personal space that apply to the North American culture (Hall, 1973). *Intimate distance* is from zero to eighteen inches and generally is reserved for lovers and people who are very involved with one another. Occasionally young children are allowed to enter the intimate zone even if they are barely known. *Personal distance* is from eighteen inches to four feet and is used for conversations between friends, relatives, and for casual business. The *social distance* is from four to eight feet and is reserved for formal, impersonal business relationships. Lastly, the *public distance* is from eight feet to the end of a person's vision or hearing. This distance is reserved for very formal, lecture-type situations (common in large lecture classes).

When the above norms are violated or your personal space is invaded, several options are available to you. First, you can **withdraw** from the situation. For example, if you don't like having your space invaded while shopping in a department store, you can leave. Second, you can learn to **avoid** situations in which you know you are likely to have your space invaded. If you don't like to be in large crowds, you can stay away from ball games and concerts where such crowding is likely to occur. Third, you can build boundaries or **insulate** yourself from others invading your personal space. For instance, you could pile your books and CDs and other items between yourself and your roommate to show where your side of the room begins and your roommate's ends. (Several years ago in our department, we had a faculty member who drew a line down the center of his office to indicate to his office mate that she was not to cross that boundary. He later installed carpeting on his side of the office.) Finally, you can **fight** or defend your space. With this option you challenge anyone who invades your space and tell him or her to move away. Of course, you must be prepared to actually physically "back up your talk" if they persist. Otherwise, it is wise to avoid this option.

When a person has occupied a particular space for such a long time that it becomes theirs or is associated with them, this is known as **territoriality**. That person becomes the owner of that space. Does someone in your family have his or her own place at the table or in front of the TV? People tend to claim territory even in public settings. For example, students often choose a favorite place to sit in class, and if they return to class the next time and someone has their territory, they are offended. We claim our territory in many ways: We designate it by use of markers (books, coats, umbrellas, and so forth); we get it by using it often enough that others grant it to us (this is called tenure); and we label our place with our name on our territory ("Don's room," for example).

How we use our personal space and territory communicates nonverbal information about us to others. For example, the faculty member who drew the line down the center of his office may have been saying that he did not like his office mate and did not want any interaction with her. He may have just been highly territorial, very possessive of his space. He was perceived negatively by others as a result. We must learn how to use our space wisely and recognize when we are being driven by territorial impulses. Otherwise we are likely to offend people without even knowing we have done so.

Touch

Haptics refers to the use of touch and how touch is used to communicate. Again, norms about this category of nonverbal behavior vary from culture to culture. For example, Northern Europeans and Americans tend to be nontactile, or non-touch-oriented, whereas Arabs and Latin Americans tend to be more touch-oriented. This is not to suggest that Americans don't like to touch or be touched; it is simply that they do not employ touch as a form of communication as much as some other cultures do.

There are five different types of touch. The first is *functional-professional* touch, which is very businesslike and tends to be cold and impersonal. A physical examination by a medical professional represents this type of touch. The *social-polite* type of touch is a way of recognizing another person according to the rules of the culture. A handshake is an example of this type of touch. The *friendship-warmth* touch is used to let people know you have a sense of their uniqueness as individuals. Hugging or putting an arm around someone is an example of this. The *love-intimacy* touch lets someone know you are committed to him or her. Stroking another's face would be an example. Lastly, *sexual-arousal* is the most intimate level of touch. This is associated with the physical attraction between two people. It is very stimulating, and an example of this would be making love.

As we stated earlier, American society tends to be nontactile. An estimated 15 percent of the population are "touch avoidants." These are people who do not like to be touched and generally avoid touching others. They are often perceived as cold and aloof. It is often quite damaging to a relationship when a very engaging, touch-oriented person is dating a touch avoidant. Neither can cope with the touching behavior of the other, and the relationship is likely to break up. This doesn't mean that touch avoidants won't or can't be intimate. It does mean that they are not likely to be as responsive to touch or to initiate touch as often as others.

Lastly, the lack of touch or touch deprivation can be devastating to infant growth and development. Infants who are not touched and held tend to be slower in developing psychomotor and cognitive skills; they read later than infants who receive touch, and they are less mature. From a very early age we need to be held, loved, and touched. The type of touch we use with others will determine to a large extent the type of communication we receive.

Environmental Factors

The environment plays a significant nonverbal role in establishing communication norms in various settings. The way the environment is arranged can determine the type and amount of communication that occurs. There are six perceptual frameworks by which we view our environment: formality, warmth, privacy, familiarity, constraint, and distance.

The *formal* environment is one in which people feel that they cannot communicate or that they should limit their communication. For example, many business establishments have very formal structures, (banks, funeral parlors). Sometimes, managers try to make the environment less formal so that people will be more relaxed and communicate more. Others may increase the formality to reduce the amount of social interaction and encourage less talking.

A *warm* environment is one that says "Stay a while and talk. Do not hurry up and eat, or step aside." Most fast-food chains do not want to create a warm environment. They have seating arrangements designed to encourage you to leave, not linger.

An environment that is conducive to *privacy* elicits a different type of conversation from one that is not private. A private environment encourages a more personal type of conversation, whereas a public environment encourages a very impersonal conversation.

Familiarity breeds contempt? Not quite. In fact, most people like being in environments with which they are familiar. They can predict who will be there and what is expected of them. The unfamiliar environment increases anxiety and makes many people uncomfortable.

Our perceptions of *constraint* depend on the duration of the restraint, its location, and the amount of privacy we have while being restrained. For example, we can all adjust to sitting in a three-hour lecture class, but not many of us could easily adjust to a jail sentence. We know we will eventually be allowed to leave class, and we have some control over the environment. However, in jail we cannot leave until the authorities say we can. In such a case we have no control over our environment.

Lastly, the *distance* established by the environment determines the type of communication. The distance can be actual or psychologically perceived distance. For example, some bosses may be only ten feet from their subordinates; however, the boss can create a much greater sense of distance by being psychologically distant with employees.

Research shows that when placed in an ugly room, people become discontented, irritable, bored, fatigued, and generally "want out" of the environment. Conversely, people placed in attractive surroundings work harder, are less fatigued, communicate more, are less irritable, and do not mind remaining in the setting for a reasonable period.

What distinguishes an attractive setting from an unattractive setting? The answer is not simple. What is agreeable to one person may not be agreeable to another. However, environmental factors seem to have a predictable impact. The color of an item or of a room will determine how someone reacts. For example, green will sell vegetables but it is not likely to sell bread. Black is associated with darkness and power, red with excitement, blue with coolness. Room lighting should be moderate, neither too bright or glaring nor too dim. Either variation will lower the effectiveness of the environment. The sound should be compatible with the environment. If it is a western dance hall, then country and western music. If it is a classroom, then have background music that won't interfere with the work by calling attention to itself. Finally, the optimal temperature for a work environment is around 68 degrees. Some would claim this is too cool; however, people are more stimulated in a cooler room than in a hot room.

The environment and its characteristics determine mostly the type and amount of communication that will take place between people. In most circumstances we should try to manipulate our environment so that it is conducive to conversation and interaction.

Smell

Our sense of smell helps us perceive the world around us and determines what communication is appropriate. For example, what is your initial response when someone with bad breath starts talking to you? It probably is to back away as fast as possible. However, if the person happens to be your teacher or your boss, you cannot leave that easily. With a loved one, you probably can mention the problem, and the suggestions might even be appreciated. For years researchers in nonverbal communication chose not to discuss smell, but more recently there has been considerable thought in the area. Scholars have concluded that our sense of smell affects our moods, attitudes about others, perceptions of others, and communication orientation toward others.

Our sense of smell is very personal, like our judgment of beauty. Some recent research has indicated that on a pleasantness/unpleasantness odor scale, the odors that were rated as unpleasant were associated with the undesirable characteristics of people such as poor health and obesity. Therefore, we will tend to judge others not only by their appearance but also by the odors we think or perceive that they emit. People tend to associate unpleasant odors with sick people and hospitals, when some hospital odors are quite pleasant. However, we have been taught from childhood that hospitals have undesirable odors and that people in hospitals smell bad. Babies don't always smell bad. When they have been lathered in baby lotion, they smell wonderful to most people. However, to many people, baby lotion is an offensive odor.

Practitioners in the medical field sometimes draw on their sense of smell to help diagnose ailments. For example, years ago doctors knew yellow fever by its butcher-shop odor, and scurvy and smallpox by their putrid odors. Typhoid fever smells like freshly baked bread, diphtheria has a very sweet odor, and the plague has the smell of apples. More recently, medical research into the area of smell has taken a more scientific turn. Some medical schools are encouraging doctors and interns to learn to identify odors associated with specific illnesses. The physician can then make a quicker diagnosis, perhaps saving precious seconds. Using their sense of smell, doctors can diagnose alcohol poisoning, diabetic coma, and general comas this way.

Our sense of smell affects how we perceive others from cultures different from our own. The general American culture is a very unnatural one in that we try to cover up or disguise our true body scents. The artificial components in perfumes, toilet paper, tissues, deodorants, toothpaste, and so on contribute to a higher rate of allergies in this country than in others. Have you ever tried to find any product that has its natural scent? These products usually say "unscented," which means that they still have probably been tampered with but not as much as the rose scented, the pine scented, or the bubble-gum scented. Scents usually have to be added to products even to make them *unscented*! Even our laundry detergents are scented. Our culture has a phobia about the natural odor of the body. People in some Middle Eastern countries, on the other hand, are taught from childhood to breathe in each other's faces. We have been socialized to find this offensive, whereas they have been socialized to find the opposite.

In summary, it can be stated that our olfactory senses affect our perceptions of others and our communication with them. Our sense of smell is a very pervasive, unconscious determiner of how we feel about others.

Time

What is this thing we call time? We cherish our time; we love to spend it, save it, give it to others; we have no time; we have free time, time limits, time tests, Central time, Eastern time, formal time, informal time, a lifetime. Time is another nonverbal element that affects us in an unconscious manner. When someone is late for a business appointment, we make judgments about that person, usually negative ones. When a student is late for class, most teachers, either consciously or unconsciously, form a negative evaluation of that person. We think our time is important and we don't like someone *wasting* it. In fact, we become very offended when someone wastes our time, and we think of that person in a very negative light.

A person's use of time communicates much about that person to others. Americans tend to be very time conscious and do not like waiting or having their time wasted. After all, "time is money." Americans like to talk faster than people in some other countries because they can get more in; they do not like waiting and are offended when they travel where they have to wait. Americans tend to be **monochronic**; that is, they like to do one thing at a time. People in many other cultures, such as some in Latin America, tend to be **polychronic**—they do several things at one time. Some Latin Americans may hold several business meetings in the same room simultaneously, and it takes American business people a long time to adjust to this. Monochronic cultures try to do one thing **well** at a time. However, they seem inflexible and insensitive to the needs of others. Polychronic cultures tend to overload people by having too much going on at once, but they seem more sensitive to the needs of others and more flexible. Besides monochronic and polychronic time orientations of cultures, there are three common cultural time orientations: technical, formal, and informal.

Technical time is concerned with the scientific measurement of time. Technical time is very precise, logical, and "Spock-like." It has no real impact on interpersonal communication, but it has a great impact on mass communication. Technical time is the scientific time used by NASA and many mass-communication projects.

Formal time is the traditional time orientation of a culture. For example, our traditional time is by days, months, years. We measure formal time by a calendar. Some cultures measure formal time by the seasons, tides, and so on. Formal time is also less associated with interpersonal communication. However, people need to be aware of the differences in formal time systems so they know how other cultures operate.

Informal time is the most difficult time orientation to understand. It is the orientation most relevant to interpersonal relationships. It is not precise and cannot be exactly measured. Informal time is the time orientation for a culture in a specific situation. Another way of defining informal time is to say it is the casual time of the culture. For example, when we say "in a minute" we probably really mean in a *few* minutes. Only the person using the expression can really be sure what he or she means. It is very difficult, if not impossible, to understand the informal time of a culture in which you have not lived for an extended period. Often you have to experience it or have an expert explain the difference in informal time orientations to you. In most parts of the United States, when we say a party will start at 7:00 P.M., most people know to arrive between 7:00 and 7:30 P.M. However, in other areas, it could mean the arrival time is anywhere from 7:30 to 9:00 P.M. It is very difficult for most Americans to adjust to the informal times in other cultures because we are so time-bound to our own.

The next major time orientation is the **psychological** time orientation. People can be past, present, or future oriented. Past-oriented cultures dwell on the past and love reliving old times. These people have a deep respect for the elderly. The Chinese culture is an example of this orientation.

Present-oriented societies are concerned with the here and now. Their philosophy is "eat, drink, and be merry, for tomorrow you might die." Latin Americans and Spanish Americans tend to be present oriented.

Lastly, a future-oriented society is concerned with what will take place tomorrow or in the future. American society is a prime example of this. For years we have studied the detrimental effects of the environment on the ozone layer. We have tried to adapt our culture to that future concern by putting proper exhaust systems on cars and eliminating spray cans. We are also currently concerned with the future of the world in the nuclear age. Many people in other parts of the world have difficulty understanding the American obsession with the future.

Psychological time orientation determines what a culture's communication will focus upon—do we talk about what was, what is, or what will be? When people with different psychological time orientations try to communicate, there is a tendency for them to talk past one another and to think the other person is not interested in "what is important."

The last major time orientation is concerned with a person's **biological** time. Our body often decides how we think, feel, and react to others throughout the day. When our body is at its peak, we function well; when it is low we function poorly. In fact, airlines have started trying to determine the peak times and low times for their pilots so they do not assign them to fly during their low times. Another way to look at this is our natural rhythms. Most of us can be classified as "owls" or "sparrows." Owls are at their peak in late afternoon and evening and at their worst in early morning. Sparrows are at their best in the early morning and at their worst in the late evening. Consider the impact on the owl student who has early morning classes. This individual is barely awake and functioning, and will probably perform more poorly in the classroom in the early morning than his or her counterparts, those chirping little sparrows. However, the sparrows are dying in their late afternoon classes while the owls are becoming lively and hooting like crazy. There are some people who are "sprowls." They never seem to run down.

Besides cultural, psychological, and biological time orientations, there are personality types, or personality orientations, that determine time orientations. For example, people with Type A personalities are very time-oriented. Everything is scheduled and time governs their lives. They tend to be very anxious people who are always clock-watching. In fact, they are compulsive in their time orientations and hate to have their routine disturbed. These people tend to have health problems because they don't take the time to rest, or when they do take a vacation they spend their time working or worrying about work. However, they get a lot accomplished and are very work-oriented.

The Type B personality person is less time-oriented and does not let time rule her or his lifestyle. These people are concerned with their jobs and will get the job done, but not at the expense of their happiness. They tend to be more relaxed and less time conscious. They also tend to have fewer health problems.

Clearly we need to understand and identify with the time orientations of others to have better communication relationships. Time is pervasive, it is always there, impacting what others think of us, and what we think of others.

In this chapter we have looked at the various types of nonverbal messages in some detail. Our focus has been on the association between nonverbal messages and the meanings stimulated by those messages in the minds of people. In the following chapter we will turn our attention to the role of messages in ongoing interpersonal relationships.

References

Addington, D. W. (1968). The relationship of selected vocal characteristics to personality perception. *Speech Monographs, 35,* 492–503.

Andersen, P. A., & Leibowitz, K. (1978). The development and nature of touch avoidance. *Environmental Psychology and Nonverbal Behavior, 3,* 89–106.

Argyle, M. (1975). *Bodily communication.* New York: International Universities Press.

Birdwhistell, R. L. (1970). *Kinesics and context.* Philadelphia: University of Pennsylvania Press.

Cortes, J. B., & Gatti, F. M. (1965). Physique and self-description of temperament. *Journal of Consulting Psychology, 29,* 434.

Davitz, J. R., & Davitz, L. (1961). Nonverbal vocal communication of feeling. *Journal of Communication, 11,* 81–86.

Eakins, B. W., & Eakins, R. G. (1978). *Sex differences in human communication.* Boston: Houghton Mifflin.

Ekman, P., & Friesen, W. V. (1975). *Unmasking the face.* Englewood Cliffs, NJ: Prentice-Hall.

Exline, R. V. (1971). Visual interaction: The glance of power and performance. In James K. Cole (Ed.), *Nebraska Symposium on Motivation,* pp. 163–206. Lincoln: University of Nebraska Press.

Fast, J. (1970). *Body language.* New York: M. Evans.

Hall, E. T. (1969). *The hidden dimension.* Garden City, NJ: Anchor Press/Doubleday.

_____. (1969). *The silent language.* Garden City, NJ: Anchor Press/Doubleday.

Henley, N. M. (1977). *Body politics: Power, sex, and nonverbal communication.* Englewood Cliffs, NJ: Prentice-Hall.

Korda, M. (1977). *Success: How every man and woman can achieve it.* New York: Random House.

_____. (1975). *Power! How to get it, how to use it.* New York: Random House.

LaFrance, M., & Mayo, C. (1978). *Moving bodies: Nonverbal communication in social relationships.* Monterey, CA: Brooks/Cole.

Maslow, A. H., & Mintz, N. L. (1956). Effects of esthetic surroundings: I. Initial effects of three esthetic conditions upon perceiving 'energy' and 'well being' in faces. *Journal of Psychology, 41,* 247–254.

McCroskey, J. C., Larson, C. E., & Knapp, M. L. (1971). *An introduction to interpersonal communication.* Englewood Cliffs, NJ: Prentice-Hall.

Mehrabian, A. (1981). *Silent messages: Implicit communication of emotions and attitudes* (2nd ed.). Belmont, CA: Wadsworth.

_____. (1972). *Nonverbal communication.* Chicago: Aldine-Atherton.

_____. (1971). *Silent messages.* Belmont, CA: Wadsworth.

Mintz, N. L. (1956). Effects of esthetic surroundings. II. Prolonged and repeated experience in the ''beautiful'' and ''ugly'' room. *Journal of Psychology, 41,* 459–466.

Morris, D. (1971). *Intimate behavior.* New York: Random House.

Richmond, V. P. (1992). *Nonverbal communication in the classroom.* Edina, MN: Burgess International Group.

Richmond, V. P., & McCroskey, J. C. (1995). *Nonverbal behavior in interpersonal relations* (3rd ed.). Boston: Allyn & Bacon.

Rosenfeld, L. B., & Plax, T. G. (1977). Clothing as communication. *Journal of Communication, 27,* 23–31.

Scheflen, A. E. (1972). *Body language and the social order: Communication as behavioral control.* Englewood Cliffs, NJ: Prentice-Hall.

Scheflen, A. E., & Aschraft, N. (1976). *Human territories: How we behave in space-time.* Englewood Cliffs, NJ: Prentice-Hall.

Sheldon, W. H. (1942). *The varieties of temperament.* New York: Hafner.

_____. (1940). *The varieties of the human physique.* New York: Harper and Brothers.

Sommer, R. (1969). *Personal space: The behavioral basis of design.* Englewood Cliffs, NJ: Prentice-Hall.

Winter, R. (1976). *The smell book: Scents, sex, and society.* Philadelphia: J.B. Lippincott Company.

MESSAGES AND RELATIONSHIPS

14

Whenever two people engage in communication, they have an interpersonal relationship. We all have dozens of relationships. Many people have hundreds. It is understood that not all relationships are alike. In fact, the **only** thing all relationships have in common is that they involve communication. Communication, then, is the foundation upon which relationships are developed. We may even go so far as to suggest that communication **is** the relationship.

If relationships are different from one another and communication defines the nature of the relationship, it follows that to understand relationships we must understand the communication that goes on in those relationships. Relationships have three important dimensions: immediacy, intimacy, and status. The variability of these three dimensions accounts for much of the difference that we recognize in the relationships we have with others. Although these three dimensions are distinct from each other, they are also frequently related. We will consider each in more detail.

Immediacy

Immediacy refers to the degree of perceived physical or psychological distance between people in a relationship. An immediate relationship is one in which the people in the relationship see themselves as close to one another. At the outset almost all relationships are nonimmediate. Some become more immediate as communication continues, but most never do.

Our feelings about others with whom we come in contact are communicated to them through both our verbal and our nonverbal messages. Thus, the verbal and nonverbal messages we send and receive in a relationship will define the level of immediacy that develops in that relationship.

Verbal Immediacy

What other people say can cause us to feel either closer to or more distant from them. Increased immediacy is produced by verbal messages that are responsive to the other person in the relationship: Messages that suggest openness to the other, friendship for the other, or empathy with the other. Such simple things as the use of the pronoun "we" rather than "you" or using "you and I" or "us" will increase feelings of immediacy.

An important method of increasing immediacy in a relationship is sending verbal messages that encourage the other person to communicate. Such comments as "I see what you mean," "Tell me more," "That is a good point," and "I think so too" will create increased immediacy. Contrast these comments with the following: "Oh, shut up," "That is stupid," "I thought of that years ago," "Frankly, I don't care what you think." If you were to hear any of the latter comments, would you want to communicate more? How close would you feel to the person who made such a comment? Clearly a direct way to modify feelings of immediacy is through verbal messages. However, there are many nonverbal messages that can accomplish the same end, although they often are much less direct. Since directness often is seen as inappropriate behavior in a nonimmediate relationship, increasing immediacy in such cases is accomplished primarily via nonverbal messages. There are many types of nonverbal messages that tend to increase (or decrease, if you wish) immediacy.

Gestures, Body Movements, and Immediacy

The position of your body when communicating with another, your posture, and the type of gestures you employ all contribute to an immediate or nonimmediate perception. The person who seems relaxed, has an open body position, leans forward when communicating, and gestures in a positive manner is much more likely to be perceived as immediate than the person who seems closed and distant.

Nonimmediate body movements are exemplified by a closed body position (arms folded), very little gesturing, and a tense posture. This type of individual makes people feel uncomfortable; communication is very limited and often even is terminated. We are unlikely even to approach a person who has a nonimmediate posture. For example, the teacher who is always distant or nonresponsive to students in her or his nonverbal body movement is saying "I don't want interaction with you." Students can subconsciously realize this based solely upon the nonimmediate body positions and gestures.

Physical Appearance, Attractiveness, and Immediacy

Ectomorphs tend to have body stances that say they are tense and perhaps afraid of communication. This can be corrected by learning to relax and present a less tense body stance. Endomorphs tend to stand in a rather uncaring, perhaps even sloppy stance. This too can be corrected. The mesomorph has the most immediate body stance. Even if your shape or general appearance does not initially present the image readily approved in this culture, you can still present an immediate or responsive image of yourself by using a more positive body stance. In fact, this will improve people's perceptions of you and your appearance. If you have a positive, open, receptive body stance, despite your body type, people will respond to you more favorably.

Dress, Artifacts, and Immediacy

These factors depend upon the communication context and the individuals involved. However, although your attire should match the context, you can still present an immediate image. For example, the teacher who dresses in casual rather than formal attire is more likely to put the class at ease than one who dresses in a very formal manner. By "casual" we mean informal, not sloppy or carelessly dressed. The supervisor who dresses in a casual fashion is more likely to be able to communicate with employees on an informal basis than the supervisor who dresses in a nonimmediate way, the way that says "I'm the boss, and you are obviously beneath me."

The effects of dress and artifacts are very important in developing an immediate relationship. We already know that how people dress predicts whether others will want to interact with them. Therefore, someone who dresses to make others feel that he or she is above them presents a non-immediate image. This is not to say that teachers should dress like students or that supervisors should dress like their employees. It does suggest that less formal attire will let people feel as if they can approach you.

Facial Expression, Eye Behavior, and Immediacy

An old adage is true, particularly with nonverbal behaviors: "You catch more flies with honey than with vinegar." The person who has a positive facial expression is more likely to be approached by others, to be communicated with by others, and to be perceived in a positive fashion by others.

Do you know someone who has had a frown line between the eyes ever since you can remember? This person probably presents a very non-responsive image to others. Your facial expressions and eye behavior are very important in establishing an immediate perception. The positive cues, such as smiling, nodding, eye contact, and an overall positive facial expression, all say to others that you like them and are interested in them, and in what they are saying. Consider the teacher who always wears a scowl, never smiles, and has very little eye contact with students. This teacher will not be perceived as immediate and will probably be perceived as unfriendly, cold, and uncaring.

Voice and Immediacy

As suggested earlier, "It's not what you say, but how you say it." The words "I love you" when said with a particular inflection can even say you *dislike* someone. To present an immediate image through your voice, you need to have vocal variety. This shows that you are interested in the other person. The person who speaks in a monotone is not only boring but may also be perceived as not caring.

Vocal variety includes sounding animated, dynamic, attentive, and using tones and inflections that suggest you like and care about what the other person says. For example, the person who has a flat voice and very little vocal variety in a conversation appears uninterested in what you have to say. In contrast, a friend who greets you with, "It's great to see you; I've been looking forward all day to hearing about your vacation" is likely to elicit an equally warm response from you.

Space and Immediacy

How do you feel when you try to stand close to someone and the person keeps backing away? Probably very uncomfortable. There are several possible explanations for this behavior: (1) the person is from a culture different from yours and feels uncomfortable when being approached, (2) the person is a touch avoidant, (3) the person is generally nonimmediate and realizes that backing away and keeping a distance makes it less likely that he or she must interact, or (4) the person is communication apprehensive and backs away realizing that this will inhibit communication.

In order for people to be perceived as more immediate, they need to reduce the distance between themselves and receivers. As the distance is reduced, the likelihood of communication increases because there is more eye contact.

In terms of territoriality, individuals need to arrange their space in a way that says "Come in, you're welcome here." Often we do the opposite because we do not want people to stay too long. For example, there are many professors who arrange their offices in a nonimmediate manner so that students will feel uncomfortable and not take up too much of their time. These professors will make sure that the student sits across their desk from them and probably in a very uncomfortable chair.

A person's territory can tell a lot about how that individual wants to interact with others. A nonimmediate environment discourages communication; an immediate territory encourages it. Supervisors also are often very aware of arranging territory to have an effect on their subordinates.

Touch and Immediacy

This nonverbal area creates a more immediate relationship than does any other. However, a person must be cautious not to interpret touching behavior by another as an overture to an intimate relationship.

As suggested earlier, touch is the most potent of nonverbal messages and is likely to stimulate very strong meanings. When a supervisor touches a subordinate on the arm or pats the subordinate on the back, the supervisor most likely is attempting to establish a more immediate relationship. However, some subordinates, particularly ones of the opposite sex, could misinterpret this. Therefore we have to learn when touch is immediate or a sign of desired intimacy. The person who avoids touch or does not like to be touched will be perceived as very nonimmediate and very unfriendly.

When possible we should touch others to show we like and respect them. The touch should be done so it is not likely to be interpreted as an overture to intimacy. With today's heightened sensitivity to sexual harassment, many people find it wiser to sacrifice a potentially improved communicative relationship to avoid being charged with inappropriate touching behavior. While touch can substantially enhance a communicative relationship, it probably is best used when a very good relationship already exists. Particularly in the workplace and the school, touch probably should be avoided in the early stages of relationship development.

Environmental Factors and Immediacy

We should strive to create an environment that stimulates feelings of familiarity, warmth, and comfort in the receiver. In this type of environment, people are more relaxed and may communicate more freely. Business executives typically have their offices arranged in one of two ways—one nonimmediate, the other immediate. The immediate environment usually consists of subdued lighting, comfortable seating, fewer barriers between the executive and client or employee, and pleasant color tones. The nonimmediate environment has many barriers built between the executive and client or employee, bright lighting, uncomfortable seating, and colors that say "go away."

Some people in the business world have constructed their offices so that they can present either environment in the same room. They usually have a seating area away from the desk so that they can have the immediate atmosphere should they choose. However, they still like to maintain a nonimmediate environment so that they can encourage people not to stay a long time if that is the desired outcome.

Smell and Immediacy

While we are probably aware that an unpleasant body odor will cause people to avoid us, we often think we smell good when others might vehemently disagree. Women and men both tend to overdo the use of perfume and cologne so that they can carry the scent all day. Heavy, opulent odors can be offensive to others and discourage interaction. People and animals alike have smell detectors called pheromones. These help us decide what odors attract and what odors repel us. Many commercial perfume companies have taken advantage of this by suggesting that their perfume will stimulate another's pheromones. We must be cautious about the scents we use and the impact these scents have on others. Remember, what attracts one person can repel another. We should not, however, underestimate the power of appropriate enhancement of an environment through smell. Many real estate agents know that the smell of bread baking in a home will substantially increase the liking of the house by potential buyers. This is an odor that increases the environmental immediacy for most (but not all!) people and gets the communication about the house off to a very good start.

Time and Immediacy

One way to alienate almost anyone in this culture is to be consistently late. Our society demands that people be on time, and we do not tolerate lateness very often. If we wish to create an immediate atmosphere, or at least set the stage for creating one, we need to adapt to the time orientations of the culture. In our culture this means that we should be on time and, if possible, a little early for appointments. Many executives will make their clients wait to establish their power and authority. This does not endear them to those clients. Few people like to be kept waiting. Time is one way we can create the atmosphere for immediacy to take place.

Outcomes of Immediacy

In this section we have defined immediacy and discussed ways to be more immediate in each of the categories of nonverbal behavior. However, we have not explicitly stated the positive outcomes from establishing immediacy. There are several, and all are related to the establishment of a more effective interpersonal relationship.

First, immediacy will usually lead to an increase in communication between participants and interactants. When people feel immediate with each other, they become more relaxed and open to communication. Second, immediacy will lead to increased attentiveness by the interactants. When we feel immediate with another person, we naturally tend to focus attention on that person. Third, immediacy will increase the likelihood that listening will improve between the interactants. Since immediacy increases openness and attentiveness, one is less likely to be defensive in response to what the other person is saying. Therefore, one's listening is directed more toward understanding what the other person is saying rather than preparing to respond to an attack. Fourth, immediacy will lead to liking between the interactants. Communication in such a positive environment is very pleasant for the individual, and these positive feelings become associated with the other person in the interaction. These four outcomes of immediacy, of course, lead to the fifth and most important outcome, more effective communication.

Considerable research on immediacy has focused on the learning environment. The results of that research strongly suggest that increased immediacy between teacher and student leads to a variety of positive outcomes. Immediacy will help the student and teacher establish a better interpersonal relationship. Immediacy will lead to students taking other courses from the teacher who is perceived as immediate. Immediacy will cause increased learning by the student because the student likes the teacher and will listen to her or him. Immediacy between teacher and student will mean fewer discipline problems. Finally, immediacy will lead to a more positive relationship between teacher and student, and thus increase communication.

There can be some disadvantages to immediacy. First, behaviors intended to increase immediacy are sometimes misinterpreted as invitations to intimacy. Second, immediacy may threaten the privacy between individuals since it fosters increased communication. This occurs often where one party perceives immediacy but the other resists or does not perceive the same degree. Third, immediacy can increase the anxiety of the touch avoidant or communication apprehensive individual. Since immediacy increases feelings of closeness and the need to communicate, these individuals may find immediate situations unpleasant. And fourth, immediacy can make people feel as if they have lost control of the situation. For example, some teachers are afraid that immediacy will lead to a loss of classroom control, when it usually has the opposite effect. Students are pleased to have an immediate, open teacher and usually behave better than in the traditional classroom. Nevertheless, people with high control needs may feel less comfortable in more immediate settings. To be open to communication with another is to relinquish some control over the relationship. Despite the benefits associated with increased immediacy, all interactions must be appropriate for both participants. If you intend to be an open, involving person, you may find it difficult to adjust your behavior so that a nonimmediate person feels comfortable. The context of every situation determines what behavior will be effective. Just as interacting with various personality types requires sensitivity to another's predispositions, so does the use of immediate behaviors.

The use of a single nonverbal behavior is not going to create the perception that you are an immediate, responsive individual. A combination of immediate nonverbal behaviors leads one to be perceived as immediate. If you want to be perceived as immediate, you should consider using such immediate nonverbal behaviors as: positive gestures, leaning forward, showing positive facial expressions, much vocal variety, touching others when appropriate, dressing casually but appropriately for the communication context, directing your body orientation toward the other person, using scents that are not overpowering, and being on time. Fortunately, you do not need to engage in all these behaviors all of the time. Rather, you should employ those which you can use comfortably and appropriately. Over time, you can develop an immediate attitude which will lead you to engage in these behaviors as a matter of course and without constant conscious attention.

If you are perceived as immediate, you will be seen in a more positive manner. You will be perceived as sociable, likable, and most of all, responsive to others. Responsiveness leads to more effective interpersonal relationships.

Intimacy

Intimacy refers to the perceived depth of a relationship between people. People in an intimate relationship see themselves as highly connected to each other. Often an individual in such a relationship is reluctant to make even a relatively minor decision that might affect the other person without first communicating with that person. People in a highly intimate relationship see their partner as an extension of themselves, and vice versa.

Very few relationships reach a point of high intimacy. Most of us will be fortunate enough to have one such relationship in a lifetime; some will have more than one; and some of us will never have one. Intimate relationships demand much of the people who are in them. Few of us have either the capacity or the willingness to extend ourselves as far as would be necessary to develop many intimate relationships.

Highly intimate relationships in the American culture provide the most common context for two things: self-disclosure and sexual relations. However, both can and do occur in relationships that are less than intimate. One focuses primarily on verbal messages, the other on nonverbal messages. Let us look at each.

Self-Disclosure

Messages of a self-disclosive nature reveal information that is private and personal. In general, people tend to self-disclose to those with whom they have much trust, confidence, and have known for a long time. However, there are exceptions to this rule. Some people will reveal anything, anytime, to anyone. These people are called high self-disclosers.

A coauthor of this text once had a female student who, on the first day of class, told the instructor how she had lost 350 pounds by having intestinal bypass surgery. In the same breath she told the instructor she had two abortions because of bad love affairs, and then revealed that she had the "hots for many of the men in class." This was all within the first five minutes of class. Not only was the instructor a bit taken aback, but the instructor did not want or *need* to know this information to communicate with the student.

High self-disclosers often cannot tell when to stop disclosing or what not to disclose, and they tend to make others feel uncomfortable by telling too much personal information about themselves. They are sending messages that are appropriate for a highly intimate relationship within a nonintimate one.

Low self-disclosers are those people who do not reveal any information about themselves unless forced to do so. They also make people feel uncomfortable, but for different reasons. Low self-disclosers reveal so little about themselves that others have a difficult time learning how to communicate with them. There is no way to reduce any uncertainty. The communication might come to a halt because one does not know how to communicate with the other. Communication apprehensives tend to be low self-disclosers because of their fear of communication. They wish to avoid communication, and the most threatening communication of all is that about the self. Avoidance of self-disclosure tends to reduce other communication as well.

In general, if one constructs verbal messages that reveal personal information to another, then reduction of uncertainty can occur and people can start interacting more comfortably. You can self-disclose about attitudes and values and be secure in the fact that you are only opening the lines of communication. However, when you start revealing very intimate information about yourself to others, don't be surprised if they start to feel uncomfortable. Only in the 1960s did North Americans buy into "letting it all hang out." However, a certain amount of self-disclosure will lead to more open and honest communication between source and receiver. It may even increase the communication between the two by finding things in common.

Think of some relationships that you have at home, work, and school. Consider the following self-disclosure statements and decide in which relationships you might be willing to state, presuming it were true: "I like bowling." "I attend Harvard University." "I have herpes." "My spouse and I are getting a divorce." "My lover and I had sex last night." "I was arrested for reckless driving yesterday." "I ran over a child when

I was sixteen." "I went to the ball game last Saturday." "I have a 3.5 GPA." "I really do not like Bill." "My boss made a pass at me this morning." "My favorite meal is steak and baked potato." "I am an alcoholic." "I am a Democrat." "I lied to you about that."

All the above statements tell something personal about the speaker. However, they are not all appropriate for all relationships. Each statement could be damaging to a relationship. Each, believe it or not, could strengthen a relationship. It all depends on the relationship. Can you provide an example (hypothetical, of course) for each statement in which it would be appropriate and helpful to a relationship? If you can, you have a feeling for the intimacy dimension of relationships.

Sexual Relations

Having a sexual relationship with another person is generally considered one of the most intimate behaviors one person can share with another. Although talking is usually associated with sexual relations, sex is primarily a set of nonverbal behaviors. Engaging in sexual relations is a highly intimate behavior, but the presence of sexual relations does not guarantee that the participants actually have a highly intimate relationship. Sexual relations can be, and are, engaged in by people who have a very nonintimate relationship.

In American society there is a strong tendency to equate sexual relations with intimate relationships. Such an equation is misleading. An intimate relationship is one in which there is considerable depth and feeling by both people. Such feelings have no necessity of being associated with sexual desire or fulfillment. Many heterosexual females have an intimate relationship with another female, but sex is not involved. Although this is not as common among heterosexual men, because such intimacy among men is viewed by many as non-masculine, it is far from unusual.

In contrast, many sexual relationships are far from intimate. One of our friends often tells us of his desire for "a short, intense, meaningless relationship." What he means is sex with no strings and no repercussions later. Such wants by both females and males lead to the phenomenon known as "instant intimacy." This was illustrated in a movie a few years ago with the following conversation in a singles bar:

Male "Hi there. I'm Bob."
Female "Hi. I'm Kim."
Bob "Come here often?"
Kim "No, this is my first time."
Bob "I'm a Virgo. What is your sign?"
Kim "I'm a Libra."
Bob "Great! Let's get out of here and go to my place."
Kim "O.K."

Although it would be easy to laugh at such a scene, or to raise serious moral questions about Bob and Kim, to do so would miss something very important. Bob and Kim probably wanted something more than sex; they probably wanted an intimate relationship but were willing to accept sex as a substitute. This is not unlike a scene that often occurs on trains, planes, and in bars. Complete strangers strike up a conversation and in minutes one or both will be revealing things that normally would be reserved for a highly intimate relationship. Humans seem to have a strong need to have an intimate relationship within which they can share some of their life with another. Not everyone has such a relationship. This leads some to engage in verbal (self-disclosures) and nonverbal (sexual relations) communication in other relationships where the behavior may not be appropriate and may even be very harmful.

Status

Status refers to a person's position in some hierarchy. The difference between people's status in a relationship is very important. This "status differential," as it is called, can have a major influence on the communication that is considered appropriate or inappropriate in a relationship.

A higher-status person in a relationship tends to control that relationship and the communication in it. The teacher in the classroom, the boss in the office, the coach on the field, and the sergeant in the barracks are all examples of this phenomenon. Where any significant status differential exists in a relationship, it is the higher-status individual who has the freedom to initiate and terminate communication encounters. Their messages are characteristically dominant, whereas the lower-status person's messages are submissive. The higher-status individual has the choice not only of what topics can be discussed but also when and for how long they can be discussed. Higher status leads to verbal dominance; lower status to verbal submission.

Status differential not only affects verbal communication in a relationship but also has a powerful impact on nonverbal communication. Status differential has an impact on eye contact, body position, posture, gestures, vocal activity, interpersonal distance, use of territory, touching, use of time, and physical appearance.

Eye Contact

People of lower status are expected to, and usually do, look more consistently at a person of higher status. However, if the status differential is very large (high school student and college president), the lower-status person is expected to lower the eyes as a sign of deference. The higher-status person is not only free to look or not look as he or she sees fit, but is even allowed to stare at the lower-status person. Such a prolonged stare by a lower-status person, however, would normally be inappropriate.

Kinesic Behaviors

A lower-status individual in a relationship is expected to face the higher-status person directly when communicating with that person. However, the higher-status person can literally face any direction he or she wants. Similarly, the higher-status individual may have as relaxed a posture as desired, but the lower-status person should always exhibit at least a somewhat more formal posture. Higher-status individuals often have much more expansive gestures than do lower-status people, although the higher-status person may choose not to gesture at all. The gestures of the lower-status person are expected to be in the direction of the higher-status person.

Vocal Behavior

Higher-status individuals are allowed to speak louder than their lower-status counterparts. Similarly, they are allowed to interrupt the lower-status person at will. Loud talking or interruptions by lower-status people generally are seen as inappropriate and may generate a hostile response.

Use of Space and Touch

Interpersonal distance and touch are almost completely controlled by the higher-status individual in a conversation. If the higher-status person does not touch the lower-status person, it is completely inappropriate for the lower-status person to initiate touch. Similarly, lower-status individuals are expected to "hold their position" so that the higher-status person can move closer or farther away as he or she chooses. Generally, the higher the status differential in a relationship, the greater the interpersonal distance that will be maintained and the less likely that there will be touching between the interactants.

In general, the higher the status of an individual, the more territory that person will command. Lower-status individuals are expected to respect that territory and not enter it unless invited. On the other hand, higher-status people are presumed to have the right to enter the territory of lower-status individuals whether invited or not. For example, students who sit on the teacher's desk are asking for trouble, but teachers are presumed to have the right to check the contents of a student's desk if they choose.

Use of Time

Higher-status people control the time for communication with those of lower status. They not only decide when it will occur but also how long it will last and what shall be discussed. Further, the higher-status person is allowed to be late if he or she chooses, but the lower-status person is expected to be on time—or early. A lower-status person who is late for a meeting may arrive to find the meeting canceled.

Dress

People of higher status tend to be better dressed than those of lower status. The higher-status person also has the added flexibility to dress as he or she sees fit when interacting with a person of lower status. In male dyads it is not uncommon to see the man with higher status remove his suit coat when talking to a lower-status person while the other man keeps his on.

We hope that you have been sensitive to the fact that in all of the descriptions outlined here, we have been considering status as a relative variable. Status differential emphasizes the *differences* in status between people. Thus, in two different relationships an individual may find vastly different status differentials present. In one case a person can be the higher-status individual, and in the other he or she may be the lower-status one. The college dean is an example. One hour he or she may be meeting with a student. There is a sizable status differential, and the dean is the higher-status person. The next hour the dean may be meeting with the university president. In that meeting the dean's position is completely reversed. The people in the relationship define the status differential, and the status differential defines the kinds of messages that one can send in that relationship.

Levels of immediacy, intimacy, and status all place boundaries on the types of verbal and nonverbal messages that can be sent in a relationship. Each dimension of the relationship contributes to determining what communication is appropriate and what is inappropriate. In addition, the culture in which the relationship exists determines the rules for interaction within the various levels of immediacy, intimacy, and status. Messages, then, stimulate different meanings in different relationships within a given culture, but they also stimulate different meanings in very similar relationships in different cultures.

References

Andersen, J. F. (1979). Teacher immediacy as a predictor of teaching effectiveness. In D. Nimmo (Ed.), *Communication Yearbook, 3*. New Brunswick, NJ: Transaction Books.

Malandro, L. A., Barker, L., & Barker, D. (1989). *Nonverbal communication* (2nd ed.). Reading, MA: Addison-Wesley.

McCroskey, J. C., Larson, C. E., & Knapp, M. L. (1971). *An introduction to interpersonal communication.* Englewood Cliffs, NJ: Prentice-Hall.

McCroskey, J. C., & Richmond, V. P. (1992). Increasing teacher influence through immediacy. In V. P. Richmond & J. C. McCroskey, *Power in the classroom: Communication, control, and concern,* pp. 101–119. Hillsdale, NJ: Lawrence Erlbaum.

McCroskey, J. C., & Wheeless, L. R. (1976). *Introduction to human communication.* Boston: Allyn & Bacon.

Mehrabian, A. (1981). *Silent messages: Implicit communication of emotions and attitudes* (2nd ed.). Belmont, CA: Wadsworth.

_____. (1971). *Silent messages.* Belmont, CA: Wadsworth.

Richmond, V. P. (1992). *Nonverbal communication in the classroom.* Edina, MN: Burgess International Press.

Richmond, V. P., & McCroskey, J. C. (1995). *Nonverbal behavior in interpersonal relations* (3rd ed.). Boston: Allyn & Bacon.

INTERPERSONAL COMMUNICATION RELATIONSHIPS

Section 5

DEVELOPING INTERPERSONAL RELATIONSHIPS

15

A fundamental component of the interpersonal communication process is the achievement of goals. Although a myriad of possible goals can be achieved through interpersonal communication, perhaps none is so central to our social survival as that of developing interpersonal relationships. We may not think of interpersonal relationship development as one of our focal concerns with communication, but it is. Just as our survival depends on the fulfillment of certain physiological and psychological needs, so too does it depend on our satisfying certain social needs.

Schutz (1960) maintains that we strive to satisfy three social needs through interpersonal communication. *Inclusion* needs are for belonging and association. Through interpersonal communication we develop relationships with others because of our need for social affiliation. To some extent, our attempt to satisfy these needs is what leads us to join fraternities, sororities, civic groups, professional associations, religious denominations, and the like.

Control needs are to have influence over others. Control is the need to take charge of various social situations and to use our leadership abilities. In trying to fulfill these needs, we are likely to take the upper hand in given situations.

Finally, *affection* needs are to be liked and to like others. When we feel this type of need, we tend to do favors for others and to show them that we care for them. We often become quite responsive to their expressions of liking and concern for us.

According to Schutz, the only way to satisfy needs for inclusion, control, and affection is by interacting with others. Largely, however, interpersonal interaction by itself is insufficient for fulfilling our social needs. What essentially allows us to satisfy these needs is the development of interpersonal relationships with others. Thus, the goal of relationship development through interpersonal communication is a major way of meeting some of our basic social needs.

In this chapter we explore interpersonal relationship development. We define and consider different characteristics of relationships. In addition, we define the stages through which relationships develop, how we go about getting people to "like" us, and various expectancies we have about our relationships.

The Nature of Interpersonal Relationships

Characteristics of Relationships

The term *relationship* as we will use it here and throughout the remainder of the book refers to a variety of social affiliations. When we mention interpersonal relationships, we are not concerned only with intimate friendships. We are also concerned with relationships such as those between siblings, parent and child, employer and employee, teacher and student, doctor and patient, and minister and churchgoer. Perhaps the biggest difference between any two of these types of relationships rests with the role played by the respective member of each relationship (for example, teacher versus student, sister versus brother). Beyond this difference, however, most interpersonal relationships are characterized by several factors. This section focuses on eight of these factors: variability, duration, frequency, revelation, meshing, support, anxiety reduction, and proximity.

Variability is that characteristic of interpersonal relationships which indicates that the partners in the relationship engage in many different types of interactions. For example, two friends who work together at the same job interact in task-related situations at work and in social situations after work. Similarly, a parishioner who has established a close friendship with her or his priest is likely to interact with the priest in a very formal way at church but in an informal way outside church.

That interpersonal relationships last over some period of time is shown by the characteristic of *duration*. Any interpersonal relationship requires a considerable amount of time to develop fully. Since the parties to the relationship continue to receive rewards from their relationship—all else being equal—their relationship should endure. Generally, the longer a relationship's duration, the stronger that relationship is. Weak relationships tend not to endure.

Closely linked with duration is *frequency*. This characteristic indicates that people involved in an interpersonal relationship engage in interactions with each other regularly and often. Both duration and frequency are important to interpersonal relationships because the more we interact with an individual, the better we come to know that person. Contrast, for example, a teacher whom you have had as an instructor for more than one class with a teacher with whom you have had only one class. Chances are you know the former much better than the latter, simply because you have interacted with that person more often and for longer periods of time.

As an interpersonal relationship develops and matures, the individuals involved in the relationship share with each other their basic as well as their more personal attitudes and beliefs. This characteristic of relationships is known as *revelation*, and it satisfies one of our more essential interpersonal needs—revealing our thoughts and feelings to others. The amount of revelation we engage in is—up to a point—determined by the duration and frequency factors mentioned above. Generally, the longer we have known someone, and the more often we have interacted with that person, the more we are willing to reveal about ourselves to that person. High self-disclosure, as we noted in the previous chapter, usually does not occur early in relationships. Thus, more revelation can be expected to occur in a long-term relationship than in a relationship in which the individuals are new acquaintances.

A fifth characteristic of interpersonal relationships is *meshing*. This refers to how the behavior of two people in a relationship is organized and interpreted with respect to each other. In some relationships each partner's behavior is *complementary* to the other person's. For example, in a relationship in which one person is a communication apprehensive and the other is not, one person's quietness complements the other person's great amount of talk, and vice-versa. In other relationships, however, each partner's behavior is *symmetrical* to that of the other person. This occurs when both individuals perceive their behavior as quite similar. For example, two communication-apprehensive individuals involved in a relationship with each other are likely to be symmetrical in their verbal behavior. Likewise, a young boy who imitates some of his father's unique behaviors exemplifies a symmetrical interpersonal relationship, one for which we have a popular cliché: "Like father, like son." Thus, meshing refers to that aspect of interpersonal relationships which conveys the complementary or symmetrical nature of the behavior of the individuals in the relationship.

A sixth characteristic of interpersonal relationships is *support*. Support occurs in a relationship when the actions of each partner are conducive to the well-being of the other person. Consider two siblings who seem to bicker with each other constantly, yet when an outsider presents some sort of threat to one of them, one sibling is quick to come to the other's aid. Support can be of several types: physical, emotional, and intellectual. One type of emotional support, anxiety reduction, is also another characteristic of interpersonal relationships.

Anxiety reduction can be thought of as a basic social need, the satisfaction of which comes through having interpersonal relationships. We all have fears, anxieties, and stresses. Sometimes these can be alleviated through the support given us by the individual with whom we have a particular relationship. For example, the anxieties we might feel about a given course can be lessened by establishing a closer relationship with the teacher or with a fellow student in the same class. Similarly, we cope with job-related stresses more easily when we seek and receive support from those who work with us.

The final characteristic of interpersonal relationships we want to discuss is that of *proximity*. This refers to the physical distance between the individuals in a relationship. An interpersonal relationship is characterized by the spatial closeness of its partners. Proximity may be the most important of the eight characteristics we have discussed. It has been found the greatest predictor of initial interaction between two people. That is, we are more likely to initiate communication, and thus to establish a relationship, with an individual who is spatially close to us than with one who is more distant from us. This may sound like common sense. However, we do tend to take proximity for granted until we are separated by a great distance from someone about whom we care very much. Have you ever had a "long-distance relationship," one in which two people carry on their relationship although separated by many miles? Such relationships are common among college students who are away from their "high school sweethearts." Lack of close proximity is perhaps the primary cause of failure in long-distance relationships. It reduces frequency and variability of interaction with the other person and complicates support and revelation from the other person.

Ongoing, well-established interpersonal relationships typically are characterized by close proximity between the partners. This is not to suggest that relationships characterized by longer distances always fail. However, greater distance does make such relationships more difficult to maintain because of its potentially negative influence on other factors. If distance limits the amount of time partners can spend together, they will not interact in as many different situations (trips to the library, grocery shopping, visits to relatives, etc.). When something happens that is moderately newsworthy, it may not be revealed if other events are judged more important to be discussed in the time available together. Meshing becomes more difficult because fewer expectations are shared.

The eight characteristics discussed above are interdependent. In other words, for any given relationship, a change in one characteristic is likely to lead to changes in several other characteristics. This is best exemplified by what happens between two partners in a relationship when there is an increase in spatial distance. These relational characteristics, along with social needs and interpersonal goals, determine in part the course any particular relationship will take in its development. In the following section we outline a general developmental path followed by most interpersonal relationships.

Stages of Relationship Development

Several communication researchers and social psychologists have offered different models of the process of relationship development. Most of these models can be broken down into three separate but related processes: relationship *building,* relationship *maintenance*, and relationship *deterioration*. One model we consider to be especially useful is that proposed by Knapp (1978). This model accounts for ten stages of relationship development. Five of these stages—*initiating, experimenting, intensifying, integrating*, and *bonding*—comprise the developmental process of "coming together." The remaining five stages—*differentiating, circumscribing, stagnating, avoiding*, and *terminating*—comprise "coming apart." We will examine these stages with emphasis on communication behavior representative of each stage.

First, however, it is important to understand that although we present the stages in a sequential, ordered fashion, many interpersonal relationships do not follow this specified sequence in their progress through the stages. Also, the amount of time necessary to complete a given stage and to move through the various stages will differ from relationship to relationship.

The first stage of "coming together" is **initiating**. This is a conventional stage and usually lasts only a few seconds, a few minutes at most. The primary decision we try to make at this stage is whether to initiate verbal communication with the other person. Thus, it involves a good deal of scanning the other person. We look at the person, consider the person's familiarity and attractiveness to us, and decide if the person is open to an interaction with us. We typically move through this stage with much caution, wanting to put our best foot forward and to make a good impression on the other person. Verbally, this stage is characterized by exchanges such as, "Hi, I'm Tom." "I'm Mary." "Pleased to meet you." "Nice to meet you too."

Once we have successfully initiated an encounter, we move to the **experimenting** stage. At this stage we try to discover how similar the other person is to us. A colleague of ours has drawn an analogy between this stage and the "sniffing-out" behavior engaged in by dogs when they greet each other. Indeed, we do engage in somewhat of a "sniffing-out" of the other person at this stage. We attempt to isolate interests we have in common, discover similarities in our backgrounds and experiences, and find a basis for deciding whether to allow the relationship to progress farther. Our verbal exchange at this stage is exemplified by such statements as, "I see you like country music." "Yeah; I used to be into rock, but I like country better now." It also involves a great amount of small talk. Knapp contends that commitment is limited at the experimenting stage and that most of our relationships do not move very far beyond this stage. One reason may be that we have only a certain amount of time to devote to each of our relationships. Therefore, we allow only a few to progress to more developed stages and let most of the others remain at the experimenting level. Here they remain noncommittal, casual, and comparatively unimportant to us.

Progress through the experimenting stage can take a relatively short time or may extend over months or years. When a relationship moves out of experimenting, it typically moves into the **intensifying** stage. Relationships with people we call "close friends" or "intimates" are maintained at this stage. Interaction here involves much deeper and broader self-disclosure or revelation. We tell the other person some of our most confidential secrets, our deepest feelings, our worst frustrations and failures.

At the intensifying stage, verbal interaction often employs the first-person plural ("We"). There are more direct expressions of commitment, such as "You really are a good friend," or "I'm in love with you." The use of nicknames and terms of endearment becomes very important for a relationship at this stage; the partners attempt to decrease formality and establish private symbols unique to their relationship. Aside from verbal cues, however, nonverbal cues become especially important at this stage as ways of communicating messages about the relationship; touch, for example, may become a substitute for many words. The partners' clothing becomes more coordinated, and they begin to share and exchange many physical possessions.

After completing the intensifying stage, a maturing relationship moves into the *integrating* stage. Occurring at this stage is a fusion of the two partners at both a psychological and a social level. Not only do they think of themselves as "one," but they also want others to recognize them as one. You probably experienced this stage with someone you dated for quite a long time. You went "everywhere" and did "everything" together as a couple. You considered the relationship special, unique, unlike any you or anyone else had before. You exchanged pictures, rings, or bracelets to emphasize your oneness with each other. Perhaps others began emphasizing your oneness by asking you to travel and do things "together," by sending you a single letter, or by giving you one gift. You began claiming common property, such as "our song," "our pizza joint," or "our car," and spoke about feeling "incomplete" or "lost without the other."

It is important to note, however, that the integrating stage does not involve complete togetherness. Although both partners commit much of themselves to the other, they still maintain a large portion of their individuality. Thus, although they want to feel like a single "unit" much of the time, there are other times they need their "selves" apart from the other.

The final stage of coming together involves a formal and contractual integration known as *bonding*. Bonding is different from integrating in several ways. First it is formal and public. Moreover, bonding recognized by society, such as marriage, is institutionalized and therefore more difficult to break off. It is a lasting commitment to a future together. Finally, bonding involves specified rules and regulations for guiding the relationship and expressing and maintaining its commitment. Much of the communication at this stage is based on the "contract," or commitment, and often entails talk about the future.

Some relationships may last until one person in the relationship dies and, at least psychologically, continue even after that for the surviving partner. Others, do not fare so well. They eventually come apart.

The first stage of "coming apart" is *differentiating*. This stage essentially is the opposite of the integrating stage of coming together. Thus, in the differentiating stage of coming apart, the individuals focus on their differences and disagreements. Verbally, the partners move away from using the "we" and "our" statements characteristic of integrating and use more "I," "me," and "mine" statements. This often is the first sign that a relationship is moving from a highly immediate or intimate status to a more nonimmediate one. Much of the communication serves to emphasize how different the people are in attitudes, beliefs, and behaviors; they talk about *not* having certain commonalities. The stage is marked by verbal exchanges such as, "I thought you liked watching 'Murphy Brown'!" "I always hated that show—I watched it just because you did!" Fighting and conflicts are obvious communicative signs of differentiating, although the stage can progress without explicit oral conflict.

A relationship that comes apart beyond differentiating may move into the *circumscribing* stage. At this stage both the quantity and the quality of communication decrease. Topics of discussion between the individuals are restrained to safe areas; touchy subjects are avoided. Interaction frequency and duration begin to decrease. This stage is marked by less revelation and fewer expressions of commitment. Statements exemplifying this stage may include: "Let's leave religion out of this." "I don't want to hear about your day at work." "Can't we just be friends?"

After circumscribing comes the *stagnating* stage of coming apart. If a dog's sniffing-out behavior is analogous to the experimenting stage, then a stagnated pond is analogous to this stage. A stagnating relationship is one that has ceased to be active and functional. Much of the communication at this stage is nonverbal and negative. The participants feel that saying anything is unnecessary because they "know" what will be said anyway. Their attitude, spoken or unspoken, says, "what is there to talk about? You know what I'll say and I know what you'll say." Many of the couple's interactions are similar to those engaged in with strangers. Their communication becomes rigid, difficult, narrow, and awkward. Just as a stagnating pond loses its means to support organic life, a stagnating relationship loses its means to support communicative life.

The process of stagnating in a relationship usually occurs while the individuals are in close proximity. The next stage, *avoiding*, involves an attempt to increase physical distance. Communication at this stage is done for the sole purpose of avoiding direct interaction with the other person. The message being conveyed is: "I don't want to see you or speak with you." Sometimes it is sent implicitly through nonverbal channels—one party simply avoids being in the same place with the other party. When physical separation is not possible, one party may simply ignore the other. Sometimes the message is sent more explicitly through verbal channels, exemplified by statements such as: "I'm too busy to talk to you." "If the phone rings, I won't answer." "Go away!"

The final stage of coming apart is *terminating*. This stage can occur any time and for any number of reasons. Two people may simply "grow apart." One person may die. Long distances between the individuals may perpetuate deterioration of their relationship. Or one party may suddenly say "Goodbye." Messages exchanged at this stage can vary as widely as the reasons. Knapp contends, however, that communication during termination is generally characterized by messages of distance and disassociation. Messages of *distance* put psychological and physical barriers between the two individuals. Such messages may take the form of actual physical separation, or they may be conveyed through certain other nonverbal behaviors and verbal expressions. A statement like "I just don't think we have anything in common anymore" would serve to express distance. Messages of *disassociation* convey concern for one's own interests while emphasizing differences from the other person. A message such as, "You never did appreciate what I'm doing; I've got my own life to live," would convey disassociation.

As already mentioned, termination can occur anywhere within the general process of relationship development. It can happen just as easily after a single "Hello" as it can after a twenty-year marriage. Like the termination stage, any stage beyond initiation can begin after any other stage. Indeed, in their developmental process, most long-term interpersonal relationships fluctuate back and forth between the stages of coming together and coming apart. Thus, any given relationship may progress, for example, from experimenting straight to stagnating, back to experimenting, then to intensifying and integrating, and from there to circumscribing, back to intensifying, and finally to bonding. Some relationships cease progressing and remain at the second or third stage of their development. Others never get beyond initiating, ending with, "A great-looking guy, but his breath would kill a mule!"

We hope that the discussion to this point has given you a deeper understanding of the nature of interpersonal relationships. Specifically, by now you probably realize that all interpersonal relationships have basically the same characteristics. You should also know that interpersonal relationships develop in and out of a series of stages. Keep in mind, however, the importance and function of these characteristics and stages will differ along with differences in people, particularly their needs and goals. We want now to look a bit closer at the individual in relationships by considering what expectancies people have for their relationships.

Relational Expectancies

Think for a moment about this question: What do you expect out of your relationships with others? That may be a difficult question to answer.

Most of us do not think about "expecting" anything from our relationships. We may think about it however when it comes up in a conversation, or something happens in a given relationship that causes us to think about it. In short, we tend to take relational expectancies for granted. At best, most of us have only a stereotyped perception of what a relationship should be. We expect it to begin easily, for there to be mutual attraction, to have fun, and to "live happily ever after." In reality, however, people have some specific expectancies for their interpersonal relationships. Some of these are expectancies about a relationship in the short-term, and others are expectancies for a relationship in the long-term.

Short-Term Expectancies

When we first enter a relationship with another, we have certain expectations about how we and the other individual will behave and interact early in the relationship. Thus, short-term relational expectancies are most readily developed in the early stages of· coming together—initiating, experimenting, and intensifying. Moreover, our focus on these expectancies and the importance we place on them will affect our communication in the stages of development. Mostly, they will determine how we communicate with the other person and what we communicate about. The seven short-term relational expectancies we want to consider are interest, peace, rule obedience, amusement, appearance, presence, and affection.

Interest. Early in a relationship, we expect to be interested in what the other person says and does. We expect them to be similarly interested in what we say and do. This is the primary purpose of the experimenting stage: to communicate so that we can isolate commonalities between us and the other person. Realization of such commonalities reinforces our desire to interact with the other person. Should our expectancy for mutual interests not be met, we may find continued interaction with the individual unrewarding and dissatisfying.

Peace. When we begin a new interpersonal relationship, we expect it to be free of discord, strife, and fighting. This expectancy is likely formed in the experimenting stage where interaction has shown to us that we can get along with the other person. Thus, it may serve as a catalyst for moving into the intensifying stage. Violation of the peace expectancy in the earliest stages of coming together may quickly lead to coming apart. We neither want nor expect conflict in the short term, so when it occurs we may decide to stop interacting with the person.

Rule Obedience. In the earliest stages of a new relationship, we expect the other party and ourselves to follow certain relational rules.

Some of these rules are learned through experience and observation; others are unspecified until agreed upon by the partners to a given relationship. An example of this expectancy can be drawn from an organizational context. When you begin a new job, you and your employer expect you to follow certain rules related to the job. These rules relate to when you are to arrive at work, whom you are to work with, whom you are to report to, how to carry out given procedures, and how often you can have access to the copying machine, among other things. The purposes of many, if not all, work rules is to allow your employer to develop a basis for trust in you. Once trust has been established, you may be allowed to "bend the rules a little." Expectancies of rule obedience operate in much the same way for more personal relationships. You and a new dating partner, for example, may follow certain rules for dating. After you have dated each other for a time and have developed trust for one another, you probably can overlook some disobedience of the rules. However, when this expectancy is violated in the short term— for example, when you say hello to a new acquaintance and he or she ignores you—the outcome is apt to be dissatisfaction with and disinterest in the other person. Thus, rule obedience is an important expectancy for communication in the early stages of relationship development. We are turned off by people who cannot follow the rules for interacting, whatever they may be.

Amusement. How often have you initiated an interaction with a joke or a one-liner? We expect to have fun early in our relationships. We expect the other person to be entertaining and to find us entertaining. This expectancy is closely linked to the expectancy of interest. People find amusing people interesting. Thus, much of our communication in the initiating and experimenting stages may consist of lighthearted, comical messages. Conversely, people find nonhumorous people boring. If early in a relationship we perceive the other person to have no sense of humor, it may cause us to lose interest in that individual. Have you ever heard the line "You're just no fun anymore?" As we begin relationships, we expect to have fun. As the relationships progress and some fun disappears, we miss it.

Appearance. Most of us realize the importance of personal appearance in making a first impression on someone. Because of this, we tend to have fairly strong expectancies about physical appearance early in our relationships. This is perhaps more true when heterosexuals initiate interactions with the opposite sex. Even with members of the same sex, however, we generally expect people with whom we are establishing a relationship to dress in a way we consider appropriate. Often we expect the other to dress quite similarly to the way we dress ourselves.

How are expectancies about appearance related to interpersonal communication? As pointed out in the chapters on nonverbal communication, one's attire sends many interpersonal messages. Through our choices of clothing we can either signal acceptance or rejection. First impressions are critical for successfully establishing relationships, and the way we dress is often critical to making first impressions on others.

Presence. We mentioned earlier that proximity is a major predictor of initial interaction with others. Once we have established a relationship with someone, we develop an expectancy related to the proximity principle—we expect that person to want to be near us. Because we often establish relationships with others who must remain far away from us—occupation, school, and the like—this expectancy may be less consistent and more situational than other short-term expectancies. That is, even in relationships with people who are a great distance from us, we expect them to *want* to be with us from time to time and that they will *try* to be with us whenever possible.

This expectancy is reinforced and upheld whenever the other person communicates messages to us that show her or his desire to be in our presence—whether those messages are transmitted via phone calls, E-mail, letters, face-to-face conversations, or through third parties. When the other person fails to send such messages, we are likely to interpret this as a lack of interest and are likely to lose interest too. Realize, however, that the other person will most likely have the same expectancy for us. There is much to be said for the slogan, "Reach out and touch someone!"

Affection. In the experimenting and intensifying stages of coming together, affection may be the most important short-term expectancy. When establishing a relationship, we expect the other person to be at least moderately attentive to us and to show liking for us. During interactions with the other person, verbal expressions such as "You are so good at that" and "I like how you always know what to say" help fulfill this expectancy. It can be reinforced nonverbally through certain gestures, eye behavior, touch, and postures that convey openness and responsiveness. Our expectancy for affection stems from our social need for affection. We seek out and establish relationships with persons who are likable and who express liking for us.

Long-Term Expectancies

As a relationship enters and progresses through the latter stages of coming together—intensifying, integrating, and bonding—we develop a set of expectations about how the relationship should operate in the long term. Some of these expectancies concern the long-term value placed on the relationship by us and our partner. For example, a major expectancy might be how we expect each other to express and maintain value for the relationship. Two of these are extensions of the amusement and affection expectancies developed for the short term. Others we will discuss are commitment equity, fidelity equity, contracting, twosome, recognition, frankness, and averaging.

Amusement.   Our short-term expectancy for amusement extends to a long-term expectancy as we progress through the intensifying stage and move on to integrating. Much of what leads us to be drawn emotionally closer to another person rests with the enjoyment and fun we experience when with the person. As we look ahead to the future of our relationship, we expect the fun and enjoyment to continue. Naturally this expectancy stems from our continued interactions with the other person. We feel that because the person has expressed a positive sense of humor in the past, he or she will continue to do so for as long as the relationship lasts.

Affection.   As important as the affection expectancy is in the short term, it probably is even more so in the long term. The very nature of the latter stages of coming together requires affection. As we interact with the other person during these stages, we expect affection to be continually provided. During integrating and bonding, we expect affection to be expressed in ways that are more intimate and private than how it is expressed in earlier stages. Moreover, the messages upholding this expectancy become more powerful in the latter stages. These messages can be conveyed through such statements as "I love you" and "We have a great 'thing' going, so let's not lose it."

Commitment Equity.   As we become psychologically tied to another person, we expect each other to have an equal commitment to the relationship. This commitment can be expressed in many ways, and perhaps differently by each partner. You and your roommate, for example, expect each other to be similarly committed to your friendship. You don't expect to violate each other's trust or in any way to threaten your liking for one another. As long as each of you perceives the commitment to be equal, it matters little how you express it. When this expectancy is violated, trust is easily lost and interactions may convey distance and disassociation.

Fidelity Equity.   One way to express our commitment to a relationship is to remain faithful to our partner. Our expectancy for equal fidelity is most prominent in intimate relationships where we expect our partner to share our sexual faithfulness. We often have a similar expectancy in other relationships. On the job, for example, we might feel that our supervisor's expressed favoritism toward a co-worker is something akin to infidelity. When we assume that a relational partner is being unfaithful to us, it is often the result of misunderstanding and misinterpretation of the other's behavior. Feelings of jealousy, for example, usually occur when we perceive our partner to be showing more interest in someone else. Our partner's interest in another is in itself little cause to suspect infidelity. However, the fulfillment of our expectancy for affection is easily threatened by other relationships involving our partner. Thus, we tend to expect our partner to adhere to the idea that "I won't if you won't." In other words, we expect a mutual level and expression of fidelity.

Contracting. In the latter stages of coming together, as two people develop a sense of oneness, we expect each other to adhere to certain implicit "contracts." For example, an unspoken contract between your parents may hold that your mother cooks and your father repairs, or he buys the groceries and she fixes the car. Less intimate relationships have similar contracts. A contract exists between you and your teacher, for example. Such a contract might say that as long as you satisfactorily complete your assignments in the allotted time, he or she will assign you an appropriate grade. The formulation of such contracts is usually not discussed and agreed upon outright by two relational partners. Rather, the expectancy develops in a predominantly nonverbal way as the two parties progress through their relationship. Experience has taught you, for example, that when you do your homework you will get a grade for it. The specifics about how to do the assignments and how they will be graded may be specified verbally, but seldom do you need to be told how to keep up your end of the teacher-student contract.

Twosome. Recall that in the integrating stage two people begin to feel as one and perceive themselves as a "couple." This fusion leads to an expectancy that, as the relationship continues to grow over time, each partner will think in terms of "us" rather than "you and me." It is expected that each partner will depend on the other. This expectancy is fulfilled through interactions characteristic of integration, where expressions such as "what happens to you happens to me" predominate in the communication. Our expectancy for being a twosome strengthens our expectancies for commitment and fidelity equity. As long as we remain a couple, we will remain committed and faithful to our relationship.

Recognition. Just as we expect each other to think in terms of "us" in an integrated relationship, we expect others to see us as a couple.

We perpetuate this expectancy through various verbal and nonverbal expressions, all of which convey the message "We're a pair." We may attend social gatherings together, share the same class and study schedule, wear identical clothing, hold hands while walking down the street. The ultimate fulfillment of this expectancy is a formal bonding.

Frankness.   In the early stages of coming together, we tend to hide some facts about ourselves and feelings that we have. Often we will distort information to stimulate the other person to have a certain impression of us. As our relationship intensifies and moves into a stage of integration, however, we expect to be more honest with each other. Basically, we expect each other to be more open about feelings and opinions and to be more responsive to the feelings and opinions of the other. Moreover, we expect not only increased frankness from each other but also more honesty with each other than with other people. In an intimate dating relationship, for example, we are likely to express certain hopes, fears, and anxieties to our partner that we would not express to others. Frankness is a very critical expectancy in intensifying and integrating relationships because its fulfillment serves as the foundation for trust and solidarity between the partners. Lack of frankness and violation of its expectation may lead quickly to disintegration.

Averaging.   This expectancy concerns a balance in our relationships between the good times and the bad times. Essentially, in integrated relationships we expect that the pluses will outweigh the minuses eventually. Anyone with a sense of reality is well aware that any relationship will have its negative aspects—that there will be strife, conflict, and other threats to the relationship. Yet the very fact that we can intensify a relationship and move into a stage of integration substantiates that we expect such a relationship to offer more good than bad. If we expected otherwise, chances are we would progress no further than the experimenting stage. When we have this expectancy, we accept that our relationships will have their problems. As long as the expectancy is fulfilled—the pluses do outweigh the minuses—we are better able to cope with the problems. Many people do not have this expectancy and thus are unrealistic in their view of what should happen in a relationship. They think everything should be positive. These people are likely to find it very difficult to have other long-term expectancies met as well.

In summary, our expectancies for a given relationship help us clarify for ourselves what the nature of that relationship is now and what it is likely to be in the future. Expectancies give us a sense of how well developed a relationship is and how we can go about developing it further. Whether our relational expectancies are met depends on the nature of communication within the relationship. If our concern is with the contracting expectancy, for example, consistent messages that appear to violate the contract will violate our expectancy. Important to note here is that violation (or lack) of a single expectancy is unlikely to cause much dissatisfaction with the relationship. Dissatisfaction most often occurs when several expectancies continually fail to be met. We should emphasize also that the expectancies we have discussed are not meant to be a completion of the list—many others are bound to exist. Our list was developed through research conducted by John Daly, a colleague of ours at the University of Texas. His hope, also ours, is that future research will continue to enlighten us on the types of relational expectancies that do exist and how both affect and are affected by interpersonal communication.

To this point, we have covered the characteristics of interpersonal relationships, the stages through which relationships develop, and some expectancies we have about our relationships. We want to conclude the chapter by looking at the most fundamental aspect of establishing interpersonal relationships—how to get people to like us.

Gaining Affinity: Getting Others to Like You

The degree to which we feel social needs for affection and inclusion often manifests itself in our attempts to get other people to like and appreciate us. This is known as *affinity-seeking*. We are probably more concerned about gaining another person's affinity in the experimenting and intensifying stages of coming together. It is in these stages that our needs for affection and inclusion are likely to be high. Affinity-seeking should be of less concern in the latter stages of coming together, because these stages assume that liking and belonging already exist.

The process of affinity-seeking is important to most of our interpersonal relationships. We engage in the process when coming together in new relationships and when trying to salvage relationships that are coming apart. Often we use affinity-seeking to gain the positive regard of our teachers, co-workers, and superiors. We may try anew to seek the affinity of a dating partner whose respect for us has diminished for some reason. Affinity-seeking is quite useful in our attempts to make positive first impressions on new acquaintances. Thus, affinity-seeking is a process that has a major role in our everyday interpersonal transactions and relationships. As pervasive as this process is in our social lives, however, researchers have only recently begun to investigate what it is that people do to gain others' affinity.

Affinity-seeking was first addressed by McCroskey and Wheeless (1976). They suggested seven techniques for increasing another person's affinity for us: control physical appearance, increase positive self-disclosure, stress areas of positive similarity, provide positive reinforcement, express cooperation, comply with the other person's wishes, and fulfill the other person's needs. Each of these suggestions has been supported by subsequent research.

The research which has had the most impact on our understanding of affinity-seeking was the series of studies conducted by Bell and Daly (1984). In the first of these studies, they asked several groups of undergraduate and graduate students to produce a list of things that people can do to get others to like them. The lists generated by these groups were pooled together and then divided into categories of affinity-seeking behaviors. The results are presented in figure 15.1. Each category, such as altruism, dynamism, listening, and so forth, represents a series or combination of behaviors used to gain another's affinity. Used together, the behaviors in any given category represent an "affinity-seeking strategy."

Following their initial study, Bell and Daly conducted subsequent investigations to find out if any of the affinity-seeking strategies are used more often than other strategies. They were also concerned with which strategies have the greatest likelihood of being used, and whether people's selection and use of strategies depend on personality and sex differences. Strategies found to occur most frequently in basic interpersonal relationships are Conversational Rule-Keeping, Self-Concept Confirmation, Elicit Other's Disclosures, Nonverbal Immediacy, Self-Inclusion, Listening, Facilitate Enjoyment, and Altruism. Those strategies that respondents said they are most likely to use for gaining affinity are Optimism, Trustworthiness, Physical Attractiveness, Listening, Conversational Rule-Keeping, and Sensitivity. Thus, it appears that people will employ affinity-seeking strategies that help them form a positive impression on another person. This tendency seems to agree with what we have already discussed as communication patterns and relational expectancies that are characteristic of relationships in the early stages of coming together. That is, we have short-term expectancies for interest, rule obedience, and appearance; affinity-seeking strategies such as Elicit Other's Disclosure, Conversational Rule-Keeping, and Physical Attractiveness parallel those expectancies.

Personality and sex have an impact on people's likelihood of using particular affinity-seeking strategies. Highly communication-apprehensive individuals, it was found, prefer using more passive strategies for gaining affinity than do low apprehensives. High apprehensives in the Bell and Daly study were more likely to use the strategies of Concede Control and Supportiveness than they were other strategies. People who were identified in the study as highly Machiavellian preferred to use the strategies of Openness, Present Interesting Self, and Reward Association. These results suggest that

Figure 15.1
Typology of Affinity-Seeking Strategies

Altruism
People attempting to get another individual to like them try to be of help. For example, they hold the door for this individual, offer to get him or her something to drink, take his or her coat, and are generally available to run errands for this individual. They also give advice when it is requested.

Assume Control
People attempting to get others to like them present themselves as leaders— people with control over what goes on. For example, these people direct conversations, take charge of activities, and often explain how they have taken charge or served as leaders in the past.

Assume Equality
The person using this strategy presents self as an equal of the other person. For example, the person avoids showing off, does not act superior or snobbish, and does not play "one-upmanship" games. If the person attempting to be liked is of lower status, he or she treats the other individual as an equal rather than a superior.

Comfortable Self
The person attempting to get another individual to like him or her acts comfortable in the setting, comfortable with himself or herself, and comfortable with the other person. He or she is relaxed, at ease, casual, and content. Distractions and disturbances in the environment are ignored (e.g., loud noises and obnoxious people). The person tries to look as if he or she is having fun, even if this is not the case. The impression this person tries to convey is that "nothing bothers me."

Concede Control
People using this strategy allow the other person to control the relationship and the situation in which the two individuals find themselves. For example, they let the other take charge of their conversations and decide what they do and where they go. The person attempting to be liked also lets the other individual influence his or her actions by not acting dominant.

Conversational Rule-Keeping
People attempting to get another individual to like them follow closely the culture's rules for how people are to socialize with one another by demonstrating cooperation, friendliness, and politeness. These people work hard at giving relevant answers to questions, saying "the right thing," acting interested and involved in the conversation, and adapting messages to the particular characteristics of the other party. They avoid changing the topic of conversation too soon, interrupting the other person, being pushy, dominating the conversation, and using excessive

self references. When talking to strangers and acquaintances, they engage in small talk rather than serious discussions. They also avoid topics that are not of common interest to both parties.

Dynamism
Here the person attempting to get another individual to like him or her presents self as a dynamic, active, and enthusiastic person. For example, the person acts physically animated and very lively when with the other person, varies his or her intonation and other vocal characteristics, and is outgoing and extroverted in the presence of the other person.

Elicit Other's Disclosures
People who use this strategy encourage others to talk by asking questions and reinforcing the other person for talking. They inquire about the other person's interests, feelings, opinions, views, etc., respond as if the answers are important and interesting, and continue to ask more questions of the other person.

Facilitate Enjoyment
In this strategy, people attempting to get another individual to like them seek to make the situations in which the two are together very enjoyable experiences. The person does the things the other will enjoy, is entertaining, tells jokes and interesting stories, talks about interesting topics, says funny things, and tries to make the environment conducive to enjoyment.

Inclusive of Other
The person attempting to get another individual to like him or her includes the other in social activities and with groups of friends. He or she enhances the other's sense of belonging and being part of the group.

Influence Perceptions of Closeness
People who want another individual to like them engage in behaviors that lead the other to perceive the relationship as closer and more established than it has been. For example, they use nicknames when addressing the other and talk about "we" rather than "you" and "I." They also mention any prior activities that include both of them.

Listening
In this strategy, individuals pay close attention to what the other person says, listening very actively and intently. They focus attention solely on this person. Moreover, the person attempting to be liked demonstrates that he or she listened by being responsive to the other's ideas, asking for clarification of ambiguities, being open-minded, and remembering things the other said.

Nonverbal Immediacy
Here the person signals interest and liking through various nonverbal cues. For example, the person frequently tries to make eye contact with the other, stands or sits close to him or her, smiles, leans forward, indicates agreement by head nodding, and directs frequent looks toward the other person. All of these indicate interest in the other and in what he or she has to say.

Openness

In this strategy, people are open about themselves. They disclose information about their background, interests, and views. They may even disclose very personal information about their insecurities, weaknesses, and fears to make the other individual feel very special and trusted (e.g., "Just between you and me").

Optimism

People attempting to get another individual to like them present themselves as positive individuals; they appear cheerful and optimistic. They avoid complaining about things, talking about depressing topics, and being critical of themselves and others. In short, the person makes a concerted effort to avoid being "a drag."

Personal Autonomy

The person attempting to get another individual to like him or her presents self as an independent, free-thinking person—the kind of person who stands on one's own, speaks one's mind regardless of the consequences, refuses to change behavior to meet the expectations of others, and knows where he or she is going in life. For instance, if the person attempting to be liked finds that he or she disagrees with the other individual on some issue, that person states an opinion anyway, is confident that his or her view is right, and may even try to change the mind of the other person.

Physical Attractiveness

People employing this strategy try to look as attractive as possible in appearance and attire. They wear fashionable clothes, practice good grooming, show concern for proper hygiene, stand up straight, and monitor their appearance.

Present Interesting Self

In this strategy, the person presents self as a person who would be interesting to know. For example, he or she highlights past accomplishments and positive qualities, emphasizes things that make him or her especially interesting, expresses unique ideas, and demonstrates intelligence and knowledge. The person may also try to discreetly drop the names of impressive people he or she knows. Such individuals may even do outlandish things to appear unpredictable, wild, or offbeat.

Reward Association

People who use this strategy in getting another individual to like them present themselves as important figures who can reward others for associating with them. For instance, they offer to do favors, and they give gifts and valuable information. The message to this individual is: "If you like me, you will gain something."

Self-Concept Confirmation

People attempting to get another individual to like them demonstrate respect for and help the other feel good about him- or herself. For example, they treat the individual as a very important person, give compliments, say only positive things about him or her, and view the things this individual says as very important. They may also tell third parties what a great person this individual is, hoping that the comment will eventually get back to the other.

Self-Inclusion
In this strategy, the person attempting to get another individual to like him or her sets up frequent encounters. For example, he or she initiates casual encounters with the other, attempts to schedule future encounters, places himself or herself physically close to the other, and is available to be invited to participate in the other person's social activities.

Sensitivity
The person attempting to get another individual to like him or her acts in a warm, empathic manner in order to communicate concern and caring. He or she also shows sympathy for the other's problems and anxieties, works at understanding how this individual sees life, and accepts what the individual says as an honest response. The message sent is "I care about you as a person."

Similarity
In this strategy, the person tries to make the other individual think that the two of them are similar in attitudes, values, interests, preferences, personality, and so forth. He or she expresses views that are similar to the views the other holds, agrees with what the other says, and points out things that the two have in common. Moreover, the person deliberately avoids engaging in behaviors that would suggest differences between the two parties.

Supportiveness
The person is supportive of the other and his or her positions by being encouraging, agreeable, and reinforcing. The person also avoids criticizing or saying anything that might hurt the other's feelings, and sides with the other in any disagreements he or she has with other parties.

Trustworthiness
People using this strategy present themselves as trustworthy and reliable. They emphasize their responsibility, reliability, fairness, dedication, honesty, and sincerity. They also maintain consistency in their stated beliefs and behaviors, fulfill any commitments made to the individual, and avoid "false fronts" by acting natural at all times.

Based on the work of Bell and Daly (1984).

highly manipulative individuals attempt to gain affinity by emphasizing how rewarding interaction with them can be. Finally, in terms of sex differences, Bell and Daly found that females are more likely than males to use relatively passive and other-directed strategies for gaining affinity. Females showed much greater preference than did males for the strategies of Conversational Rule-Keeping, Elicit Other's Disclosures, Listening, Sensitivity, and Similarity.

The research findings collected by Bell and Daly suggest that, although people generally prefer some affinity-seeking strategies over others, a person's personality and sex play a part in the choice of which strategies to use. Thus, it can be expected that if you exhibit certain personality characteristics, you will use affinity-seeking strategies that are different from those of someone whose personality is unlike yours. If you are a relatively quiet and reserved person, you are likely to use more passive strategies than someone who is more outgoing and talkative. Similarly, if you are a male we can expect that your strategies for getting others to like you are somewhat more aggressive than those used by a female.

The research cited above also found that people's choices of affinity-seeking strategies differ from situation to situation. In a social situation, for example, people seem more likely to use strategies such as Inclusion of Other, Assume Equality, and Concede Control. Whereas in a task situation, they are more likely to use the strategies of Openness and Dynamism. These results suggest that strategies used to gain affinity with others may differ not only according to our specific personal characteristics but also according to the situation in which we and the other person are interacting. Thus, you are likely to vary in your use of strategies for gaining affinity with a new acquaintance—the student sitting next to you, your teacher, and someone you would like to date. Other research has confirmed many observations reported by Bell and Daly. This research has pointed to similarities and differences in effectiveness of different strategies between general peer relationships and those involving teacher/student and supervisor/subordinate relationships.

To summarize, the process of getting others to like us has its greatest impact in the early stages of relationship development. The process is related both to how we communicate in those stages and to the expectancies we have about a given relationship. The studies by Bell and Daly have identified twenty-five strategies that people choose from for gaining affinity with others. People tend generally to prefer several strategies over others. However, people's ultimate likelihood of using various strategies depends on their personalities, their gender, and the context. Since people strive to satisfy their needs for inclusion and affection, they will engage in the process of affinity-seeking. This tendency is a fundamental reason for establishing and maintaining interpersonal relationships.

References

Baxter, L. A. (1984). Trajectories of relationship disengagement. *Journal of Social and Personal Relationships, 1*, 29–48.

Bell, R. A., & Daly, J. A. (1984). The affinity-seeking function of communication. *Communication Monographs, 51*, 91–115.

Daly, J. A., & Kreiser, P. O. (1992). Affinity in the classroom. In V. P. Richmond & J. C. McCroskey, *Power in the classroom: Communication, concern, and control*. Hillsdale, NJ: Lawrence Erlbaum.

Davis, M. S. (1973). *Intimate relations*. New York: The Free Press.

Derlaga, V. J., & Chaikin, A. L. (1975). *Sharing intimacy: What we reveal to others and why*. Englewood Cliffs, NJ: Prentice-Hall.

Fitzpatrick, M. A., & Best, P. (1979). Dyadic adjustment in relational types: Consensus, cohesion, affectional expression, and satisfaction in enduring relationships. *Communication Monographs, 47,* 167–178.

Harre, R., Morgan, J., & O'Neill, C. (1979). *Nicknames: Their origins and social consequences*. London: Routledge & Kegan Paul.

Knapp, M. L. (1983). *Interpersonal communication and human relationships*. Boston: Allyn & Bacon.

_____. (1978). *Social intercourse: From greeting to good-bye*. Boston: Allyn & Bacon.

McCroskey, J. C., & McCroskey, L. L. (1986). The affinity-seeking of classroom teachers. *Communication Research Reports, 3,* 158–167.

McCroskey, J. C., & Richmond, V. P. (1992). *Communication in educational organizations*, ch. 9. Edina, MN: Burgess International Group.

McCroskey, J. C., & Wheeless, L. R. (1976). *An introduction to human communication*, chs. 12–13. Boston: Allyn & Bacon.

Pearce, W. B. (1974). Trust in interpersonal communication. *Speech Monographs, 41,* 236–244.

Phillips, G. M., & Wood, J. T. (1983). *Communication and human relationships: The study of interpersonal communication*. New York: Macmillan.

Richmond, V. P., & McCroskey, J. C. (1992). *Organizational communication for survival*, ch. 12. Englewood Cliffs, NJ: Prentice-Hall.

Richmond, V. P., McCroskey, J. C., & Davis, L. M. (1992). The relationship of supervisor use of power and affinity seeking strategies with subordinate satisfaction. *Communication Quarterly, 34,* 178–193.

Rubin, W. C. (1966). *The interpersonal underworld*. Palo Alto, CA: Science & Behavior Books.

Schutz, W. C. (1960). *FIRO: A three dimensional theory of interpersonal behavior*. New York: Holt, Rinehart & Winston.

POWER AND INTERPERSONAL INFLUENCE

16

A primary reason we communicate is to influence others. People have to learn to cooperate to achieve common goals. People also have to learn that influence through interpersonal communication is a primary means of getting people to work together toward common goals. We have already learned that having high credibility, being attractive, and being similar are all prerequisites for influencing another's attitude. When we attempt to influence others, our ultimate goal is to modify their attitudes and behaviors. To meet this goal, the best means of communication is interpersonal. Because of its personal nature and opportunity to supply feedback, interpersonal communication is the most effective type of communication for influencing people and causing behavior change. This chapter examines different strategies that can be employed when trying to influence another. First we need to examine the types of behavior change we want and the advantages and disadvantages of each.

Levels of Influence

Three levels of influence are possible through interpersonal communication. We can get people to *comply* with, to *identify* with, or to *internalize* recommended behaviors. For example, an instructor might say that he or she does not expect any cheating during a class exam. Many students only comply when the teacher is watching. However, many others identify with the behavior requested and are self-motivated to comply. Some students understand the importance of learning on one's own and have internalized this model. The ultimate goal in many influence situations is to get the other person to internalize the recommended behavior. For the students who have internalized the value, cheating is simply not considered an alternative at all.

Compliance

Compliance is the most transitory level of influence. People comply with another's request because they can see either some potential reward for complying or some potential punishment for not complying. Individuals temporarily accept the idea to gain specific rewards or avoid specific punishments—not because they believe in it. Therefore, compliance is mainly a superficial response to an influence attempt.

The compliant individual does not necessarily believe the behavior is a good one. This is quite common in the classroom. Often students yield to a teacher's demands because they feel they will be rewarded or can avoid punishment. However, the student's behavior is totally dependent on whether the teacher is capable of carrying out the rewards or punishments. In addition, the demand must be salient or important to students, or they will not comply. If the teacher threatens a student with a poor grade if the student does not stop talking, but the student does not care about the grade, the student is not likely to stop talking. Therefore, the request and the source of the request, must be perceived as relevant to the receiver in orde. for the receiver to consider complying.

The amount of attitude change in the compliance model is usually very minimal, often short-lived, and generally does not lead to motivation to continue the behavior. It simply leads to movement by the receiver. To guarantee compliance, the source can illustrate concern, control, and scrutiny to the receiver. *Concern* refers to the source indicating he/she really cares whether the receiver complies, *control* refers to the source indicating he/she can really do something to or for the receiver, and *scrutiny* refers to the source indicating he/she has ways of knowing whether the receiver complies.

Law-enforcement agencies of this country have shown their concern about speeding by reducing the speed limit to 55 or 65 MPH. They have shown that they can control speeding with road monitors and that they can watch for speeders by using radar. When the above methods are available, compliance with speed laws will probably occur. However, when one of them is missing, compliance may not occur. For example, if the radar is turned off for a day, speeders know that they are not being scrutinized by the police. They will speed even if concern and control are present. Teachers who say they do not want cheating on a test, but then leave the classroom, have just told the class they are not really concerned about the possibility of cheating.

Compliance is the lowest level or outcome of interpersonal influence. Compliance gets people only to conform, not to identify with or internalize a specific behavior. People who comply "just do it." They don't have to like it.

Identification

When people change a behavior because they think the change is a good idea, they are changing at the identification level. This is a more lasting level of influence. Often people will identify with behavior changes because they also identify with the person recommending the change. "If Martha thinks it is a good idea, that is good enough for me." In other cases the rationale for the change convinces the person that it is a good idea. In either case, the person influenced now "owns" the behavior.

Change achieved at the identification level is much more persistent than that achieved at the compliance level. Changes tend to be long-term, and the person who changes may even attempt to influence others to make the same change.

Whereas compliance depends primarily on the source's ability to mediate rewards and punishments, identification depends more on the relationship between the source and the receiver. Although people still conform to a source's recommendation at the identification level, they do so because they believe they are making a good decision. The perception of the source's character or competence (or both) is positive and leads the receiver to "buy into" the recommended change.

Internalization

This is the most lasting level of influence. It involves making the new behavior a habit; its desirability becomes meshed with the person's value system. When an idea or behavior is internalized, it is integrated into the individual's existing value system and is a part of the way the person thinks or behaves. It is indistinguishable from the person's already existing behaviors in the same area. For example, if we do not believe in cheating on exams, we take little notice when the teacher says not to cheat, for the idea of cheating is simply foreign to us. We engage in the recommended behavior because of who we are, not because someone else promises rewards or threatens punishments. It is already just the way we behave.

When internalization is achieved, the individual is induced to perform the behaviors despite the scrutiny of the source. The behavior will be performed because the person is internally motivated and feels this is the good or right thing to do. In interpersonal relationships, when internalization is present, individuals will do things for the other person without even being asked to do so. They will do something because they believe it right and good and will help in establishing an effective interpersonal relationship. They will engage in desired behaviors without the need for additional communication.

It is not always important that we exert influence to such an extent that we produce internalized behavior change. In most of our interpersonal relationships, simple compliance may be all we will ever want or need. However, if lasting change is wanted, it is very important that the influence be at either the identification or internalization level. Without a very positive relationship with the other person, we will not have the power to produce change at these levels.

Power

Power, as we will use the term in this chapter, refers to an individual's ability to have an effect on the behavior of another person or group. When we exert interpersonal influence, we are exerting our power.

Power is a word that is used in many ways, so we need to make clear that we are not talking here about raw, physical power. The use of guns, fists, and bombs is not what we mean by interpersonal influence. That type of power can reasonably be described as destructive and evil. Not all power is of that type. The power we are concerned with is the power freely granted to one communicator by another.

We believe the most useful model of power is the one advanced by French and Raven (1959) in which they explicated the five bases of power: assigned, coercive, reward, referent, and expert.

Assigned Power

Assigned power, sometimes called "legitimate power" stems from the assigned role of a person in a relationship (parent, supervisor, teacher). Assigned power is based on your perception that the other individual has the **right** to make certain demands and requests as a function of her or his position or assigned role. This type of power can have very explicit rules ("You are not allowed to date until you are fifteen"). This type of power can have implicit rules ("I expect you to do the best work you can"). Either way you will comply because they are seen as "legitimate" demands from the other person because of her or his relationship with you.

Assigned power usually only engenders compliance from the other person. However, in a parental relationship an individual is likely to identify with some legitimate demands of the other person. In other environments this may not be the case. For example, in the work and school environment, most legitimate demands only lead to compliance. Often in these environments legitimate power is associated with the power to reward or punish; therefore, many people dislike the use of legitimate power.

Coercive Power

Coercive power relates to an individual's capacity to inflict punishment if another does not conform to that person's requests or demands. For example, a teacher's coercive power is contingent upon the student's perceptions of how probable it is that the teacher will exact punishment for nonconformance and the degree of negative consequences such punishment would entail, minus the probability of punishment from other sources (peers, for example) if the student **does** comply with the teacher.

Coercive power provides the best example of how power must be granted by one person to another for the power to exist. For example, teachers are assigned the right to grade students. However, students who really do not care whether they pass or fail do not grant the teacher the power to coerce. If threats to fail fall on deaf ears, the teacher is left powerless. In short, if we are willing to accept the punishment, the other person has no coercive power over us. Of course, the reverse is also true. If the other person is willing "to take our best shot," we have no coercive power over them either. Power must be granted, it cannot just be assumed.

Even when used, coercive power will only gain *compliance* on the part of the other individual; it will not create motivation to continue the new behavior. Therefore, for an effective interpersonal relationship, the coercive power model should be avoided at all costs or employed only if necessary to get someone to do something you absolutely must have done. (See figure 16.1.)

Figure 16.1
Bases of Power and Impact on Levels of Influence

Five Bases of Power	Compliance	Levels of Influence Identification	Internalization
Legitimate	X		
Coercive	X		
Reward	X		
Referent	X	X	X
Expert	X	X	X

Reward Power

When an individual has the potential to provide rewards to another for compliance, this is known as reward power. For example, if your boyfriend or girlfriend wants you to do something and promises to take you to dinner as a reward, you might engage in the behavior. However, this does not mean that you identify with or internalize the behavior.

Rewards can be effective if they are ongoing, positive, and consistent. If a reward is used once in a situation, it has to be used again in that situation or the person will feel as if he or she is being punished (for children under ten this may vary). For example, if you do something for your friend and he or she takes you to dinner, the next time you are asked to do a similar favor, you will expect to be taken to dinner again. If you aren't, you will feel you were cheated and will not engage in similar behavior again.

Although it often is not recognized, coercive and reward power essentially are the flip side of the same coin. Coercive power involves introducing something unpleasant or removing something pleasant if the person fails to comply. Reward power involves introducing something pleasant or removing something unpleasant if the person does comply. Neither one provides a solid basis for identification or internalization. However, reward is a much friendlier means of inducing movement than coercion and at least opens the door to further cooperation.

Referent Power

An individual's identification with a specific person or group is called referent power. It is sometimes called the power of association. Specifically, it is based on the desire of the less powerful person to identify with and please the more powerful person. The less powerful person wants to be liked by and/or to become more like the more powerful person, which means adopting that person's attitudes and behaviors. The stronger the less powerful person's attraction to and identification with the more powerful person, the stronger that person's power is.

Whatever the context of the communication, referent power will lead not only to compliance but also to identification and internalization. This means that in the interpersonal relationship, referent power can cause significant behavior change. Referent power in a strong relationship can be a reciprocal process for the persons involved. For example, if your best friend does not cheat on exams, then you may model this behavior and eventually internalize it. At another point in the relationship your friend might model the way you dress or talk. Thus, the more referent power between two people, the stronger the relationship is likely to become.

Expert Power

Expert power results from an individual's perceiving the other person to be competent and knowledgeable in specific areas. Expert power stems from source credibility. The more one perceives another to be knowledgeable, the more likely one is to go to that person for information or advice. The person whose advice is asked has the potential to be very influential, particularly in terms of being able to direct another person's way of thinking. Expert power leads to compliance, identification, and finally internalization. If the conveyed knowledge is put to use, then the receiver of the information has identified with the person giving the information, and possibly will internalize the information.

Communicating Influence

The use of power requires communication. Often, power is used to influence without explicit verbal communication. When a teacher tells students to do their homework, it is usually not necessary to add "or I will punish you by lowering your grade," "because I am the teacher and I have the right to demand that you do this," or "because you like me and want to please me." Such appeals to power are implied and are generally recognized by the student without being directly stated.

In other instances, direct power appeals are stated. Coercive power, for example, may be invoked when a teacher says, "If you don't turn your work in on time, I will give you an F for the assignment." Similarly, reward power may be invoked when a teacher says, "If you do this extra problem, I will give you five bonus points." An appeal to referent power may take the form of the teacher saying "I need help setting up this VCR."

Whether power appeals are stated directly or implied, in order for a source to influence behavior, the receiver must associate the requested behavior with the power held by the source. All power is based on the receiver's perceptions. If the receiver does not perceive the source to have a certain type of power, a source's appeal to that power, whether direct or implied, is not likely to result in influence. Similarly, even if the receiver perceives the source to have the power, if the influence attempt is not associated with the power, the attempt is likely to be unsuccessful.

Behavior Alteration Techniques

More recently, the five bases of power have been expanded. A range and diversity of power strategies or Behavior Alteration Techniques (BATs) available for personal influence have been identified. All of the BATs are concerned with getting others to do what you want them to do. Twenty-two representative BATs, or categories, have been identified. Each category is best represented by a combination of messages, or BAMs (Behavior Alteration Messages; see figure 16.2).

Most of the BATs and respective BAMs represent the previously defined five power strategies. The first five BATs fall in the Reward category. BATs 6-9 are associated with Punishment (coercion). BATs 12 and 13 comprise the Referent category. The Assigned or Legitimate category is represented by BATs 14 and 15. The Expert category

Figure 16.2
Behavior Alteration Messages

Category (BATs)	Sample Statements (BAMs)
1. Immediate Reward from Behavior	You will enjoy it. It will make you happy. Because it's fun. You'll find it rewarding/interesting. It's a good experience.
2. Deferred Reward from Behavior	It will help you later on in life. It will prepare you for college (or high school, job, etc.). It will prepare you for your future. It will help you with upcoming relationships.
3. Reward from Source	I will give you a reward if you do. I will make it beneficial to you. You will be rewarded if you do this.
4. Reward from Others	Others will respect you if you do. Others will be proud of you. Your friends will like you if you do. Your parents will be pleased.
5. Internal Reward: Self-Esteem	You will feel good about yourself if you do. You are the best person to do it. You are good at it. You always do such a good job. Because you're capable!
6. Punishment from Behavior	You will lose if you don't. You will be unhappy if you don't. You will be hurt if you don't. It's your loss. You'll feel bad if you don't.
7. Punishment from Source	I will punish you if you don't. I will make it miserable for you. I'll get others to punish you. You will be an outcast.
8. Punishment from Others	No one will like you. Your friends will make fun of you. Your parents will punish you if you don't. Your friends will reject you.
9. Internal Punishment: Guilt	If you don't, others will be hurt. You'll make others unhappy if you don't. Your parents will feel bad if you don't. Others will be punished if you don't.
10. Source/Receiver Relationship: Positive	I will like you better if you do. I will respect you. I will think more highly of you. I will appreciate you more if you do. I will be proud of you.
11. Source/Receiver Relationship: Negative	I will dislike you if you don't. I will lose respect for you. I will think less of you if you don't. I won't be proud of you. I'll be disappointed in you.
12. Peer Modeling	Your friends do it. People you respect do it. The friends you admire do it. Other students you like do it. All your friends are doing it.

*Power and
Interpersonal
Influence*

13. Source Modeling	This is the way I always do it. When I was your age, I did it. People who are like me do it. I had to do this when I was in school. People you respect do it.
14. Legitimate-Higher Authority	Do it; I'm just telling you what I was told. It is a rule; I have to do it and so do you. Others expect you to do it.
15. Legitimate-Source Authority	Because I told you to. You don't have a choice. You're here to work? I'm the person you answer to. I'm in charge, not you. Don't ask; just do it.
16. Receiver Responsibility	It is your obligation. It is your turn. Everyone has to do his or her share. It's your job. Everyone has to pull his or her own weight.
17. Responsibility to Referent Group	Your group needs it done. The class depends on you. All your friends are counting on you. Don't let your group down. You'll ruin it for the rest of the group.
18. Responsibility to System— Normative Rules	We voted, and the majority rules. All of your friends are doing it. Everyone else has to do it. The rest of the group is doing it. It's part of growing up.
19. Debt to Source	You owe me one. Pay your debt. You promised to do it. I did it the last time. You said you'd try this time.
20. Altruism toward Others	If you do this it will help others. Others will benefit if you do. It will make others happy if you do. I'm not asking you to do it for yourself; do it for the good of the group or others.
21. Source Identification with Receiver or Source Responsiveness	Because I need to know how well you understand this. To see how well I've told you. To see how well you can do it. It will help me know your problem areas. Let me verify if I told you the right things to do.
22. Source Expertness	From my experience, it is a good idea. From what I have learned, it is what you should do. This has always worked for me. Trust me—I know what I'm doing. I had to do this before and I got good at this.

Kearney, Plax, Richmond, & McCroskey (1984).

is represented by BATs 21 and 22. The two new categories are Relational (BATs 10 and 11) and Moral Responsibility (BATS 16-20).

Figure 16.3 presents the individual BATs and the level of influence that we believe probably can be obtained by using each. The remainder of this section examines each BAT and discusses its implications. They are ordered according to the power basis upon which they presumably draw.

Reward BATs

Immediate Reward from Behavior. Based on the typology of BAMs, this BAT promotes a source's attempts to elicit specific receiver behaviors by suggesting that such behaviors will be inherently rewarding and fulfilling. This BAT points out to the receiver that rewarding consequences can be derived from engaging in the desired behavior. This "try it, you'll like it" approach is likely in situations in which receivers are reluctant to engage in behaviors that represent deviations from the old way of doing things. This approach is particularly relevant in a new relationship in which the people are determining each other's likes and dislikes. This BAT would be a way to develop some similarity between two people and helps in the development of a trusting relationship. The key is to make sure the receiver is rewarded for engaging in the new behavior, or else it may be discontinued. For example, an author of this text was told by a close friend that a martini is the best drink around. She tried one, believing the reward would be the adoption of a new, good-tasting drink. However, she did not like the martini and to this day has not had another. The author's trust for that person as an opinion leader on alcoholic beverages was lowered. Remember, what is a reward for one person may not be a reward for another.

This BAT usually is not likely to go much beyond the compliance level of influence. Reward usually leads only to movement, not to motivation to adopt and continue the new idea, unless the reward is highly wanted and is always obtained when the behavior is performed.

Deferred Reward from Behavior. The BAMs that reflect this BAT combine into another type of reward appeal. People who use this BAT are concerned with the reward coming later, later in life, or later in the relationship. This BAT is supposed to prepare one to cope with similar circumstances later in life. The main problem with this BAT is that it is not immediately reinforcing; therefore, the receiver may not engage in the behavior because he or she cannot see how it will help in future relationships. For example, the teacher who says to students "This will help you on tests in college" is trying to get the student to comply now with the understanding that it will help later. Often this

Figure 16.3
Behavior Alteration Techniques and Levels of Influence

BATs	LEVELS OF INFLUENCE		
	Compliance	Identification	Internalization
1. Punishment from Behavior	X		
2. Punishment from Source	X		
3. Punishment from Others	X		
4. Internal Punishment: Guilt	X		
5. Immediate Reward from Behavior	X		
6. Deferred Reward from Behavior	X	X	
7. Reward from Source	X		
8. Reward from Others	X		
9. Internal Reward: Self-Esteem	X	X	X
10. Source/Receiver Relationship: Positive	X	X	X
11. Source/Receiver Relationship: Negative	X		
12. Peer Modeling	X	X	X
13. Source Modeling	X	X	X
14. Legitimate-Higher Authority	X		
15. Legitimate-Source Authority	X		
16. Receiver Responsibility	X		
17. Responsibility to Referent Group	X	X	
18. Responsibility to System— Normative Rules	X		
19. Debt to Source	X		
20. Altruism toward Others	X	X	
21. Source Identification with Receiver or Source Responsiveness	X	X	
22. Source Expertness	X	X	X

V. P. Richmond and J. C. McCroskey, "Interpersonal Influence in Relationships." Unpublished manuscript, West Virginia University, 1983.

simply does not work. To make some future reward appealing, one must give exact circumstances in which the behavior will be rewarded in the future. For example, if you want to change the way someone dresses, show that person how this will help in getting the job he or she wants in the future and then the person might adopt. Generally, this BAT will lead to compliance only at a particular point and time, not to identification and internalization, because many people cannot see the future reward.

Reward from Source. This BAT reflects another reward-type appeal. It should be noted that this BAT most closely resembles French and Raven's reward power. It is primarily concerned with giving receivers a reward if they comply with the source's request. Some might consider this the "bribe" category: If you do something I want you to do, I will reward you. Parents use this frequently with small children, but after a while the children learn to ask for bigger and better rewards. This type of power leads only to movement, not to motivation to continue the behavior; therefore, only compliance will be obtained.

Reward from Others. This BAT is another one of the reward-type appeals. It is concerned with others being proud of the receiver or respecting the receiver for engaging in some desired behavior. In this BAT the receiver will do something because others will be pleased, which may or may not be reinforcing for the receiver. This BAT generally leads to movement to please others; therefore, there is little chance for identification and internalization.

Internal Reward: Self-Esteem. This reward appeal centers on feeling good about engaging in a new behavior. It says, "you will feel good about yourself if you do this." Generally, if you feel good about something you have done, you are likely to continue it; this will lead to compliance, and sometimes to identification or internalization. However, until receivers have engaged in the desired behavior and felt good about themselves, there will be no identification or internalization.

Punishment BATs

Punishment from Behavior. This BAT is an appeal either to do something or to lose and be unhappy. It says if the behavior is not engaged in, the receiver will feel a loss and be hurt by his or her lack of compliance with another. This BAT, as with the punishment-coercive power, leads only to compliance, not to identification or internalization. Receivers may engage in the behavior, but only because there is an implied threat; they will not internalize the behavior.

Punishment from Source. This BAT is the flip side of the Reward from Source. By using this BAT the source has said the receiver will be punished if he or she does not engage in the behavior the source wants. For example, the mother says to the small child, "Clean up your room, or I will not allow you to watch TV." In interpersonal relationships, people use this BAT frequently, and then they cannot understand why the other person does not identify with the behavior. For example, a partner might say, "I want to date others and if you don't agree, I will stop dating you." In effect, the statement is, "I will punish you if you don't agree with this decision." This strategy is not likely to convince the partner that changing the exclusive status of the relationship is a mutual decision. If someone is going to use the above strategy on another, then he or she should make sure that the threatened punishment can be carried out and that it is perceived as punishment by the receiver. If it is not perceived as punishment, it is totally useless in gaining compliance. Obviously this strategy leads only to compliance, not to internalization.

Punishment from Others. The plea of this BAT is that others will not like the receiver if he or she does not engage in the desired behavior. The underlying premise is that others (friends) will reject the receiver for not engaging in the behavior. This BAT is very powerful for getting people to do something they don't want to do, but it does not lead to identification or internalization. People will do many things they wouldn't normally do to please others; however, it is only **movement** on their part to please the other—it will not be internalized. A person should be wary about overusing this BAT because it loses its appeal quickly. After a while, the receiver will say, "So what—if they don't like me, I don't like them anyway."

Internal Punishment: Guilt. BAMs in this category suggest that the receiver will comply because others will be hurt or unhappy if he or she does not. This BAT is commonly used by college professors: "How will your parents feel when you bring home an F in Communication 1?" The appeal is to the receiver's inner self. It is an appeal to guilt about how one's significant others will feel if one does not comply. This BAT will lead to compliance, but it generally does not lead to identification or internalization. If the receiver complies with a source's request because others will be hurt, that is little more than compliance. The receiver is doing it for someone else and may not even buy into the request except to keep others happy. When those others (parents, friends) are not involved, the receiver will not comply with the request.

The use of punishment-oriented BATs will gain only compliance, not identification or internalization. Punishment BATs are negatively associated with identification and internalization. Coercive BATs should be avoided at all cost in any interpersonal relationship and, if used, should only be used as a last resort. Generally, the use of punishment BATs leads only to negative outcomes—dislike for the source, mistrust, and maybe even a breakup in the friendship.

Relational BATs

Source/Receiver Relationship: Positive. BAMs in this BAT category suggest that the source will like the receiver more if the receiver will comply. Essentially this BAT is concerned with the source's increased respect for the receiver. This BAT tends to be very powerful, particularly if the source is a referent model or a significant other for the receiver. This means that the receiver will not only comply but may also identify with and internalize the behavior.

Source/Receiver Relationship: Negative. This BAT is the flip side of the previous one. It suggests that the source will dislike and lose respect for the receiver if the receiver does not comply with the source's request. This is negative referent power, which is akin to some punishment strategies, and this type of power may lead only to compliance, not to identification and internalization. After a while the receiver will start thinking that the relationship is negative if he or she has to comply with the source's request in order not to disappoint the source. Receivers will feel unfairly manipulated by the source. The relationship could be destroyed by this negative use of referent power.

Referent BATs

Peer Modeling. The BAMs within this category suggest that the receiver should comply with the source's demands because the receiver's friends and admired peers are already engaging in the behavior. It suggests that people who are liked and respected by their peer group engage in this behavior. This is a very potent power strategy because it leads to modeling of the peer group. From this modeling, much reinforcement will be given by the peer group, and often internalization takes place.

Source Modeling. This BAT suggests that the receiver should model the source because of the receiver's respect for the source. If the receiver respects the source as an opinion leader, the receiver is likely to model the source and identify with and internalize the source's ways of thinking and acting. This power strategy obviously may lead to identification and internalization by the receiver, but only if the receiver respects the source.

Assigned or Legitimate BATs

Legitimate-Higher Authority. The BAMs in this category suggest that the receiver should do what the source asks because both the source and others in the system are expected to do it by some higher authority. Often, people will comply with higher authority (students comply with teachers who comply with principals) if the request seems reasonable. However, if the request is unreasonable, the receiver will try to find a way not to comply. Then the source has to resort to punishment-oriented types of power, which are very detrimental to an effective interpersonal relationship. This BAT will lead only to compliance, not to identification or internalization.

Legitimate-Source Authority. The BAMs that reflect this BAT are source-oriented. This BAT says that the receiver should comply with the source's demands because the source has the legitimate right to ask the receiver to comply. For example, the teacher has the legitimate right to ask students to be on time for class. This BAT will guarantee only compliance, not identification and internalization.

In conclusion, the authority BATs just discussed are concerned with the use of assigned power. Assigned power, although not perceived as negatively as the punishment types, is still perceived by receivers in a somewhat negative light. The positiveness or negativeness of assigned power is primarily decided by the respect the receiver has for the source of higher authority and for the source. If the source is respected by the receiver, compliance will be obtained without resorting to threats. However, if the receiver does not respect and like the source, the legitimate power often must be accompanied by threats or the punishment-oriented strategies.

Moral Responsibility BATs

Receiver Responsibility. The BAMs within this category suggest that compliance is derived from the receiver's sense of responsibility. The source tries to get the receiver to conform by pointing out that everyone has to do his or her share and "It's your turn to do your share." This obligatory type of power generally leads only to compliance by the receiver. However, it does not so often lead to negative feelings toward the source as do the punishment-oriented or legitimate strategies.

Responsibility to Referent Group. This appeal is made when the source suggests that the receiver's referent group is depending on the receiver's compliance. It suggests that the receiver will let friends or the group down if he or she does not comply with the source's demands. This BAT may get receivers to comply and even identify with the source's demands, but they may not internalize. The appeal is dependent on how receivers feel about their referent group. Because it is a referent group, the receiver probably feels very close to it and will comply and perhaps identify with the value of the source's demands on behalf of the referent group, but the receiver may never internalize. For example, athletes know they should not smoke; therefore, they will comply for many reasons. They may identify with the no-smoking rule because it is their obligation to the group. However, they may never internalize the no-smoking rule. When they no longer are on the team, they may smoke.

Responsibility to System—Normative Rules. This BAT is concerned with majority rule, or the idea that the receiver should conform because friends are doing it. Many people will conform to demands because these are the norm during that period in their lives; however, they may never really identify with or internalize the demands. First-year college students often take their first drink based on this premise; it is the norm to drink to be accepted by the group, so they drink. They never identify with or internalize drinking. When they leave college, they drop the habit and pick up habits of their primary work group.

Debt to Source. Similar to the previous responsibility BATs, this BAT is concerned with the receiver's feelings that he or she owes it to the source to carry out the source's requests. The source might even go as far as to say to the receiver, ''You owe it to me to do this.'' Paying back a debt leads only to compliance, not to identification and internalization.

Altruism toward Others. This BAT suggests that if the receiver complies with the source, others will benefit and be happier. The motto here is, ''Try it; others will benefit from it.'' This BAT asks the receiver to comply for the good of others; there is no particular benefit to the receiver other than seeing others pleased. This is similar to Responsibility and Referent Group in that it could lead to compliance, and perhaps identification, because it will benefit someone.

These five responsibility BATs have all dealt with the feeling of responsibility by the receiver to comply for the benefit of the source or some other people. As we can see from the above, the only responsibility BATs that are likely to lead beyond compliance are Responsibility to Referent Group and Altruism toward Others. These two may lead to identification because we tend to identify with particular groups and see them as an extension of ourselves. As has been suggested before, altruism may be little more than enlightened self-interest.

Source Responsiveness. As indicated by the BAMs, the receiver must comply by either performing the request or at least by explaining his or her perception of the request to the source. Then the source knows whether the receiver understood what he or she was expected to do. If the source can get verification about whether the receiver understood the request, then the source can help the receiver with any problem areas in carrying out the request. This technique is really more for clarification of the request than it is to encourage the receiver to carry out the request. However, this technique lets the receiver realize how important it is to carry out the request. Therefore, compliance and identification could result.

Source Expertness. Like French and Raven's notion of expert power, the BAMs in this category suggest that the receiver should comply with the source's request because the source is an expert and has had previous experience in this area. As in French and Raven's expert power strategy, this BAT may lead to compliance, identification, or internalization.

It is important to stress that an individual should avoid the use of the Punishment (coercive) BATs. An individual should also refrain as much as possible from using the Assigned (legitimate) BATs in establishing and maintaining effective interpersonal relationships. Although the Reward BATs may not lead to internalization, they can be used initially to induce movement or to establish the Referent and Expert BATs.

The BATs presented here are valuable tools for the establishment and maintenance of effective interpersonal relationships. However, one must remember to try to communicate only with the more desirable BATs. Personal influence is fairly easy to achieve without sacrificing friendship if only pro-social BATs are used. If you choose to employ the more anti-social BATs, you can expect to have your relationship deteriorate sharply or disintegrate completely. Compliance with a specific behavioral request is rarely worth such extremely negative relational side effects.

References

French, J. R. P., & Raven, B. (1959). The bases for social power. In D. Cartwright (Ed.), *Studies in social power.* Ann Arbor: Institute for Social Research.
Kearney, P., Plax, T. G., Richmond, V. P., & McCroskey, J. C. (1985). Power in the classroom III: Teacher communication techniques and messages. *Communication Education, 34,* 19–28.
_____. (1984). Power in the classroom IV: Teacher communication techniques as alternatives to discipline. In R. N. Bostrom (Ed.), *Communication Yearbook 8,* pp. 724–746. Beverly Hills: Sage Publications.

McCroskey, J. C. (1992). *An introduction to communication in the classroom*, ch. 8. Edina, MN: Burgess International Group.

McCroskey, J. C., & Richmond, V. P. (1983). Power in the classroom I: Teacher and student perceptions. *Communication Education, 32*, 175–184.

Richmond, V. P., & McCroskey, J. C. (1992). *Power in the classroom: Communication, control, and concern.* Hillsdale, NJ: Lawrence Erlbaum.

_____. (1984). Power in the classroom II: Power and learning. *Communication Education, 33*, 125–136.

Richmond, V. P., Davis, L. M., Saylor, K., & McCroskey, J. C. (1984). Power in organizations: Communication techniques and messages. *Human Communication Research, 11*, 85–108.

Richmond, V. P., McCroskey, J. C., & Davis, L. M. (1986). The relationship of supervisor use of power and affinity-seeking strategies with subordinate satisfaction. *Communication Quarterly, 34*, 178–193.

_____. (1982). Individual differences among employees, management communication style, and employee satisfaction: Replication and satisfaction. *Human Communication Research, 8*, 170–188.

Richmond, V. P., Wagner, J. P., & McCroskey, J. C. (1983). The impact of perceptions of leadership style, use of power, and conflict management style on organizational outcomes. *Communication Quarterly, 31*, 27–36.

Wheeless, L. R., Barraclough, R., & Stewart, R. (1983). Compliance-gaining and power in persuasion. In R.N. Bostrom (Ed.), *Communication Yearbook 7*, pp. 105–145. Beverly Hills: Sage Publications.

MANAGING CONFLICT

17

It is often said that only two things are inevitable in the human experience—death and taxes. Another fact of human experience is equally inevitable—conflict. Aggression was the biological drive which helped our ancestors compete when vital resources were scarce. In advanced cultures, the means for conflict are structured into society; thus we have adversarial legislative and judicial systems. In fact, the study of communication developed in ancient Greece to help citizens argue their positions in the newly created courts.

Communication is the means for structuring conflict in our interpersonal relationships. Whether the results will be constructive or destructive depends on our skills. All the concepts highlighted in previous chapters become vitally important in the context of conflict: perception, expectations, selection, attribution, and immediacy. Conflict is also fertile ground for exploring many of the misconceptions highlighted in chapter 3, particularly "the more communication, the better."

Conflict often leaves the feeling of impending disaster. When facing uncertain situations (and conflict is marked by uncertainty), many people cling to learned responses. In this culture, a common reaction to conflict is either attack or avoidance. If your parents suffered differences of opinion in strained silence, you probably avoid conflict; if they ended up shouting, you probably do the same. In a frantic effort to avoid calamity, we often say and do the least appropriate things. Since all conflicts are unique, knee-jerk responses rarely provide the best approach. One of the first steps to managing conflict is to analyze exactly what conflict means—in what context, with what people, in what relationship, and with what consequences.

Have you ever used the term conflict to describe an internal struggle? For instance, you could be wavering over whether to take a skiing trip with friends or to study for the entrance exam to graduate school. The opposing choices present a conflict; however, it is not an interpersonal conflict because you are the only person involved.

Now imagine yourself at lunch with an acquaintance. You're discussing proposition 187 in California which limits public aid to illegal immigrants. You think the issue is straightforward; if someone is not a citizen of this country, why should tax monies be spent on that person? You are astounded to learn that your luncheon companion characterizes this position as inhumane. Is this a conflict? As we will learn later, that depends on a number of factors.

Finally, suppose your friends Jess and Dale are married. Dale grew up in Chicago, has been offered a job there, and wants to move back. Jess has always lived in the South, has just received a promotion to the home office in Atlanta, and does not get along with Dale's family in Chicago. How does this differ from the example above? In this chapter, we will identify various elements to be considered in conflict situations. Although we will discuss similarities, remember that no two situations are identical. Because no two people are alike, no two conflicts are alike.

Conflict is an inherent part of interpersonal relationships, whether those relationships are between parent and child, teacher and student, supervisor and subordinate, or between lovers. Although the occurrence of conflict in interpersonal relationships is inevitable, the frequency with which it occurs, and the severity of the conflict, can be reduced by effective communicators. Thus, although we cannot reasonably expect to eliminate conflict from our interpersonal communication, we can learn to manage it and to keep it under control.

Disagreement vs. Conflict

To understand the nature of conflict, one needs to distinguish between conflict and disagreement. Disagreement is simply a difference of opinion. We may disagree on facts, on what the facts imply, or on what we might wish to do about those facts. Disagreement does not necessarily lead to conflict. People may disagree, even disagree extremely strongly, without entering into conflict.

Conflict is often characterized by hostility, distrust, suspicion, and antagonism. Disagreement can lead to conflict, but this will occur mainly when the level of affinity between the communicators is not high. If we really like another person and that feeling is reciprocal, the incidence of conflict is greatly reduced. When it does occur, it is usually short-lived. Consequently, conflict is sometimes defined as "disagreement plus negative affect."

According to McCroskey and Wheeless (1976, p. 247) "Conflict between people can be viewed as the opposite or antithesis of affinity. In this sense, interpersonal conflict is the breaking down of attraction and the development of repulsion, the dissolution of perceived homophily (similarity) and the increased perception of incompatible, irreconcilable differences, the loss of perceptions of credibility and the development of disrespect."

Disagreement is a critical component in conflict. However, the way a person habitually deals with disagreement has more to do with whether disagreement will lead to conflict than with the simple presence or absence of disagreement. People differ in the extent to which they can tolerate disagreement and, thus, avoid entering conflict.

Tolerance for Disagreement

Perhaps you have noticed that some people with whom you interact tend to become hostile whenever you disagree with anything they say; others tend to remain relatively unemotional even when you take a view directly counter to theirs. If these people maintain a customary pattern of response in similar situations, they are evidencing differing levels of tolerance for disagreement.

Figure 17.1 provides a basic illustration of the tolerance for disagreement construct, and it notes the distinction between disagreement and conflict. This figure shows that, other things being equal (see figures below), the lower the degree of difference of opinion and/or the higher the degree of positive affect, the less likely it is that communication between people will enter into conflict. Thus, if little difference of opinion is expressed, or high affinity is present, the likelihood of conflict occurring is greatly reduced. The pattern illustrated in figure 17.1 represents the general relationship between conflict and disagreement and notes that tolerance for disagreement separates those two conditions.

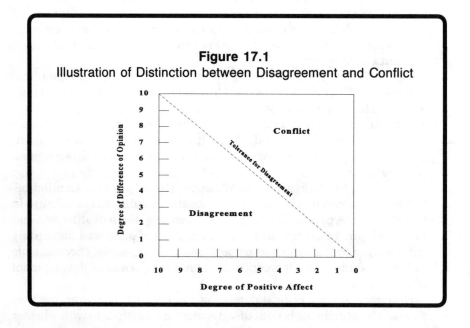

Figure 17.1
Illustration of Distinction between Disagreement and Conflict

People differ in terms of how much disagreement they can tolerate. They differ even when degree of difference of opinion and degree of positive affect are held constant. Figure 17.2 presents the type of situation in which people in an interaction have a low tolerance for disagreement. As indicated by the placement of the line, even an average level of difference of opinion will lead to conflict, as will even an average reduction in positive affect. People with this type of personality orientation are likely to be in conflict much of the time. Other people must work very hard to structure their communication to avoid conflict with such people because of their low tolerance for disagreement. In many communication contexts, people do not feel this is worth the effort, therefore conflict will most likely occur.

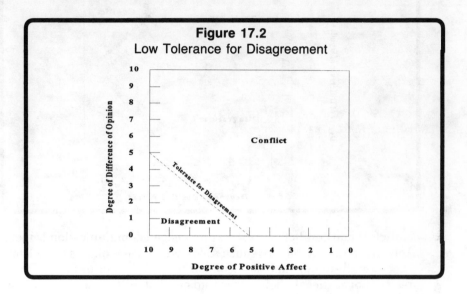

Figure 17.2
Low Tolerance for Disagreement

Figure 17.3 represents exactly the opposite type of situation. For conflict to occur, a major degree of difference of opinion must be expressed or a substantial reduction in positive affect must be present. People with this type of personality orientation are likely to experience very little conflict in their everyday communication.

What is not illustrated in any of the figures discussed here is what happens when conflict is experienced by only one individual in the dyad. Suppose Kerry perceives a high degree of conflict, while Chris experiences no conflict at all. When this occurs, the probability that Chris will eventually experience conflict increases substantially. Kerry is likely to react harshly toward Chris, who inadvertently (unaware that the two are in a sensitive area) may voice statements that exacerbate the conflict. This scenario illustrates a basic principle concerning conflict: *Conflict feeds on communication*; that is, communication interchanges **are** the conflict. Without communication, the conflict is not expressed. We can dislike someone, but if our communication—verbal and/or nonverbal— does not reveal those feelings, there is no interpersonal conflict. Just as we can't form friendships until we act on our initial attraction by engaging in communication, neither can we be involved in interpersonal

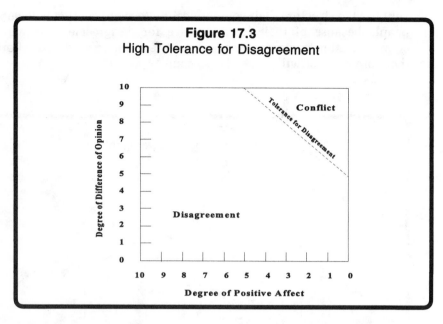

Figure 17.3
High Tolerance for Disagreement

conflict. When conflict is present, unmanaged communication is more likely to *increase* it than to reduce it. We will expand on this point later.

Let's return to our luncheon conversation. Whether or not the disagreement over illegal aliens turns into conflict will depend heavily on the level of affinity between you and your acquaintance and on how much disagreement each of you can tolerate.

Preventing Conflict

Although it is not always possible (nor always desirable) to prevent conflict from occurring, there are times when we can take steps to control our communication behaviors which might otherwise cause dissension. Three options are: (1) raise a person's level of tolerance for disagreement, (2) reduce the importance of issues in your communication, and (3) increase the level of affinity between communicators. The first option has very limited potential. We can have little effect on the basic personalities of others, and rarely does our own personality change radically. As for the second option, sometimes it is possible to de-emphasize or reduce the importance of issues in our communication. It is not uncommon for people to get into heated over arguments over issues that are not worth their time to discuss. However, issues are the very reason for the existence of much of our communication, and issues are important.

While eliminating the significance of our opinions is not itself a viable option, we should determine whether an issue is actually causing the conflict. Sometimes, we allow ourselves to be drawn into strife without knowing why. Earlier we discussed learned patterns of responses. In our society, sports is an arena where competition and conflict are endorsed. Over the last decade, football players have moved from athletes performing anonymously to celebratory dances in the end zone to posturing over their "prey" after every tackle. It has become almost obligatory to celebrate one's success directly in the face of the "vanquished." Basketball games are marked by trash-talking, in-your-face confrontations. (Note how communication accelerates the conflict even in the athletic field.) Fans in the stands increasingly engage in taunts of the opposition. Patterning communication behavior on such confrontational behavior will virtually guarantee that we become involved in destructive conflict. Randolph J. May editorialized in the *Wall Street Journal* that our society is increasingly expressing "outrage" at any perceived affront. "Have we learned that we are unlikely to get attention, particularly from the media, with expressions of milder forms of concern? . . . There is a definite correlation between the heightened use of the language of outrage and the general loss of civility that now permeates our society. A correlation between the obligatory outburst and the inevitable even-more-calculated counterburst. Between the felt need to shout and the diminished ability to listen."

A better model for managing conflict is to pause and think about what we are feeling. What words are we mentally using to characterize the person who has disagreed with us? Enemy, bully, stupid? Do we care about voicing our opinion or silencing our opponent? Do we want to be right at any cost? Was it what was said or the way in which it was said? Did our adversary intend to communicate disrespect, or does his or her conversational style differ from ours and the difference is causing our uneasiness? Check your perceptions. Are you perceiving what really happened or is your interpretation colored by insecurity or anger? We don't have to devalue issues to help prevent conflict, but we should make sure that the conflict itself has not become the only issue.

Our third option, increasing the level of affinity between communicators, holds the most promise for preventing conflict in our everyday lives. Remember from our discussion in chapter 15 that affinity-seeking often involves stressing areas of similarity, expressing cooperation, and self-disclosure. Self-disclosure is an invitation to others. It shows we trust them with important information and invites them to trust us. We're much more likely to become friends with someone we trust and someone who appears cooperative. Without affinity, communicators do not have a sufficient basis for understanding one another; therefore, discord is much more likely.

The importance of affinity is dramatically illustrated by the use of hate words. The offensive potency of such words depends on who says them and where. If gay activists choose to call their organization Queer Nation, the effect is far removed from the use of the same term by strangers whose motives are unknown. As we have seen, words are not logical instruments; they are symbols. Our reactions to the symbols depend on how we view the person using them.

We have substantial control over the way in which others view us. We can, in other words, determine to a major extent the affinity others have for us. Therefore, we have at our disposal a method for greatly reducing the amount of conflict we will experience in our lives and for increasing the amount of influence we have over the attitudes and behaviors of others. The basis for this control is our use of communication to seek affinity directly and to influence others.

Behavior Alteration Techniques

In chapter 16 we outlined twenty-two behavior alteration techniques (BATs) that we generated from a series of research projects. These are essentially the options we have available for getting others to change their behaviors or their attitudes. When employing such techniques, our primary concern is behavior change on the part of the other person. However, a secondary concern should not be overlooked—maintaining affinity for us in the person we are attempting to influence.

Our research suggests that attempting to alter another's behavior generally is not an effective method of increasing affect. That is really not surprising. People generally do not want to change their behavior. Thus, to try to change them causes some stress, at best.

Only two of the twenty-two BATs have been found consistently related to increased affinity. These are Deferred Reward from Behavior and Internal Reward: Self-Esteem. In other words, if you try to get people to change their behavior by indicating they will be rewarded sometime in the future and/or that they will feel better about themselves, they are likely to increase their regard for you.

In contrast, eight of the twenty-two BATs have been found consistently related to *decreased* affinity. These are Punishment from Source ("I will punish you if you don't"); Punishment from Others ("Others will dislike you if you don't"); Guilt ("If you don't, others will be hurt"); Source/Receiver Relationship: Negative ("I will dislike you if you don't); Legitimate-Higher Authority ("Do it; I'm just telling you what I was told"); Legitimate-Source Authority ("Because I told you to"); Receiver Responsibility ("It is your obligation"); and Debt to Source ("You owe me one"). Clearly, use of these techniques leads to a reduction in affinity and an increased probability that conflict will occur. Other techniques should be chosen whenever possible, and usually it *is* possible to use others.

The remaining twelve BATs have not been found consistently related to affinity, either positively or negatively. Thus, it is not necessary to use only Deferred Reward from Behavior or Internal Reward: Self-Esteem to influence others. The remaining twelve BATs are based primarily upon one's ability to reward others, or upon a positive affinity relationship between the communicators. Thus, if a good relationship is built initially, efforts to modify another person's behavior need not lead to either increased conflict or decreased affinity. The eight BATs that we cited in the preceding paragraph, those that are most associated with decreased affinity, are most likely to be used when there is already a bad relationship between people. Their use only leads to a worse one. The key, then, is to build affinity directly at the outset and continue to cultivate it as the relationship continues.

Building Affinity

In chapter 15 we outlined twenty-five affinity-seeking strategies. Our research suggests that most of these are associated with increased affinity between communicators, although they do not all appear to be equally effective.

Two of the strategies, Dynamism and Personal Autonomy, seem helpful in building affinity only if used in moderation. Extensive use leads to negative results. Six of the strategies seem only modestly helpful. These are Altruism, Concede Control, Influence Perceptions of Closeness, Reward Association, Self-Inclusion, and Similarity.

The remaining seventeen strategies are all strongly associated with increased affinity. Thus, one has a substantial array of choices when seeking to increase affinity with others. We will go so far as to suggest that the primary reason a person will not build affinity with another must be that the person doesn't *want* to!

Let's pause a moment to assess the conflict factors we have considered thus far. Disagreements differ from conflict because they center on facts, whereas conflict is frequently marked by negative feelings attached to the disagreement. People have varying tolerances for disagreement, thus they are more or less likely to allow differences to pull them into conflict. We can exercise control over our communication to try to limit misunderstandings from escalating into conflict. The amount of affinity in relationships is a prime factor in determining how an interaction develops.

To this point we have discussed relationships and issues where differences are expressed but the outcome does not significantly affect the participant's lives, other than lost opportunity. In such situations, our individual needs often override the relationship, and personalities may figure more prominently than the issue. Our earlier example of Jess and Dale involves a relationship and an issue of a different nature. A decision about where to live and work is required. That decision may affect the marriage, depending on how it is handled. We have reached a point on the conflict continuum where a communicated dispute involving at least two people seeking contrary goals must come to a conclusion which will have a major impact on both parties. Before looking at techniques which will help us face such challenges, let's take another look at the nature of conflict.

Just as communication is both the conflict and sometimes the best solution, conflict is also paradoxically both the source of growth or the destruction of relationships. The techniques described below are useful for seeking a resolution to conflict. Note that we did not use the term solution. Conflict is composed of multiple realities—it is not a mathematical problem with a single answer. In fact, we most often are dealing with two perceptions of the same event. Whether one perception is more ''real'' than the other is frequently not relevant. To resolve the conflict, the perceptions must be addressed. The word resolve means to separate, to analyze a complex notion into simpler components. The key concept here is that if the relationship is to be preserved, both parties need examine the conflict by breaking it down into manageable parts, with **both** participants' goals in mind.

Both participants need to assess the nature of the conflict carefully. Is it about real disagreement over an issue or a misunderstanding? Is it worth the energy (and risk to the relationship) to engage in conflict? Will the relationship suffer if the issue is avoided or buried? Will sharing more information help? Is there a power imbalance in the relationship? Will that affect the resolution? Is it possible to reach a compromise or to cooperate so that both parties perceive a gain?

Sometimes there will be no satisfactory resolution. As an extreme example, Sandy and Alex have been married for ten years. Sandy desperately wants to have children; Alex does not. They have buried the conflict, using finances and work as an excuse not to address it. Sandy refuses to avoid the conflict any longer. If neither party agrees to change, the marriage will end.

There are numerous situations which do not reach that stage. Conflict serves very useful purposes. It helps us achieve a more accurate picture of ourselves and others. It focuses our attention so that we are more aware of exactly what we think and why. It tests the strength of relationships and ideas and encourages reflection and ingenuity. It shocks us into action to investigate previously unexplored paths and leads us to notice things of which we were unaware. The ability to withstand the tension and stress of conflict and to reach a good compromise increases our self-esteem. Cooperative conflict improves the sense of solidarity in the relationship.

One of the most important tools for dissecting conflict in order to find some similarity in the expressed dissimilarity is listening. In any context, effective listening requires hearing without judgment or preconceived notions about what will be said. This is even more difficult in conflict situations when emotions are heightened. If we have labelled the speaker as an adversary, we will probably listen to find "evidence" of short-comings. It's difficult to listen objectively if you have another purpose. At best, we are listening selectively. If we're just waiting to tell our side, we probably aren't listening at all. The most important factor in listening is being interested in understanding what is being said. Put aside your own agenda; do not attribute ideas, values, or motives to the other. Try paraphrasing what you heard so that the other can correct any misinter-pretations. Another major stumbling block to achieving objective listening is a lack of self-awareness. We all have sensitive areas that make our defenses spring into action. Try to monitor your reactions so that your response is to what was actually said not a retaliation against a perceived threat. Learn to read nonverbal cues. Is the other attempting to create a climate of interest and cooperation? Are they using an open body stance and maintaining eye contact? If you listen to all the com-munication—verbal and nonverbal—you will, at a minimum, have more reliable information to begin your search for a satisfactory resolution. Listening increases our awareness of the issues, the other, and ourselves. In conflict situations, it helps us to have more realistic expectations.

Conflict-Management Techniques

Whether or not the conflict is productive depends on how the struggle is expressed, both participants' perception of goals and possible rewards, the degree of interdependence, the amount of cooperation, and the maintenance of connection in the relationship. We are going to find ourselves in conflict from time to time in spite of our best efforts. It is important, then, to understand the options we have when such situations arise. We will consider four of these.

Leaving the Field

Because conflict feeds on certain types of communication, one of the first options we should consider is *leaving the field*. By this we mean halting the communication that is stimulating the conflict. One method of doing this is to leave physically—to break off communication and to leave the presence of the other person. Although this approach may not reduce the conflict, it may prevent it from escalating further. Be careful to try to determine how your partner will interpret this behavior. How will the withdrawal be interpreted? If it will be viewed as indifference or lack of caring, expect escalation of negative feelings and feelings of being misunderstood. A person who craves contact with others will prefer even argument to being left alone.

A second leaving-the-field method is to leave psychologically. By this we mean to stop communication (at least verbally) about the topic with the other person. When employing this method, one lets the other person have her or his say but does not respond with a contrary opinion. If you do this, you may continue to disagree privately but not say so. Therefore, the communication that would allow the conflict to escalate is not present. This is a method employed by many married couples. One person knows the other person's views and disagrees with them. If the topic is not absolutely critical, one may simply not express the contrary views. Then, because disagreement is not voiced in the communication, the potential for conflict is greatly reduced.

The final leaving-the-field method is to change the topic of discussion. Sometimes we can simply note that the present disagreement cannot be resolved. Thus, there is no useful purpose served by discussing the topic further. A person skillfully employing this technique will shift the topic of discussion to one that the parties agree on. Because disagreement is no longer being expressed, the level of conflict can drop sharply in a relatively brief period.

It must be stressed that the leaving-the-field option is *not* a method of resolving disagreement. Rather, it is an effective method for putting the disagreement out of sight for a time. Withdrawal decreases all interaction; it eliminates escalation of the conflict but also all opportunity to find common ground. Thus, this method should be seen only as a first step toward easing tensions, thus paving the way for future attempts to reach a mutually satisfactory agreement.

Restoring Trust

When serious interpersonal conflict has developed, one way of breaking out of a self-perpetuating cycle is to deal with suspicion and distrust. The problem is to restore a sufficient amount of trust so that effective communication can occur. Trust exists when someone feels free to make a risky decision, to self-disclose, to stick one's neck out. When trust is present, we are willing to give a little, to take a chance that could potentially result in harm to us.

Trust is more likely to be present when people have had previous experiences of positive orientations toward each other's welfare. If husband and wife, father and son, or student and teacher have previously acted positively toward each other, then the restoration of trust is more likely. Trust can be developed even when the people in conflict have not previously had a positive relationship; it is just more difficult to achieve.

By setting up certain conditions, we can help the restoration or establishment of trust. Trust may develop when each person has some guarantee, or knows with some certainty, what the other person will do before each makes an irreversible decision to trust the other. For example, in marital problems, the promise or "solemn oath" not to repeat some behavior is often sought. Labor unions seek legal contracts before they return to work after a labor dispute. Trust may also develop when there is both the opportunity to communicate about mutual responsibilities and the means to deal with violations of trust. Marriage counselors often focus upon these elements. Two people having conflict over a class project they are working on together may discuss mutual responsibilities and actions that will be taken if trust is violated.

In addition, we can facilitate trust if we have the power to influence other people's choice to trust by rewarding their trustworthy decisions and punishing their untrustworthy ones. This technique is often used in child rearing. At times, parents inform children of their responsibility to return home from a date by a particular hour, especially if their trust has been violated in the past. Actions that will be taken when this trust is violated are also frequently noted. We have a similar ability, if we hold the right position or rank, in complex business organizations or in the military.

Finally, we can facilitate trust with the use of a third party. A third person or agency can point out how losses to either party because of violations of trust are detrimental to both people in the conflict. Interpersonal disputes and personal marital problems are often solved by the instigation of trust through a third party.

An important part of restoring trust is to communicate that a struggle over values or resources does not necessarily involve destroying the other. Confront issues, not each other. Don't make someone else wrong. Try to convey any criticism of the opposing ideas in a spirit of cooperation and with the intention of reaching an understanding, not as a put down of the other person. If trust is restored and the conflict discussed with respect for both parties, there is less chance of a residue of negative feelings affecting the relationship and future interactions.

Reinstating Communication

A major problem in conflict management is reinstating communication between the two parties involved. Here's our paradox again. Communication probably initiated the conflict in the first place—some verbal statement or nonverbal behavior was interpreted in a way that increased hostility, competition, or distrust. On the other hand, lack of communication may perpetuate the conflict.

For example, imagine that Lee and Whitney are members of a group assigned to find ways to improve customer service. In the last three meetings, Lee has started to speak, and Whitney has interrupted to present the very same ideas. Lee was initially annoyed but has now decided that Whitney is trying to look good in front of the group. Two concrete things have happened. Whitney interrupted Lee, and Lee stopped speaking. Lee has attributed certain motives to Whitney but those have not been confirmed. Before the conflict escalates further, Lee should ask Whitney about the interruptions. Whitney could be unaware of the interrupting behavior, could apologize, and could ask why Lee just didn't say something like, "Hold that thought. I'll be finished with mine in just a minute."

The restoration of communication is no guarantee that the conflict will be reduced. Perhaps the interruption took place because Whitney thinks Lee wastes the group's time. If that is voiced, the conflict will increase. There is some evidence to suggest that too much communication may often be detrimental to interpersonal relationships. For example, disclosure patterns in marriage may focus on undesirable elements, and high disclosure is often associated with marriages in conflict. Further, in negotiation, completely free communication may be used to convey information such as threats and insults, which intensify hostilities rather than reduce them. Consequently, reinstatement of communication must be carefully planned and, to some extent, controlled.

To be useful in managing conflict, communication must be limited and directed toward actions that are vital to reduction of the conflict.

1. Direct communication toward restoring trust. Note the ways we have proposed to accomplish this. Some evidence suggests that reinstated communication without trust is not very useful.

2. Focus communication on common goals. From our previous discussion of factors related to affinity and attraction, we would expect common goals to have an effect.

3. Direct communication toward other areas of similarity, such as common attitudes, beliefs, and values.

4. Keep communication positive and reinforcing. This is particularly true of self-disclosure in conflict situations. Care should be given to positive and reinforcing disclosures. The opposite of this is often referred to as "gunnysacking"—the tendency to stockpile irritations and unleash them when angry.

5. Communicate cooperation and compliance in areas indirectly related to the dispute. Avoid assessing blame.

6. Stress past behaviors which brought people together to help recreate a climate of trust.

Free ventilation and disclosure of feelings should not be the essential nature of the communication exchange. These can lead to greater conflict. Recitation of platitudes and principles is seldom helpful. In fact, statements such as "Let's be rational" usually mean "I'm right and you're emotional." In conflict situations we are seldom influenced by injunctions to "turn the other cheek," or that "it is better to give than receive." The conflict itself shows that we have abandoned these as working axioms in this situation. Similarly, communication that focuses upon the common enemy has only a temporary effect in resolving the conflict and merely transfers the conflict to others.

A now classic study conducted under the direction of social psychologist Muzafer Sherif experimented with some conflict variables in a secluded boys' camp. The experimenters created two groups in the camp that were in conflict with each other. They tested most of the above methods of resolving conflict and found that the most successful was the common goal approach. When the boys were brought together in the accomplishment of a superordinate goal (survival) the process of conflict resolution was begun. Their cooperation was necessary for achieving the goal, which in turn built strong bonds. Successive experiences further strengthened common bonds and eventual resolution of the conflict between the two groups.

Compromise and Negotiation

Even when some measure of trust has been restored and communication has been reinstated and directed, it is likely that conflict will still not be completely eliminated, except in very minor problem situations. The ground has been prepared for compromise and negotiation. Compromise and negotiation assume that sufficiently strong mutual interests are at stake. Some common goals must be established at the outset. Marriage partners in conflict frequently compromise by both "giving in a little" or both changing their behaviors because of underlying strong bonds and common goals, such as children.

In the negotiation phase, communication should be directed toward discovering the ranges or latitudes of acceptable and unacceptable solutions to both parties involved. If there is an overlap of acceptable solutions (although not the most desired by either) then compromise in this area of overlap can produce resolution. This frequently occurs in labor-management disputes that are settled fairly quickly. When there is no overlap between each party's range of acceptable solutions further communication must follow. The two parties must be influenced to expand their range of acceptable solutions so that there is an area of overlap in which compromise can be reached.

Communication in this setting functions in three ways: (1) communication is used to discover what settlements both parties are likely to accept; (2) communication is used to influence or persuade both parties to modify their range of acceptable solutions; (3) communication is used to provide both parties with rationalizations for acceptance of previously unacceptable positions or solutions.

In the compromise and negotiation setting there is usually mutual pressure for reaching agreement early in the exchange. Communication is usually less threatening and more cooperative at that point. As time goes on, however, there is less tendency to agree. Communication may become more competitive and lose sight of common goals. Again, too much communication, especially free ventilation between conflicting parties, may be detrimental to compromise and the restoration of affinity. In the last analysis, some level of tolerance may always be needed.

In summary, we have attempted to explain the nature of conflict and its relationship to communication. We have stressed the strong relationship between the possibility that conflict will occur and the level of affinity between communicators. If you work to build affinity with others and use your knowledge about people and communication, you can probably prevent a number of conflicts from occurring. However, it is impossible to build a conflict-free existence. We have suggested options to manage conflict when it occurs. Following these suggestions can lead to resolutions where both parties are satisfied—and to creating a climate where future conflicts can be addressed constructively. Even in truly irreconcilable situations, conflict will—at a minimum—clearly define that circumstance and free the interactants to pursue more promising avenues.

References

Bell, R. A., & Daly, J. A. (1984). The affinity-seeking function of communication. *Communication Monographs, 51*, 91–115.

McCroskey, J. C., & Richmond, V. P. (1992). *Communication in educational organizations*. Edina, MN: Burgess International Group.

McCroskey, J. C., & Wheeless, L. R. (1976). *Introduction to human communication*. Boston: Allyn & Bacon.

May, R. J. (1995). Such outrage is outrageous. *Wall Street Journal*, January 13, p. 1.

Newcomb, T. M. (1953). An approach to the study of communicative acts. *Psychological Review, 60*, 393–404.

Richmond, V. P., & McCroskey, J. C. (1992). *Organizational communication for survival*. Englewood Cliffs, NJ: Prentice-Hall.

_____. (1979). Management communication style, tolerance for disagreement, and innovativeness as predictors of employee satisfaction: A comparison of single-factor, two-factor, and multiple-factor approaches. In D. Nimmo (Ed.), *Communication Yearbook 3*, pp. 359–373. New Brunswick, NJ: Transaction Books.

Richmond, V. P., Wagner, J. P., & McCroskey, J. C. (1983). The impact of perceptions of leadership style, use of power, and conflict management style on organizational outcomes. *Communication Quarterly, 31*, 27–36.

INTERCULTURAL COMMUNICATION

18

Context is one of the critical components of the communication process. As we noted in chapter 2, context focuses on **roles** and **rules**. Since culture is the largest (and often most important) aspect of context, it is primarily responsible for defining communication roles and setting forth the rules we must follow in our communication with others.

When we are communicating with people from our own culture in everyday interactions, we seldom recognize the extent to which we depend on our socialized understandings of how and when to communicate. Only when we try to communicate with someone from another culture (with whom we do not share enculturated prescriptions) do we realize how helpless we become when we don't understand where the other person is "coming from."

Sensitivity to cultural differences is increasing in the United States. While there are many areas in the United States which remain very homogeneous, this has never been true in large cities and is becoming less true in other communities across the country. The United States was built on the "melting pot" model, where people from multiple cultures came here and formed one new "American" culture. The degree to which this has effectively occurred is now subject to considerable debate, far beyond the scope of this text. The melting pot metaphor now shares the stage with calls for the acceptance of "diversity" of cultural perspectives. As a consequence, there are multiple sets of roles and rules employed by people with whom we are likely to come in contact.

Of course, there have always been many cultures with many different views of appropriate roles and rules for communication. Anyone living in other countries quickly learned the necessity of adapting to other customs. Today, however, **all** of us are highly likely to find ourselves in intercultural communication contexts on any given day. In fact many of us are finding such contacts increasingly routine. When contact with other cultures was primarily the province of the wealthy who could afford the expense of a trip by ship to a foreign land, the impetus to study the problems of intercultural communication was not strong. Now such contacts can be had by driving a few blocks, or flying a few hundred miles for a few hundred dollars, or by connecting to the internet system and communicating with a person from thousands of miles away virtually for free. Today, intercultural communication is everybody's concern.

The Nature of Culture

When we use the term "culture" we are referring to "a learned set of shared perceptions about beliefs, values, and norms, which affect the behaviors of a relatively large group of people" (Lustig & Koester, 1993, p. 41). Culture, as defined here, "refers to the relatively specialized life-style of a group of people—consisting of their values, beliefs, artifacts, ways of behaving, and ways of communicating—that is passed on from one generation to the next. Included in culture would be all that members of a social group have produced and developed—their language, modes of thinking, art, laws, and religion" (DeVito, 1994, p. 420). According to Paul Bohannan, "Culture is an interlinked web of symbols" (1992, p. 12). It consists of intimately related parts (knowledge, beliefs, custom, morals, language, myths, art, law, religion, economics, education, family, communication, tools, and any other capability) of a complex whole learned by humans as members of a society. It is also a storehouse of knowledge; that is, culture consists of choices made over long periods of time. It allows us to learn from others and to know what choices are suitable in specific circumstances. Bohannan tells us that certain behaviors work "because they get expected results or because they are acceptable to others. . . . Culture is thus a means of standardizing choices and of sharing successful results of choices made by others in the past" (Bohannan, 1992, p. 13).

Bohannan also points out that culture must exist both in people's minds (the meaning they attach to symbols) and in the environment, either as behavior or as artifact. If any item is not in both places, it is not culture. Transforming the culture (meaning) in our minds to the outside world is behavior. Transforming the culture from the outside world to our minds is learning (Bohannan, 1992, p. 14). In addition, Bohannan notes that every human activity is culturized; it carries a cultural overload. "It is evaluated for good or bad, right or wrong—both by the individual person and by everybody in his or her presence. This evaluation grows out of cultural convictions and multi-generational experience about efficiency, appropriateness or moral suitability" (Bohannan, 1992, p. 13).

A culture may be thought of as "a set of rules for constructing, interpreting, and adapting to the world (Klopf, 1995, p. 26). It is useful to think of a culture like a living thing. Cultures grow and change very slowly and have many means of protecting themselves. They have very high "self-esteem" and their devotees are fiercely loyal. A culture is cumulative, it grows, expands, and adapts to changes. A group's culture is passed on to its children through a learning process called "enculturation." While schools are the most obvious instrument of enculturation for children, religious groups, parents, peers, senior members of communities, writers and artists, the mass media, and even government agents function to enculturate the young. When new people move into a culture, the host people attempt to "acculturate" the newcomers by directly and indirectly influencing them to adopt new ways of thinking and doing things—the ways of the host culture.

Acculturation is almost always in this direction—host culture influencing newcomer. Efforts by newcomers to change the host culture are usually rejected, and often newcomers who persist in making such attempts will be ejected from the host culture or at least made to feel extremely unwelcome.

Although you may have grown up in one of the many "less sophisticated" areas in North America, even if you hate opera and classical music, fear not—you are cultured! You are a part of the general North American culture. You probably take certain things pretty much for granted, such as "American" music in one or more of its various forms (jazz, rock, country, Broadway, rap, gospel, etc), supermarkets, cinemaplexes, fast food, interstate highways, talk radio, commercial TV, cable TV, free public education, Dr. Pepper, diet soft drinks, apple pie, grits, black eyed peas, tacos, barbecue, public colleges and universities, football (not soccer!), basketball, baseball, pickup trucks, rodeo, cowboy boots, jeans, aloha shirts, button-down collars, deodorants. You might be surprised to learn that some cultures have *none* of these things! That is the way culture is—it is so omnipresent that we seldom notice our own culture except when we are somewhere where it *isn't!*

But culture is not just about things like fast food and jeans. It is about much more serious things, like how people think. People in the general North American culture tend to have certain beliefs ingrained in them, although some people in the culture may not identify with all of the beliefs and attitudes of the general culture. Some common beliefs in this culture are that everyone should have an opportunity to achieve a better life, that working hard will eventually pay off, that people should strive to do well and succeed, that one should help people who are poor or less fortunate than themselves, that democracy is the best form of government, that people should be free to worship as they please, that everyone should learn to communicate in American English, and that "the American way is the best way, and if everyone were like us, the world would be a much better place."

Subculture is a term we need to consider before we go much farther, for you may have looked at the list of "things American" above and found some that just don't fit into what you see as your culture, while many others do. Within all very large cultural groups exist sub-groups which share many of the characteristics of the larger culture but also share characteristics within their group which are not shared by the larger culture. The most commonly recognized subcultures within the general North American culture stem from ancestry and/or geographical residency.

The number of "hyphenated" Americans in the United States is enormous. In fact, most United States citizens have some identification with an ancestry group, whether it be German-American, Asian-American, African-American, Japanese-American, Chinese-American,

Mexican-American, Irish-American, English-American, Italian-American, Cuban-American, Swedish-American or one of dozens of others. Members of each of these subcultures share important similarities with each other that are not shared with the larger culture. However, while each person's identification with that subculture may be strong, odds are very good that culturally the person is more like people in one of the other hyphenated American groups than he or she is like the people who currently live in the country of origin. The exception to this general rule, of course, is people who are very recent immigrants to this country.

Geographical residency also represents potential for important subcultural groupings. Certainly Canadians don't like being mistaken for United States residents, and within Canada the distinction between the French-speaking and English-speaking groups is very important. Within the United States there are important regional subcultural groupings—such as New England, West Coast, Midwestern, Great Plains, Southern, Eastern, and Texas (as their tourist bureau says, "A Whole Other Country!"). While people in any two of these regions are far more alike than they are like Rumanians, they have unique cultural characteristics in which they take pride and which makes them prefer their subculture over others.

The Cultural Context of Communication

A central tenet of modern communication theory, which we advanced and discussed early in this book, is that "meanings are in people, not words (or nonverbal behaviors)." Consequently, if we are to communicate effectively with you about the area of intercultural communication, it is important that we explain how some terms related to intercultural communication are commonly used in this field. While culture provides the general context for all communicative encounters, the nature of that context may take many forms.

Intracultural Communication

Intracultural communication refers to communication between members of the same cultural or subcultural group. In this form of communication (the most common for most people) the proportion of shared meanings for words and nonverbal behaviors (i.e., communicative messages) is quite high. Meanings develop differently within cultures, but people within a given culture learn through schooling and experience in everyday interaction what messages are intended to mean.

When most of us think about communicating with others around us, this is the communication context we have in mind. However, we must keep in mind that even within this context, major differences may be present as a function of membership in different groupings within the same general culture. Consider the differences in orientations within a single culture between females and males, heterosexuals and homosexuals, teenagers and senior citizens, blind and sighted, hearing and deaf, physically handicapped and non-handicapped, Christians and Jews, doctors and patients, teachers and students, even people employed in two different organizations (which are often referred to as having different "organizational cultures"). Some people prefer to consider all of these to be instances of "intercultural" communication. While we understand this view, we prefer to reserve the term "intercultural" for contexts where the basic culture is not the same. This is not meant to trivialize the differences between people in these categories, for they can be large and very important and are deserving of study in their own right. Here, however, our attention is directed toward the larger cultural context.

Intercultural Communication

"Intercultural" communication refers to communication between members of different cultural groups. This term is also used to refer to communication between members of two subcultures within a larger culture, particularly when the subcultural differences as seen as quite substantial.

Cross-Cultural Communication

"Cross-cultural" often is used interchangeably with "intercultural" to reference communication between members of different cultural groups. However, it is more commonly used to reference comparisons of communication behaviors across different cultures in different nations and the study of specific communication issues on a comparative basis in such cultures. We make "cross-cultural" comparisons of nonverbal communication behaviors, for example, in chapter 13.

International Communication

"International" communication refers to communication between governmental representatives of different countries. Such contacts can represent very great cultural differences (England and Japan) or comparatively small differences (Canada and United States). Most international communication, however, is plagued with all of the problems that individuals face in intercultural communication, plus the added ones produced by governmental concerns. This is thought by some to be the most difficult context for communication that humans regularly encounter.

Interethnic Communication

"Interethnic" communication is communication between members of different ethnic groups which represent subcultures within a larger, overall culture. For example, an Irish-American communicating with an Italian-American would be engaging in interethnic communication. Similarly, an African-American communicating with a Korean-American would be considered interethnic communication.

Interracial Communication

"Interracial" communication is communication between members of different racial groups. Most interracial communication is also interethnic communication, as exemplified by our African-American/Korean-American example above. However, the reverse is not true. That is, much interethnic communication involves members of the same racial group, as in our Irish-American/Italian-American example above.

Whatever the cultural context for communication, the level of a person's ethnocentrism plays a critical role in determining the effectiveness of that communication. While ethnocentrism tends to make *intracultural* communication *more* effective, it raises severe problems for communication in all other cultural contexts.

Ethnocentrism

The view that the customs and practices of one's own culture are superior to those of other cultures is known as **ethnocentrism**. There are few things that have been found to be truly "pancultural" (the same across all cultures), but the view of one's own culture being superior to all the rest does seem to be fairly universal. People in all cultures are ethnocentric in varying degrees. Even if they move to a new culture, they tend to retain their ethnocentric attitude about their former culture—which often makes them far less than welcome in the new culture!

Ethnocentrism comes from the combination of two Greek words. **Ethnos** is Greek for "nation" and **kentron** is Greek for "center." In combination they suggest that our own nation is the center of the universe. When one holds ethnocentric views, as virtually everyone does, one's own culture is used as the standard by which all other cultures will be evaluated. Most importantly, any deviation from that standard is most likely (but not always) to be seen as negative and an indication of the inferiority of the other culture and the people from that culture. Thus, since in North America we play "American" (or Canadian) football, another form of football (soccer) is inferior, and athletes who play that game are not equivalent to those who play "real" football.

Positive Aspects of Ethnocentrism

We have implied above that ethnocentrism may have negative implications, and we will return to that consideration later. However, if its impact were only negative there would be no reason for it to continue to exist, and it would die out. Ethnocentrism performs a valuable function for cultures and subcultures. It helps maintain the integrity of the culture in the face of external threats and when interfacing with other cultures or subcultures (whose members also think their culture is superior).

Ethnocentrism gives the people of a culture an identity and helps make them more homogeneous and cohesive. As a result, it promotes positive and effective communication among members of the culture. This makes people more willing to go along with the formal and informal rules of the culture. After all, those rules are **right** and the **best** rules around! When things go wrong in communication with people from other cultures, blame can be placed externally and there is less need for internal conflict. Ethnocentrism serves as the foundation for such values as patriotism—for if our system is the best, it certainly is worth defending, and possibly even worth dying for! Wars have been fought to "preserve democracy." And more people have been killed in wars to protect or advance someone else's religion than for all other reasons combined throughout human history.

Ethnocentrism, then, is the first line of defense for a culture. Without ethnocentric views in its people, a culture is open to rapid and extreme changes and is subject to losing its very existence. For this reason, people who lead subcultural groups within a larger general culture often resort to very militant communication in the ethnocentric defense of their subculture and their attacks on the larger culture. They recognize that in the absence of high ethnocentrism among the members of the subculture, it will lose its distinctiveness and blend into the larger culture (and the leaders will lose their leadership status). If no one thinks a subculture is worth preserving, it will not be preserved.

Negative Aspects of Ethnocentrism

Like most things, ethnocentrism in moderation can be positive. If taken too far, ethnocentrism can become a very negative orientation. Equally as dangerous is for people to have strongly ethnocentric beliefs and not recognize that they do. It is always easy to see ethnocentrism in others, but it usually is difficult to see in oneself. Let us examine three potential problems for communication which can emanate from ethnocentrism: culture shock, stereotyping, and prejudice.

Culture Shock. First described by Oberg (1960), culture shock is something almost everyone experiences when they move to a new cultural environment. Whether the move is from one continent to another, one state to another, or just from home to a nearby college, some degree of trauma is likely to be experienced. That trauma has been dubbed "culture shock." If you ever have experienced it, "shock" will not seem too strong a word to describe it.

Most people go through stages when they move to a new culture. The move is often preceded by considerable anticipation and great enthusiasm. This excitement and pleasure usually is enhanced in the early days after arrival in the new environment. All of the newness is exciting, and one enjoys being introduced to new ideas, people, places, and ways of doing things. Not too much later, however, the person has to deal with the new world he or she is in—has to deal with problems relating to housing, what to eat, where to shop, how to get to work or school, where to get money, what is expected by neighbors. In short, one has to deal with an everyday world that just is not like what he or she is used to. Frequently, people feel like *everything* is different, even if only a small portion really is. This is the point at which culture shock is experienced. Often it is experienced through depression and fear of everything—other people, the water, the food, the bedding, the buildings, the weather, the traffic. This may be accompanied by severe loneliness, a longing to be "back home," and a desperate need for things that one is used to—their favorite soft drink, a pizza, some peanut butter or other familiar food, and someone to talk to "who makes sense."

This period of shock is a critical period for the individual. Many cannot survive it, flee as rapidly as they can, and return to their home culture. Others, who want to leave but cannot, often become resentful and irritable. They are apt to withdraw from contact and become very lethargic. When they come in contact with members of the new culture, they are likely to view friendly suggestions as criticisms and lash out or communicate in very negative ways at the least provocation. This is an extremely unpleasant experience for the individual, or the family if it has moved as a group. It increases self-doubt and feelings of inadequacy. Some people even go so far as to commit suicide during this stage. Others communicate in such negative ways that they alienate those around them in the new culture with whom they might otherwise have become friends.

While individuals often don't think so at the time, most people pass through this stage in a few weeks, or a few months for the more extreme sufferers. Gradually most people begin to adapt to the new cultural environment. Some even come to view the new culture as their home and the new culture as their own; but the latter typically only happens over many years.

A person's level of ethnocentrism is a very good predictor of the severity of the culture shock he or she is likely to experience. The more ethnocentric the person, the more severe the shock. This makes sense, for if the old ways are perfect and all the good people live in those ways, that must mean that the new ways are defective and the people who live like that are not good people, right? That really is what ethnocentrism is all about. If you want to experience other cultures, reduce your ethnocentrism first, or your intercultural experience may be one of the worst experiences of your life.

Stereotyping.   When we view a group of people from a culture or subculture as sharing one or several common characteristics, we have formed a generalization commonly known as a "stereotype." Such generalizations are a means of organizing our experiences and interactions with others. We need these kinds of generalizations so that we may better predict how people around us are likely to behave in response to our communicative efforts or everyday behavior.

It is simply impossible to respond to every input and to adjust our perceptions and communication to every different nuance. We know so little about most people, any responses we attempt to individualize are likely to be wrong because we don't know enough about the person to adapt appropriately.

Stereotypes are a way of making sense out of the infinite variations in our environment. Such generalizations are necessary for thinking and communicating. We initiate interaction with those fitting our stereotypes of either "probably interesting" or "likely pleasant to be with." We match our communication and other behavior to our stereotypes of various types of people as we come in contact with them: professor, student, male, female, server, police officer, parking attendant, store clerk, child. While each one we meet will certainly be at least somewhat different than others we have met before, we must depend on our stereotype to get us started in our initial encounter.

There is no question, then, whether a person will make the kinds of generalizations we call stereotypes. All people do, and must in order to function. The problem comes when we stereotype within the context of high ethnocentrism. If we are highly ethnocentric, it is likely that we positively evaluate those who are very much like ourselves—are good representatives of our culture, and negatively evaluate others—all, or nearly all, others. This is why we hear so many negative expressions about stereotypes. People who do not fit into the stereotype of "a lot like me" tend to be placed in a variety of very negative stereotypical categories.

When we stereotype, we tend to make three kinds of errors: over-estimate differences, under-estimate differences, see what we expect to see. We will consider each in turn.

The first common error we make when stereotyping is over-estimating the differences between groups. Stereotypes typically exaggerate differences between cultural groups. They emphasize a few obvious differences while ignoring many similarities, therefore the other group is seen as odd, unfamiliar, even dangerous because it is so much "not like us." Such stereotypes lead to avoiding communication with people from other groups because of fear or distrust. It is only a short step from there to disliking or even hating the stereotyped group.

The second type of error is to under-estimate differences among people from another culture. While we usually recognize that there are great differences among people in our own culture (some of whom are wonderful people, and others who are really rotten eggs!), we tend to stereotype people from other cultures as all being the same. We fail to acknowledge within our stereotype that such variability is probably present in the other culture's people as well. One rude taxi driver or hotel clerk and our stereotype of New Yorkers becomes that of "rude people." One bad meal in a French restaurant, and "French food is terrible"—we don't acknowledge that restaurants probably range from great to awful in France just like they do "back home." We meet one group of tourists from Japan all carrying cameras and wearing aloha shirts, and our image of Japanese people takes on those characteristics.

The final type of error is the one that lets us keep our stereotype even though we have evidence of its weakness right before us. We tend to selectively perceive what our stereotype causes us to expect to perceive. If we see evidence that the stereotype is wrong, we just consider this observation as an exceptional one and discount it. If our stereotype is that women who live on farms are fat, we will center our attention on the ones we see who are indeed fat and look at the others as exceptions—even if the "fat" ones account for only a small percentage of the farm women we meet.

Given these common errors to which we are all prone, it is no wonder that once stereotypes are formed, they are highly resistant to change. In fact, if we enter a culture with stereotypes firmly in place, we are likely to reinforce those stereotypes through our selective perceptions of those around us and our choices of people with whom to communicate in that culture—for those that fit our stereotype will be easier for us to deal with in many cases.

Prejudice. Essentially, **prejudice** refers to *a priori judgements based on stereotypes*. The term "a priori judgements" references judgements which are made in advance of the time when they are employed. That is, we may form the judgement today but not have cause to use it for days or months into the future. When we say the judgement is based on stereotypes, we indicate that the judgements are not based on the best information. The judgement may be applied to a person we have never even met or a behavior we have never observed, and it was determined on the basis of limited information about a group of people about whom we knew very little and whose behavioral tendencies were only the subject of conjecture. In short, prejudice means to pre-judge a person or a person's behavior on the basis of limited information about the culture or subculture of which that person is a member.

While it is quite possible for such pre-judgements to be positive, in actual practice most prejudice is very negative. While most people can come up with an example or two of positive prejudices, the availability of negative examples runs far beyond those that are positive. Hence, it is appropriate to think of prejudice in negative terms. It seldom helps anyone, and it usually is harmful to all it touches.

Like stereotyping, the root cause of prejudice is ethnocentrism. Since it is normal to be at least somewhat ethnocentric, and it is normal to need to place people around us into groups and then generalize about those groups in order to make sense of our environment, most (if not all) people have prejudices about some groups of people and their culturally based behaviors, including communication behaviors. Most of these prejudices are very negative and put people in those groups in a very negative light.

Coping with Ethnocentrism—Yours and Mine

The problems which stem from ethnocentrism, as we have seen, can be very severe. Communication can be problematic, at best, in the presence of even moderate levels of ethnocentrism—even if only one person in an interaction is behaving ethnocentrically. Communication can become absolutely destructive under circumstances where more ethnocentrism is present, either one person being highly ethnocentric or both people being moderately ethnocentric with regard to each other's culture. Intercultural communication, then, is fraught with potential problems, for at least some ethnocentrism is likely to exist in any intercultural communication encounter. Your ethnocentrism added to my ethnocentrism equals our communicative disaster!

DeVito (1994) has outlined an ethnocentrism continuum and identified five steps along that continuum. Each step has considerable implications for the nature of intercultural communication. We will examine each of these steps.

Equality. This is the lowest level of ethnocentrism. The person at this level communicates with others on the basis of equality. While differences in cultural practices and ways of behaving are acknowledged, they are not considered inferior to one's own, just different. If both interactants approach the communication situation with this orientation, the probability of effective communication is quite high. Unfortunately, this is the least common circumstance under which intercultural communication is likely to be undertaken.

Sensitivity. This is a moderately low level of ethnocentrism. The person at this level is sensitive to the fact that he/she is somewhat ethnocentric and wants to communicate without offending the person from another culture. If both people in an intercultural communication encounter are at this level of ethnocentrism or lower, the likelihood of successful communication is good. This is the type of intercultural communication encounter which is likely to occur at international conferences where everyone is "on their best behavior" and highly sensitive to the potential problems which intercultural communication encounters may confront.

Indifference. This is a moderate level of ethnocentrism, the amount a typical person would have in a typical culture. Such people are happy with their own culture, or at least they don't think negatively about it. Such people really don't know or care much about how people from other cultures or subcultures differ from people in their own culture. They prefer to communicate with people who are very much like themselves, and prefer not to think about people with different attitudes and values at all. If they are forced to interact with people from other cultures or subcultures, they are likely to become much **more** ethnocentric as a result. The likelihood of a successful intercultural encounter when even one of the participants has this level of ethnocentrism is low.

Avoidance. This is a moderately high level of ethnocentrism. At this level, people know they are ethnocentric (although they may not have ever heard the term!), and they want little to do with people from other cultures or subcultures. While they may be in contact with people from other cultures in everyday life, they will have a very difficult time communicating effectively enough with them to have a good working relationship, much less a personal relationship. Avoiding communication with people from other cultures and subcultures is the primary orientation and that is a wise choice, for the chances of effective intercultural communication with this level of ethnocentrism are very low.

Disparagement.   This is a very high level of ethnocentrism. A person with this high a level is likely to be thought of by others as a racist, sexist, and/or jerk. The communication of this person with one from another culture or subculture is most likely to involve hostility. He/she is likely to belittle the other person and their culture and make a major point of talking about the positive qualities of her/his own culture, particularly in contrast to that of the other person. The probability of effective intercultural communication with this person is nil.

Many people suggest that we learn to assume a position of ***cultural relativism*** when entering intercultural communication encounters in order to keep our own ethnocentrism under control. While we can still maintain our preference for our own culture (remain ethnocentric, in other words), we need to learn to understand how other cultures see things from their vantage point rather than through the evaluative filter of our own belief system. Understanding another culture does not mandate that we personally approve of it or even that we think it to be reasonable. Understanding the other culture simply means that we are aware of what attitudes, beliefs, and values are held by members of that culture and what implications that has for the behavior of people in that culture.

The ability to take on a culturally relativistic position is vital to our capacity to engage in effective intercultural communication. It is what makes it possible for us to function at the "sensitivity" level of ethnocentrism, the highest level at which successful interpersonal communication is likely to occur (and the lowest level most of us will ever be able to achieve!).

If cultural and subcultural groups are to maintain positive civil relationships with each other, it is critical that children in all such groups be taught how to assume the culturally relativistic position. This position means that we accept other people ***as they are,*** and not expect them to change to what we would prefer them to be. We must leave our "missionary zeal" at home when we enter into intercultural communication encounters. People are not likely to change their cultural orientation as a function of others pushing them to do so, and certainly are even less likely to do so when those others are stating or implying that the people's culture is somehow inferior to that of the persuader.

For children (or adults) to learn the skill of assuming a culturally relativistic position, the skill most central to being an effective intercultural communicator, it is vital that they be taught the nature of culture and its influence on people's behavior. Most societies do a very good job of enculturating their children, but a very poor job of preparing those children to communicate in a world of people who do not share the same culture.

Improving Intercultural Communication

In a sense, everything we have talked about in the previous chapters of this book can be employed to improve your intercultural communication. At the bottom line, competent intracultural communicators have the best opportunity to become competent intercultural communicators. However, that achievement will not come without special effort and attention to the unique problems relating to communication in intercultural contexts.

Our purpose in this section is to provide several suggestions you should consider if you wish to become a more effective intercultural communicator. Attention directed to even a few of these suggestions should result in meaningful improvement.

1. *Recognize your own ethnocentrism.* As we have noted above, ethnocentrism is the number one enemy of effective intercultural communication. While you are entitled to think that your culture is the best culture in the world, it is vital that you also recognize such judgements are a matter of opinion, not a matter of fact, and that a person from *any* other culture is most likely not to agree with you.

2. *Avoid derogating anyone else's culture.* Be sensitive to the ethnocentric feelings of people of other cultures. They, like you, are proud of their culture. You can gain nothing by making negative references to the other person's cultural views or practices. Such references will only serve to "make an enemy" and ruin your chances for establishing effective intercultural communication. Remember: The more someone attacks a person's culture, the more ethnocentric that person will become.

3. *Demonstrate respect for the other person and her/his culture.* The principle of reciprocity, which also applies in intracultural communication, suggests that if you show respect and sensitivity to the other person and her/his culture, it is more likely you will be shown similar respect in return. Remember: Intercultural communicators do not have to like one another's cultural orientations, but they do need to be sensitive to them and show respect for them if there is to be effective intercultural communication.

4. **Be empathic.** Try to see things from the vantage point of the other person's culture. You may see them differently, but if you can empathize with the other person and understand why he or she has a view different from your own, it is more likely that the two of you can reach some common ground through your communication.

5. **Develop a higher tolerance for ambiguity**. Intercultural communication encounters often present one with situations for which one has no previous experience. Imagine being invited to a person's home and shown throughout the rooms of what we would call a mansion in this country. Then, after seeing a beautifully appointed bathroom, you request to use it but are shuttled out back to an "outhouse." If you were not aware that it was common in that culture to have fancy bathrooms that are for show only, for there is no sewer system in most areas, you could be very offended and reciprocate in very negative ways. If, however, you develop a high tolerance for ambiguity, you are more likely to presume that there is some good reason for this strange behavior, go along with it, and find out later what was going on.

6. **Reduce the level of evaluation in your messages.** People in the general North American culture tend to be highly evaluative in observations of the world around them. When people from this culture communicate with people from other cultures, most of whom are far less openly evaluative, it is important that this level of evaluation be reduced. Try to be more descriptive—"That seems somewhat strange to me; can you explain why it is done?"—in contrast to "I hate that."

7. **Be exceptionally careful in interaction management.** The cues that people follow for turn-taking, initiating communication, and terminating communication are all culturally determined. You can be reasonably certain that the way you have learned to manage interaction is not the same as the way a person from another culture has learned to do so. In order not to offend, the best rule is: When in doubt, defer to the other person.

8. **Be sensitive to relational/social needs.** North Americans tend to be very straightforward and business-like. After the business is over, it is time to socialize and relate to others. That approach is not shared by many other cultures. In many cases the cultural norm is to avoid business until people have established a very good social relationship. If that cannot be done, no business will be allowed! In many cases, moving toward business too quickly will guarantee failure of the communication. In general, it is wise to assume that the needs for a social relationship are at least as

important as the task relationship, and to attend to those needs before moving on to business.

9. ***Do not assume that nonverbal messages are pancultural.*** We learn our nonverbal behavior from our culture, and we learn it so well we assume it is "natural human behavior" that every human uses. It isn't. In fact, some of the most innocuous nonverbal behaviors in one culture are obscene in other cultures. Nodding the head in some cultures means "yes," while in others it means "no." Standing or sitting very close to someone while communicating is normal in some cultures, but offensive in others. When anticipating an intercultural encounter, such as traveling to another country, it is wise to read about the nonverbal behaviors characteristic of people in that culture. Otherwise, the probability of misunderstanding and/or offense is very high.

10. ***Be sensitive to both differences and similarities.*** In intercultural encounters it is easy to become overly focused on the differences between people. It is, indeed, important to recognize those differences, as we have noted above, but it is equally as important to look for real similarities between you and the other person. Just as is the case in intracultural communication, in intercultural communication homophily is a powerful influence toward effective communication. In some cases a small number of important similarities will go a long way toward overcoming problems caused by less important differences. International mediation and conflict resolution often boils down to the search for important similarities upon which to build common understandings.

11. ***Work to build better stereotypes.*** You are going to find it necessary to build generalizations about how to expect people to behave in various cultures. The more you read and study a culture, the better generalizations you will be able to make. Similarly, the more contact with people from a given culture you have, the more your stereotypes can be refined.

12. ***Never forget that meanings are in people, not in cultures.*** Remember that people in any culture do not all behave alike. Therefore, while it is fine to start with cultural stereotypes, try to monitor the behavior of the individual with whom you are communicating in order to identify the important ways that person is different from the cultural stereotype.

The twelve suggestions above are not the "Twelve Commandments," but if followed they will increase the likelihood that your intercultural communication experiences will be more positive and effective. Unfortunately, the other person's ethnocentrism could be so high that nothing you do could overcome it and permit the two of you to communicate effectively. All we can expect of one person is to meet the other person half way. If you follow these suggestions, you will at least have some assurance that you have done what you could.

References

Bohannan, P. (1992). *We, the alien: An introduction to cultural anthropology.* Prospect Heights, IL: Waveland Press.

DeVito, J. A. (1994). *Human communication: The basic course* (6th ed.). New York: HarperCollins.

Klopf, D. W. (1995). *Intercultural encounters: The fundamentals of intercultural communication.* Englewood, CO: Morton.

Lustig, M. W., & Koester, J. (1993). *Intercultural competence: Interpersonal communication across cultures.* New York: HarperCollins.

Oberg, K. (1960). Cultural shock: Adjustment to new cultural environments. *Practical Anthropology, 7,* 176–182.

Richmond, V. P., & McCroskey, J. C. (1995). *Nonverbal behavior in interpersonal relationships* (3rd ed.). Boston: Allyn & Bacon.

Samovar, L. A., & Porter, R. E. (1991). *Communication between cultures.* Belmont, CA: Wadsworth.

GENDER AND COMMUNICATION

19

Culture is the foundation upon which systems of communication are built. As we noted in the previous chapter, each culture builds its own system of communication. Culture determines the roles each of us must play in our everyday lives, and the rules that we must follow. Culture is a major portion of the contextual variation from one communication situation to another. Its impact, though often not recognized immediately, is overpowering.

Possibly the most important impact of culture, which frequently is not recognized, is its impact on the way we see males and females in our society. From early childhood we know how boys differ from girls, and how each is expected to behave (or **mis**behave). If we don't behave in the expected ways, parents, teachers, peers, and even strangers are quick to point out the discrepancies.

While we grow up thinking that biology determines how boys and girls (later men and women) behave, the reality is that biology has very little to do with it. The culture in which children are raised determines how they will be shaped to behave as men and women. Most important in that shaping process is how children are taught to communicate according to their gender.

As we noted in chapter 2, communication changes from one context to another and how we must communicate in various contexts depends on our **roles** in different interactions and the **rules** associated with those interactions. Roles pertain to the "part" we play in a given situation (friend, lover, teacher, student, parent, child, and so forth). Rules are the generally unspoken cultural norms that dictate how we are to play our part as a communicator in that situation. To the extent that our roles change from situation to situation—which in turn calls for a different set of rules by which to carry out interaction—communication also changes.

The way that roles are defined and rules are established in any given culture depends heavily on how that culture determines appropriate behavior differentially for females and males. These **gender roles** and how they impact on our communication behaviors are the central focus of this chapter. We believe it is important to consider gender roles because they have significant impact on how each of us communicates with others in our environment. Specifically, we will look at how gender roles develop, our psychological orientations toward femininity and masculinity, how males and females differ in their use of verbal and nonverbal communication behaviors, and at how they differ respective to their attitudes about, and behavior in, both intimate and non-intimate communicative relationships.

Since culture so dominates how we see male and female communicative behaviors, as well as communication between males and females, it is important that we make clear at the outset the framework in which this chapter is presented. We are looking at gender and communication from the vantage point of the dominant North American culture. That culture has its distant heritage in Europe and is centered on heterosexual orientations. It should not be expected, therefore, that masculine and feminine distinctions which are noted here will be equally applicable to people with other cultural backgrounds and/or orientations, including many North Americans representing diverse subcultures. Each reader, however, is invited to compare her/his own cultural orientations with those outlined here.

The Development of Gender Roles

One of the first distinctions we should make is between sex and gender. Sex is genetically determined. If a Y chromosome is present, the sex is male; if it isn't, the sex is female. Sex is a biological difference. The significance attached to biological sex is a cultural construct. Gender is about roles and attributes our culture assigns to one sex or the other. We learn those roles; we are not born with them. Paul Bohannan describes this as becoming "gendercentric" and shows that the learning process begins immediately. "In exactly the same way that we become ethnocentric as we learn culture, we also become gendercentric. . . . When nurses in hospital maternity wards talk to girl babies, they raise the pitch of their voices—as much as a third higher than when they talk to boys. Studies show that nurses actually handle boy babies with larger gestures than they do girls" (Bohannan, 1992, p. 57). We learn gender through what we are taught combined with our experiences of being male and female and the way people react to us.

As mentioned above, we often confuse the impact of biology with the impact of culture. Biology involves reproductive capabilities and anatomical differences. Beyond these few physical differences, few other "natural differences" exist between males and females. Generic attributions and generalizations—such as "women are the weaker sex" or "men aren't intuitive"—assume a constancy both in a given female's or male's behavior and across people of the same gender which simply has no biological basis. They are usually based on certain expectations that we have for each sex. In other words, we have different expectations about how females and males are "supposed to be" based on their actual or presumed physical differences. However, it does not suddenly occur to us that males and females are different kinds of people simply because they differ physically. Rather, our expectations for females and males derive from our cultural, societal, and interpersonal background and experiences.

At the *cultural* level, we expect each sex to behave in certain ways based on our cultural background. Most of us know, for example, that females and males in many Asian and African countries interact and are perceived differently than those in North America. At the *societal* level, our expectations for the behavior of each sex are based on the norms currently prevalent within our given society. They involve such things as what clothing a person is expected to wear, what kind of job one is expected to have (if any), what kind of leisure activities one is expected to find enjoyable, and how much education one is expected to have. Because such norms are subject to change over time, societal expectancies also may change. In this society, for example, only recently has it been generally accepted in some areas that females and males are "equal" in their intellectual and emotional capacities. Earlier, males were seen as more intellectual and less emotional than females. Expectations such as these are generated through the general social (educational, occupational, religious, and political) norms characterizing our society.

Expectations at the *interpersonal* level are based on our individual interactions with "significant others"—our family, close friends, and opinion leaders. These people help to shape not only our morals, beliefs, and values about life in general, but also our views about appropriate gender roles in particular. Thus, you may have been raised believing that males and females are equal in every aspect and should be treated in that way, or you may have been raised with the view that "a woman's place is in the home" and that "the man is expected to bring home the bacon."

All of these expectations are generated through our interpersonal and mass communication experiences with others and are reflective of the culture as it exists around us. Most of us never have really *chosen* how we view the roles of men and women. We have just *acquired* a view, and unless we encounter someone who has a view which is strongly divergent from our own, we probably have never really thought much about the differences between men and women at all. After all, such differences are just *natural*, right?

The types of expectations just described are important to understanding perceptions of female-male differences because they lead to stereotypical perceptions of what roles males and females should fill. When these perceptions become strong enough and prevalent enough, they become, in effect, norms for gender roles. Since its beginnings, the general North American culture has assigned a primarily *instrumental* role for males and a primarily *expressive* role for females. The instrumental male role is task-oriented, concerned with getting things done—complete an education, compete with others, be an occupational success, and so forth. The female expressive role is other-oriented, concerned with developing socially—show care for others, share self with others, be a mother and a wife, and so forth. In terms of communication differences, then, norms imply that male communication behavior will be mostly task-oriented (much talk about work, future goals, making money, sports) and that female communication will be mostly other-oriented (much talk about social affairs, the family, interpersonal relations, and so forth).

While much has been made of greater equality between the sexes over the past three decades, the primary socialization of children today is not greatly different than it was several decades earlier. In particular, socialization of males still focuses on the instrumental and generally ignores, for the most part, the expressive. In many communities in North America, however, females are receiving more socialization toward the instrumental than they have in the past. Thus, males continue to be socialized toward the single, instrumental role, but females are frequently being socialized toward dual (instrumental and expressive) roles.

It is important at this point to make a distinction between two general kinds of roles. *Ascribed roles* are those we are born into and cannot avoid, such as our ethnic group, nationality, family position (e.g., first born or later born), and biological sex. *Achieved roles* are those we fill by earning a particular position, such as college student, supervisor, professor, foreperson, lieutenant, and husband or wife. Although we have no control over our ascribed roles, we can influence the achieved roles we fill. If you want to earn your Ph.D. in psychology, you will work and study to do so. If you want to marry and become a husband or wife, you will structure your social life so as to find a suitable mate. Essentially, and this is the major point here, females can achieve a normative instrumental male role, and males can achieve a normative expressive female role, if they individually choose to do so. But society will not push either the female or the male in these directions. Females and males today are achieving non-prescribed roles. Contemporary examples include females who are filling traditionally male-dominated positions in business and industry, government, the military, and politics. Also, males are achieving expressive roles as elementary teachers, nurses, secretaries, and "house-husbands."

Gender-role norms thus can be and often are violated. This is much more acceptable today than it was two or three generations ago. Inasmuch as these violations lead to changes in gender-role norms, they also lead to changes in perceptions of appropriate communication behavior. Hence, we are becoming accustomed to visiting with female physicians, voting for (or against) female politicians, talking with our child's male first grade teacher, and asking a male telephone operator for assistance. Our perceptions are changing such that it is becoming "acceptable" for males to be more expressive and other-oriented in their communication behavior and for females to be more assertive and task-oriented. Changes in gender-role expectations lead to changes in our orientations toward females and males and the differences between them. Essentially, these orientations are psychological in nature and relate to our self-identification with femininity and masculinity.

Psychological Gender Orientation

When researchers and scholars in the social sciences use the terms *male* and *female*, they usually are referring to anatomical sex. When the terms *feminine* and *masculine* are used, however, reference is being made to *gender*, a type of personality orientation. Thus, describing someone as *feminine* does not necessarily mean a person is female nor does describing a person as *masculine* mean they are male. Rather, masculinity and femininity concern one's identification with and use of behaviors that are generally characterized in the culture as either masculine or feminine behaviors. This identification is called one's *psychological gender orientation*.

A person's psychological gender orientation is her or his level of self-identification with both assertiveness (instrumentality) and responsiveness (expressiveness) in interactions with others. That is, it is the person's overall orientation represented by communication behaviors which reflect assertiveness or responsiveness toward those with whom he or she interacts. A person with a highly feminine gender orientation is one who employs mostly responsive communication behaviors. The person's communication behaviors will express helpfulness, cheerfulness, affection, sympathy, sensitivity to others' needs, understanding, compassion, sincerity, an eagerness to soothe hurt feelings, warmth, tenderness, and gentleness. On the other hand, a person with a highly masculine gender orientation is one who employs mostly assertive communication behaviors. The person's communication behaviors will express competitiveness, aggressiveness, a willingness to lead, self-sufficiency, forcefulness, assertiveness, and independence. In short, a very masculine individual expresses strong control needs, and a very feminine individual expresses strong affection needs.

The development of gender orientation is related to the development of self-concept (the way one views oneself as a person) and stems from our social experiences and background. Essentially, how others respond to us as either a female or a male affects how we view ourselves. As little girls or boys, for example, we are dressed in either pink or blue, play with either dolls or balls, and pretend that we are either "mommies" or "daddies." A little girl may further observe and be taught that girls are supposed to be nice, are not to get dirty, are supposed to learn piano, are not to hit or play rough with others, and are to portray appropriate manners. A little boy is likely to be taught that he should play with action toys, should play to win, should defend his honor in a fight or by taking risks, and that he should never cry. Thus, males and females at an early age develop masculine and feminine role expectations and learn behaviors associated with each of these roles.

Generally, boys develop masculine behaviors and receive reinforcement for them. Likewise, girls generally develop and receive reinforcement for feminine behaviors. To the extent that these expectations are fulfilled through interactions with others, individuals will develop a view of themselves that indicates "this is the way I am supposed to be." This self-view eventually develops into a particular gender orientation that is manifested in the types of assertive or responsive communicative behaviors we have mentioned. That is, females tend to be taught to communicate in responsive, nurturing, and expressive ways while males typically are taught to communicate in assertive, instrumental, and competitive ways.

Females who have a high feminine orientation and males who have a high masculine orientation are said to be *sex-typed*. Sex-typed females, then, are those who exhibit mostly responsive communication behaviors when interacting with others, and sex-typed males are those who display mostly assertive communication behaviors. However, you may know people of both sexes who most exhibit behaviors typically thought to be those of the opposite sex. A "tomboy," for example, is a female who generally exhibits assertive, competitive, "masculine" behaviors, and a "sissy" is a male who most often displays responsive, expressive, "feminine" behaviors. These individuals are said to be *sex-reversed* because their behaviors indicate a gender orientation opposite of their biological sex. It is likely that they have developed such an orientation because, like the sex-typed individual, they have some need to engage in their respective behaviors and have received reinforcement for doing so.

You may be thinking by now that there are times when you feel that you exhibit mostly responsive behaviors, other times when you show more assertive behaviors, and still other times when you feel that you express a combination of both. In other words, you may be the type of person who engages in specific behaviors according to the demands of the given situation. If so, you may have an *androgynous* gender orientation.

The term *androgyny* is a combination of the Greek words *andros*, meaning "man," and *gyne* meaning "woman." Thus, an androgynous person is one who can exhibit both masculine and feminine characteristics. In terms of psychological gender orientation, this type of individual is able to adapt to a variety of roles by engaging in either instrumental or expressive behaviors, depending on the situation.

Essentially, then, the androgynous individual can be warm, compassionate, sincere, helpful, sympathetic, and submissive in one situation, and turn right around and be competitive, risk-taking, aggressive, independent, and dominant in another situation. An example of an androgynous female might be the college student majoring in petroleum engineering (a traditionally male major) who spends her Saturdays and Sundays watching college and professional football (a typically masculine recreation), but who also enjoys going shopping (a typically feminine recreation) and studying dance (a traditionally feminine interest). An androgynous male might be exemplified by the firefighter (a traditionally male occupation) who spends one of his days off each month doing volunteer work at a day-care center (a typically feminine, nurturing activity).

Generally, then, the person with an androgynous gender orientation is highly flexible in her or his behavior. These individuals do not feel limited in their communication with others and are fully aware of and adaptable to their affection and control needs. Thus, androgynous individuals are able to sense another person's needs to be dominant in a given situation and, if they deem it appropriate, will engage in submissive behaviors. Similarly, this type of individual recognizes when the partner in an interaction requires compassion and warmth and is quite able to meet those needs. On the other hand, persons who are either highly sex-typed or highly sex-reversed are quite limited in their behavior. Specifically, they are not as adaptable to varying situational demands as are androgynous people. The highly masculine person, for example, may have difficulty expressing sympathy for another, whereas the highly feminine individual might have trouble coping with a very competitive and aggressive interaction. In sum, our psychological gender orientation develops from our social interactions—the way others respond to us affects how we see ourselves and our roles as females or males, and these effects appear in our interpersonal communication behavior.

Now that you have a basic understanding of psychological gender orientation, we can turn to a more general discussion of female-male difference in communication behavior. We wish to reiterate at this point that males and females communicate differently not because they are anatomically different but because they are taught to accept certain gender orientations which are proscribed by their culture. Each gender orientation represents certain communication patterns which the culture determines are appropriate means of expressing masculinity or femininity. In short, we do what we are taught to do, not what we are biologically predetermined to do.

In our discussion of communicative differences between females and males below, we will be making comparisons which have been found to exist in the general North American culture. Such differences should not be expected to exist to the same extent, or even in the same direction, in other cultures—nor even in all subcultures within the general North American culture. Remember: gender differences are primarily a function of cultural conditioning—different cultures produce different differences.

By this point, you most likely have recognized that gender differences are highly associated with the three components of basic communication competence which we discussed in chapter 7—assertiveness, responsiveness, and versatility. In the general North American culture males are taught to be more assertive, and this is taken in this culture to be a positive sign of masculinity. In contrast, females are taught to be more responsive, and this is taken to be a positive sign of femininity. They are also taught to avoid engaging in the behaviors of the other sex—to be consistently masculine or feminine, not versatile. Thus, children of both genders are taught to be ''half-competent.'' They are encouraged to exhibit the communication behaviors culturally appropriate for their sex and avoid those behaviors which are culturally inappropriate for their sex. These differences in behavior are reflected in both verbal and nonverbal communication behaviors.

Gender Differences in Verbal Communication

Differences between males and females in verbal communication are most evident in the type and amount of information they disclose, the language they use, and the subject matter they discuss. We consider each of these areas below.

Self-Disclosure

According to most of the research in the general North American culture, females disclose more information about themselves than do males. Although several studies in this area of communication have found women *not* to be significantly more disclosive than men, none have found men to be more disclosive. Women sometimes self-disclose a greater amount of information, with longer duration, and with more intimate topics than do men. Moreover, females are less guarded and more honest about disclosing negative information about themselves than are males. Females also disclose more intimate information to other females than they do to males. On the other hand, males tend to reserve their most intimate disclosures for females with whom they are close, being quite nonintimate in self-disclosure to other males. Males typically do not self-disclose much negative information to either sex. Some research suggests that sex differences in disclosure may be related to socioeconomic level and geographic region. For example, studies utilizing students from some "prestigious" universities show no difference in the amount of disclosure between females and males.

Language Use

Have you ever felt that your male friends use different types of words and phrases than do your female friends? Such differences do indeed exist. As we have already noted in earlier chapters, the language we use both constructs and reflects our perceptions of reality. Thus, much research in recent years has sought to determine the effects of certain word usages on perceptions of the sexes. This body of research has examined the use of particular nouns, verbs, and pronouns and found that some do indeed affect how we perceive males and females. For example, studies have found females to be (1) referred to more frequently than males by informal terms (first names or nicknames), (2) referred to more often in terms of the men with whom they are associated rather than by their own identity ("Bill's wife," "Mrs. Jones," "Mr. Smith's girl"), and (3) identified more than males as sex objects ("fox," "doll," "babe"). Studies have found that females, on the other hand, use more euphemisms (substituting more acceptable or polite terms for embarrassing terms; for example, "He is intellectually challenged" instead of "He really is stupid"), more emotional terms ("I just *love* that!" instead of "That is very nice"), and more intensifiers ("enormous" as opposed to "large" or "big") than do males.

A great deal of research in this area has looked at the use of *generic* pronouns, those used to refer to people in general rather than gender-specific references. The most notable of these terms in the English language is the generic *he*. For centuries in both written and oral communication, this pronoun has referred to both males and females, particularly when the actual referent is unknown. When a female referent is known, however, the pronoun *she* is used instead, although *he* remains when a male referent is known. It is perhaps because of this dual usage of *he* that it has been found to be an unsatisfactory generic for many readers and listeners. Not surprisingly, studies have shown that the use of masculine terms as generics causes readers and listeners to think of the referent as male. Such language use shapes our perceptions in unintended ways—we read or hear a generic such as *he* and envision something specifically sex-typed, which is what use of generic terms is specifically designed to avoid in the first place.

Finally, we tend to use different types of verbs in reference to females and males. For males we generally use verbs expressed in the active voice; for females however, we more often use verbs expressed in the passive voice. Talking about Becky and Phillip going to the market, for example, we are more likely to say "Phillip took Becky to the market" (active verb "took") or "Becky was taken to the market" (passive verb was "taken") as opposed to "Becky rode to the market with Phillip."

Thus, males and females both use and are referenced by different types of words and word patterns. Again, the source of this differential usage most likely stems from the differences in gender-role expectations we have for masculine and feminine behavior. Different language usage allows us to fulfill and maintain those culturally based expectations.

Subject Matter

We have already noted that males and females differ in the types of information which they disclose to others. On a more basic and less intimate level, males and females also differ relative to the types of topics with which they most frequently begin conversations. These differences occur in both same-sex and opposite-sex interactions. Some of the patterns may surprise you. When females initiate conversation with other females, the most likely subjects they will discuss are men, clothing, and other women. When men initiate conversation with other men, the most likely topics of discussion will be business, money, and sports or other amusements. In opposite-sex dyads, when females initiate conversation with males, they are most likely to discuss men and other women. When males initiate conversation with females, however, they are most likely to begin with a discussion of sports or other amusements. When such differences occur, they can probably be attributed to the instrumental, external orientation of males in contrast to the expressive, internal orientation of females. These orientations, of course, are remnants of cultural norms and expectations. Thus, normative expressive behavior of females explains their likelihood of beginning and carrying on conversations about other people, both men and women. Clothing, by the way, is a highly expressive subject for females. Similarly, the normative instrumental behavior of males explains their likelihood of initiating interactions on the subjects of work, money, or amusements.

Females and males do indeed differ in their verbal communication with others. Most of these differences stem from cultural norms and expectations we have developed about male and female behavior. Perhaps more noticeable than the verbal differences on an interpersonal level, however, are the nonverbal differences between the sexes.

Gender Differences in Nonverbal Communication

Differences between females and males in nonverbal communication have been consistently reported in research on eye behavior and facial expressions, posture, use of personal space, and touching behavior. Because these areas were considered more fully in chapters 13 and 14, this section focuses solely on how the sexes differ in their use and interpretation of them.

Eye Behavior and Facial Expressions

Eye behavior differs for males and females in terms of the frequency, duration, and distance of eye contact between interactants. Generally, females have a greater frequency and longer duration of eye contact with others than do males. Females also look more when talking and when others are talking to them. Males tend to share gaze with a partner at greater distances, whereas females maintain mutual gaze at closer distances. Although these findings seem rather straightforward, several factors impinge on male and female gaze behavior. When interacting with an opposite-sex acquaintance, for example, both sexes tend to try to increase physical distance between themselves and their partner in an apparent effort to reduce eye contact. Other factors that affect differences in eye behavior are verbal intimacy, anxiety, body orientation (posture), age, and degree of friendship.

Relative to facial expressions, gender differences appear in the amount of emotion a person reveals. Because they are inhibited in our society from showing their emotions, males tend not to display as much facial emotion as females do. Both females and males smile more when they are seeking social approval from others. Generally, however, females smile more often than do males, particularly females from the southern United States subculture. Males are highly unlikely to exhibit crying and are more likely than females to display displeasure through their facial expressions.

Posture and Gestures

The next time you are sitting in a classroom, look around and see if you notice any differences in the way males and females sit. Make a similar observation the next time you are in or near a mixed-sex group of people; take note if there are any differences between the sexes in their use of gestures. Typically, you will find that males sit or stand with their legs apart, hold their hands against their hips, keep their heads erect, maintain an upright stance, and take up space to a greater extent than females. Although males are more likely to use pointing gestures in an interaction, females are more likely to clasp their hands together, fold their arms across their midsections, or pat their hair. Finally, when seated during a dyadic interaction, males are likely to engage in many more seat-shifting movements than are females.

Personal Space

In general, females maintain closer physical distances in their interactions than do males. As with eye behavior, however, several variables seem to affect this trend. The sex of the interaction partner is perhaps the most influential of these. Several studies have shown that females tend to sit closer to other females than do males. It seems that males simply require more space than females. They are, however, likely to sit closer to females than to other males. The direction of the other person's approach also affects use of space. For example, females let others approach them more closely from the sides, whereas males let people approach them more closely from the front. In terms of their own approach, females are likely to approach closer to a "best friend" and to remain farther away than males from "mere friends."

Touching Behavior

Several interesting relationships have been found between touching behavior and one's sex. First, the norm for adults of both sexes in our society is one of very limited and infrequent physical contact. Touching behavior appears to be much more frequent for both sexes early in life, with frequency of touch steadily decreasing as the individual gets older. Studies show that the greatest frequency of touch occurs during infancy, when much consistent contact is maintained between mother and infant. Generally, however, male infants receive more touch during the first six months of life, and thereafter females increasingly receive more touch from both parents.

An interesting facet of this research, one that has recently received attention, is touch avoidance, a person's unwillingness or lack of desire to have much physical contact with others. Research has discovered gender differences in touch avoidance. Specifically, males tend to show much higher levels of touch avoidance toward other males than do females toward other females. Conversely, females show a tendency toward higher touch avoidance toward males than do males toward females. Moreover, both of these trends are consistent over various age groupings.

Finally, it is interesting to consider how males and females interpret different types of touch. Studies show that both females and males view a "pat" as the most friendly and playful form of touch, and a "stroke" as the most loving, sexual, and pleasant form. Although both sexes indicate that touch to the genital areas communicates a sexual meaning, differences between the sexes appear in that males are more likely to view genital/sexual touch by females as positive, whereas females view such touch more negatively. One important note: These findings were for unmarried females; married females perceived sexual touch quite positively. It is likely that the research environment had a major impact on the results of this research.

Many differences exist in the nonverbal behavior of males and females. In most cases the origin of the differences can be traced back to cultural norms and general sex stereotypes. To the extent that nonverbal behaviors are expressive and self-disclosive we can expect, based on cultural norms, that females will display more emotional nonverbal behaviors than will males. Conversely, to the extent that nonverbal behaviors indicate dominance and interaction control, we can expect that males will exhibit more of them. It is equally likely, however, that an individual with an androgynous gender orientation will be able to adapt to and utilize a variety of nonverbal communication behaviors across numerous interaction situations. Inasmuch as people's communication behavior is a function of their gender, their perspectives toward interpersonal relationships are also a function of gender.

Gender and Interpersonal Relationships

Men and women tend to perceive interpersonal relationships differently. Their differing perspectives on relationships coincide with the varied expectancies and norms that society has for men and women. In general, then, relationships for females revolve around an expressive function, whereas relationships for males revolve around an instrumental function. This section discusses female and male perspectives on friendships and intimate communicative relationships.

Friendships between Females

Females tend to develop friendships with other females in terms of an expressive function. They seek out friendships that enable them to satisfy their needs for affection and belonging. Phillips and Wood (1983) have identified three primary reasons why females develop friendships. One is *recreation*. Many female friendships are based on shared activities and events. Examples would be friendships developed at an aerobics class, at PTA meetings, or at the hairstylist. These types of friendships serve especially to provide conversation and noncommittal association with another. Thus, the friends who greet and interact with one another in aerobics class will not likely have an association outside that class.

Another reason females develop friendships is for ***personal support***. This type of friendship stems from a need to have a confidante with whom to share one's deepest thoughts, feelings, and concerns. Females are more likely to share this kind of information with another female than they are with a male. Moreover, females maintain this type of relationship much longer than do males—females are much more likely than males to have associations with "lifelong" friends. In short, a female's greater expressed need for personal support leads her to expend more energy maintaining close associations with certain other females.

The third reason females develop friendships is for **problem solving**. This type of friendship serves to provide a female with information and experience she might not be able to acquire from anyone else. Mothers of young children, for example, develop friendships with others in the same situation; most interactions might deal with child-rearing problems and activities to interest the children. Similarly, women employed outside the home tend to develop friendships with other women similarly employed, and many of their interactions concern, for example, career goals, sexism, equal pay and opportunity, and corporate responsibility.

One feature of female-female friendships that is less apparent in male-male friendships is **reciprocation**. Females, more so than males, view friendships as dependent on mutual exchange, a give and take. Thus, females tend to put into their friendships with others what they expect to get out of them, and vice versa. Interestingly, however, females are likely to give up a female friendship for a relationship with a male. Whether the fact that females sustain a number of female-female relationships makes the sacrifice of one more likely or whether cultural expectations override other values has yet to be determined.

Friendships between Males

Most male-male friendships develop through an instrumental function. This coincides with a male's predominantly task-oriented perspective toward relationships. Males typically develop and maintain relationships with other males that satisfy the social need for control and also the need for belonging. Contrary to female-female friendships, male-male friendships tend to be quite superficial. Males do not share their deepest feelings and problems with each other; they are more likely to turn to females for such disclosure—or not disclose such things at all.

Male friendships develop mostly around activities. A male's closest male friendships are likely to be with men with whom he works, who have the same hobbies he has, or who belong to the same social organization or club. College males, for example, find their closest friendships to be with fraternity brothers or roommates. Moreover, Phillips and Wood have found that males define friendship in terms of allies and team members. Friends for a male are those who share mutual favors and take sides with each other. Males, perhaps more so than females, socialize with those who are most like themselves. That is why in college you may notice that many male friendships are among people who have the same major, are from the same home town, are members of the same athletic team, or frequent the same night spots.

Like female friendships, male friendships develop because of recreational, personal support, and problem-solving concerns. Unlike females, however, males are unlikely to disclose much about their values, fears, or troubles associated with these concerns. Also, male friendships are less reciprocal than female friendships. In fact, many males refrain from using the term *friend* to describe or refer to their male associations. It would seem, then, that males develop friendships with other males in order to get from the relationships what they can, and they think less about what they can put into the relationship. This isn't to suggest that males are selfish, egocentric ogres. Rather, it is a reflection of their instrumental orientation. Males have a culturally engendered need to be dominant, competitive, and to develop their leadership qualities. It is through their friendships with other males that males are best able to develop and satisfy these needs.

Intimate Female-Male Relationships

No type of interpersonal relationship is as central to a heterosexual's social concerns and desires as is an intimate interpersonal relationship with a member of the opposite sex. However, females and males differ in their perspectives on what intimacy is and how it should be expressed.

Men equate intimacy with sexual activity much more so than do women. In their survey of female and male attitudes toward intimate interpersonal relationships published in 1983, Phillips and Wood found that males desire an intimate relationship with a female who provides not only nurturance and support but also good sex. For the males studied, intimacy with females could not be discussed without reference to sex, and many males reported that their first thoughts when meeting a female in a work environment were about her possibilities as a sexual partner. Were that research to be replicated today, results might be different. Even if males still have the same perceptions, they might be less willing to disclose them to a researcher today. Unlike males, females do not openly admit to seeing sex as highly important in male-female relationships. They tend to feel that opposite-sex relationships can develop and be sustained without implications for sex. As a result, heterosexual females often find non-sexual relationships with male homosexuals to be particularly pleasant. Although females were unlikely to state it openly, the Phillips and Wood survey revealed that most females do perceive sex as an important issue in their relationships with heterosexual males. Given these discrepant views of male-female relationships, it is no wonder that considerable tension exists in many organizations. When even the definition of what constitutes sexual harassment might vary according to one's socialization, the prevention of it becomes even more difficult.

Given the expressive and instrumental orientations of females and males, respectively, it would appear that most intimate opposite-sex relationships evolve in a complementary fashion. Males seek to develop intimate relationships with a female who will enable them to maintain their self-definition of dominance, self-sufficiency, and independence, but who will also provide them with needed compassion, empathy, affection, understanding, and help. Females desire intimate relationships with a male who will enable them to express their nurturance, compassion, and affection, and who in turn will provide responsibility and leadership where it is needed. These orientations may appear boringly traditional and may seem to leave out the independent woman and the compassionate man. They do, however, represent the norm for complementary opposite-sex relationships in our society, and they stem from the expectancies formed by the cultural norms for males and females.

Many intimate female-male relationships are symmetrical. These are relationships in which the partners are "balanced" in most ways. Thus, some male-female relationships may involve partners who share equal orientations toward issues, share interests and activities, perceive themselves equal in status and ability, and perhaps even have the same career objectives and goals. The advantage of this type of relationship is that it allows both partners a wide margin of independence and power in the relationship.

Where does communication come into play with intimate opposite-sex relationships? As chapter 15 on relationship development emphasized, communication *is* the relationship. Thus, the level of intimacy experienced between two partners in a relationship is a function of their communication. To the extent that communication is intimate, the relationship will be intimate. Intimacy is, of course, communicated in different ways among people and relationships. Much intimacy is communicated verbally ("I love you"; "We are meant for each other"), but a great deal of it is communicated nonverbally through such general modes as touch, eye contact, and facial expression. For intimacy to be fully and adequately expressed between two partners, however, it should be conveyed through both verbal *and* nonverbal messages. That is, for most partners it will not be sufficient to be told "I love you" without actions to back it up, nor will the actions stand alone without appropriate verbal support.

In many opposite-sex relationships, sexual activity serves as an important indicator of intimacy. Moreover, a person's satisfaction with sexual relations within the relationship may be important to general satisfaction with her or his partner and their association. Communication researchers have attended to this aspect of intimacy and have developed the concept of *sexual communication satisfaction*. This is defined as "satisfaction with communication about sexual behavior and the satisfaction that sexual behavior itself communicates" (Wheeless, Wheeless, & Baus, 1981, p. 2).

Sexual communication satisfaction is reflected by (1) satisfaction with communication about sexual behavior, (2) communication about what kind of sexual behavior is satisfying, (3) satisfaction from what is communicated by certain sexual behaviors, and (4) willingness and/or ability to communicate about sex with one's partner. From this conceptualization it can be deduced that sexual behavior is both a verbal and a nonverbal form of communication. It involves not only engaging in sexual activity but also talking about those activities with one's partner. Also, sexual communication satisfaction pertains to a wide variety of sexual activities ranging from winking at one's partner to having sexual intercourse. That it is indicative of the level of intimacy is substantiated by research that has shown sexual satisfaction to be highest for partners whose relationships are highly developed and lowest in relationships that are just beginning and those that are completing termination ((Wheeless, Wheeless, & Baus, 1981).

In summary, different expectancies and norms for males and females manifest themselves in the sexes' different perspectives on relationships. Males view friendships as mostly instrumental; females view them mainly in an expressive way. Females and males conceive of intimate opposite-sex relationships in somewhat opposing ways, but both feel that sex should be an integral concern within such relationships. Indeed, sexual activity and one's satisfaction with it may be one of the major factors determining the level of intimacy in some relationships, but certainly not all relationships.

Gender and culture are intertwined in framing the context for communication among humans. While biological differences exist between the sexes, every culture tells its members how to interpret and react to those differences. The culture determines the nature of relationships between members of both the same sex and the opposite sex. While differences between what is considered appropriate masculine and feminine communication behaviors exist in all cultures, it is important to remember that males and females in a given culture are likely to communicate *more like one another* than they are to communicate like members of their own sex from another culture.

References

Bate, B. (1988). *Communication and the sexes.* New York: Harper & Row.

Bem, S. L. (1974). The measurement of psychological androgyny. *Journal of Consulting and Clinical Psychology, 47,* 155–162.

Bohannan, P. (1992). *We, the alien: An introduction to cultural anthropology.* Prospect Heights, IL: Waveland Press.

Carlson, J. (1976). The sexual role. In F. I. Nye (Ed.), *Role structure and analysis of the family.* Beverly Hills: Sage.

Cline, R. J. (1982). Revealing and relating: A review of self-disclosure theory and research. Paper presented at the International Communication Association convention, Boston.

_____. (1983). The politics of intimacy: Costs and benefits determining disclosure intimacy in male-female dyads. Paper presented at the Speech Communication Association convention, Washington, D.C.

Exline, R. V., Gray, D., & Schwette, D. (1965). Visual behavior in a dyad as affected by interview context and sex of respondent. *Journal of Personality and Social Psychology, 1,* 201–209.

Exline, R. V., & Winters., L. C. (1965). Affective relations and mutual glances in dyads. In S. S. Tomkins & C. E. Izard (Eds.), *Affect, cognition, and personality.* New York: Springer.

Galvin, K. M., & Brommel, B. J. (1982). *Family communication: Cohesion and change.* Glenview, IL: Scott, Foresman.

Hays, R. B. (1984). The development and maintenance of friendship. *Journal of Social and Personal Relationships, 1,* 75–98.

Kendon, A., & Look, M. (1969). The consistency of gaze patterns in social interaction. *British Journal of Psychology, 60,* 481–494.

Leibman, M. (1970). The effects of sex and race norms on personal space. *Environment and Behavior, 2,* 208–246.

Leibowitz, K., & Andersen, P. (1978). The development and nature of the construct touch avoidance. *Environmental Psychology and Nonverbal Behavior, 3,* 89–106.

McCroskey, J. C., & Wheeless, L. R. (1976). *Introduction to human communication.* Boston: Allyn & Bacon.

Pearson, J. C. (1985). *Gender and communication.* Dubuque, IA: Wm. C. Brown.

Phillips, G. M., & Wood, J. T. (1983). *Communication and human relationships: The study of interpersonal communication.* New York: Macmillan.

Richmond, V. P., & McCroskey, J. C. (1995). *Nonverbal behavior in interpersonal relationships* (3rd ed.). Boston: Allyn & Bacon.

Rosenfeld, L. B., Kartvs, S., & Ray, C. (1976). Body accessibility revisited. *Journal of Communication, 26,* 27–30.

Sommer, R. (1959). Studies in personal space. *Sociometry, 22,* 247–260.

Wheeless, L. R., Wheeless, V. E., & Baus, R. (1981). Communication satisfaction and interpersonal solidarity in relationship development. Paper presented at the annual convention of the Speech Communication Association of Puerto Rico, San Juan.

Willis, F. N. (1966). Initial speaking distance as a function of the speakers' relationship. *Psychonomic Science, 5,* 221–222.

INDEX

and relationship, 225–226
Pictographic writing system, 39
Pilkonis, P., 55
Plato, 104
Plax, T. G., 248
Political campaigns, 104
Polychronic cultures, 193
Positional cues, 181
Posture, gender and, 304
Power, 242–245
  bases of, 244
  and interpersonal influence, 240–257
  of source, 117–122
PRCA. See Personal Report of
  Communication Apprehension
  Scale
Predispositions, traits as, 160
Preening behavior, 181
Prejudice, 286
Presence, in relationship, 226
Primacy, selective retention and,
  150–151
Privacy, 190
Problem solving, female friendships
  and, 307
Process, communication as, 6–7
Pronouns, gender and, 302–303
Proxemics, 187–188
Proximity, 143–144
  in interpersonal relationships,
  218–219
Psychological androgyny, 91
Psychological level, of communication,
  32–33
Psychological time orientation,
  193–194
Psychology, gender and, 298–301
Public communication, 42. See also
  Media
  mediated, 44–45
Public distance, 187–188
Punishment, behavior alteration
  techniques and, 246
Punishment BATs, 251–253

Quiet people, perceptions about, 83–86
Quintilian, 104

Radio, 43. See also Media; Mediated

communication
Raven, B., 243
Recall, 151
Receiver(s), 8, 14, 15, 40–41
  lack of, 148
  source perception by, 104–105
Recency, selective retention and,
  150–151
Reciprocation, female friendships and,
  307
Recognition, in relationship, 228–229
Recreation, female friendship and,
  306–307
Redmond, M. K., 35
Redundancy
  in messages, 147–148
  selective retention and, 150
Reference groups, 133–134
Referent BATs, 253
Referent power, 245
Regulating, in nonverbal messages,
  174, 179–180
Reid, R., 91
Reinforcement
  childhood, 58–59
  selective exposure and, 144–145
Reinforcement theory, 132–133
Relational BATs, 253
Relational level, of message, 5
Relational needs, sensitivity to,
  290–291
Relationships
  affinity-seeking and, 230–236
  characteristics of, 216–219
  coming apart in, 219
  coming together in, 219
  development stages of, 219–223
  expectations in, 223–230
  as goal, 18, 19–20
  interpersonal, 216–237
  intimate, 22
  intimate female-male, 308–310
  messages and, 198–211
Repeating, in nonverbal messages, 174
Requests, assertiveness and, 93
Research, on affinity-seeking, 231
Responding, 8–9
Responsibility, moral, 254–255
Responsiveness, as style, 92, 93–94